D1598103

Deafness, Deprivation, and IQ

PERSPECTIVES ON INDIVIDUAL DIFFERENCES

CECIL R. REYNOLDS, *Texas A&M University, College Station*
ROBERT T. BROWN, *University of North Carolina, Wilmington*

A Continuation Order Plan is available for this series. A continuation order will bring delivery of each new volume immediately upon publication. Volumes are billed only upon actual shipment. For further information please contact the publisher.

Deafness, Deprivation, and IQ

Jeffery P. Braden

University of Wisconsin
Madison, Wisconsin

PLENUM PRESS • NEW YORK AND LONDON

Library of Congress Cataloging in Publication Data

Braden, Jeffery P.
    Deafness, deprivation, and IQ / Jeffery P. Braden.
        p.   cm.— (Perspectives on individual differences)
    Includes bibliographical references and index.
    ISBN 0-306-44686-3
    1. Deaf—Intelligence levels. 2. Deaf—Intelligence testing. 3. Deafness—
Psychological aspects. 4. Deprivation (Psychology) I. Title. II. Title: Deafness,
deprivation, and intelligence quotient. III. Series.
BF432.D4B73   1994   94-2567
155.9′16—dc20   CIP

ISBN 0-306-44686-3

© 1994 Plenum Press, New York
A Division of Plenum Publishing Corporation
233 Spring Street, New York, N.Y. 10013

Printed in the United States of America

Foreword

Deafness is a "low incidence" disability and, therefore not studied or understood in the same way as other disabilities. Historically, research in deafness has been conducted by a small group of individuals who communicated mainly with each other. That is not to say that we did not sometimes publish in the mainstream or attempt to communicate outside our small circle. Nonetheless, most research appeared in deafness-related publications where it was not likely to be seen or valued by psychologists. Those researchers did not understand what they could learn from the study of deaf people or how their knowledge of individual differences and abilites applied to that population.

In *Deafness, Deprivation, and IQ*, Jeffrey Braden pulls together two often unrelated fields: studies of intelligence and deafness. The book includes the largest single compilation of data describing deaf people's intelligence that exists. Here is a careful, well-documented, and very thorough analysis of virtually all the research available. Those who have studied human intelligence have long noted that deafness provides a "natural experiment." This book makes evident two contrary results: on the one hand, some research points to the impact deafness has on intelligence; on the other hand, the research supports the fact that deafness has very little, if any, impact on nonverbal measures of intelligence.

Braden's meta-analysis of these studies leads to some very interesting findings, the most remarkable of which are the similarities between deaf and hearing people. The book shows that the impact of deafness on intelligence is simply to depress verbal IQs and not affect nonverbal IQs. At the same time, deaf children with deaf parents have performance IQs that are above the mean for hearing people.

The natural experiment of deafness has been available for centuries. What is new here is the emphasis that deafness does not represent an experiment solely with respect to language deprivation. Previous characterizations of deafness, were often simplistic, described deafness as a condition in which the primary (and often the only) independent variable was language. What is new and important here is the very careful presentation of dysfunction and abnormal family dynamics, which would very likely have a significant impact on intellectual development.

Much of the discussion in this book about group differences in intelligence is controversial. No single area within psychology has generated more debate than group differences in intelligence. Similarly, in the study of deafness, the field continues to be divided as to whether or not differences exist between deaf and hearing people that are due solely to deafness. While the literature reflects extensive research and theorizing about intelligence, much of the research on deafness is atheoretical and descriptive. Braden brings an important scientific rigor to the analysis of deafness research. His book has the potential to serve both deafness and psychology research in the areas where they overlap.

As a psychologist who has spent my entire career working in the field of deafness, I have been terribly disappointed that the value of studying our community has been overlooked by mainstream psychology. Some of this disregard has been difficult for me to understand. How, for example, can anyone continue to discount differences between verbal and nonverbal intelligence measures after seeing the differences that exist among deaf people? This book clearly shows that by studying deaf people we can learn a great deal about nature and nurture and about the genetic and environmental influences on intelligence.

Reading this book will reveal much of the debate that still exists in these fields. More importantly, it will reveal some light. Braden has done a remarkable job of bringing these two disparate fields together.

Little is more valued within the academy than the achievements of one's student. All of us believe, on some level, that within each of the students lies the potential to rise high above the norm. Each of us is quick to take some credit when one of our students stands out. It is a special privilege for me to write an introduction to a book written by just such a former student.

I first came to know Jeff Braden when he attended Gallaudet University for a year as an undergraduate. The drive and potential in him were clear. As a student in my course on Psychological Design and Statistics, Jeff proceeded through the materials so rapidly that he and I soon agreed he would become more of a teaching assistant than a student. He quickly learned that to teach something one must really understand it. *Deafness, Deprivation, and IQ* is the work of a researcher, a scholar, and a teacher.

I. KING JORDAN

President
Gallaudet University
Washington, D.C.

Preface

I can think of no psychological issue that has generated more controversy than the effect of nature and nurture on the development of human intelligence. The relative contributions of genetics (nature) and environment (nurture) to the differences in IQ found among ethnic, racial, and gender groups is hotly debated. This debate has been carried forward with more passion than precision; with more conviction than caution. Even careful scholarly research (e.g., Flynn, 1986; cf. Jensen, 1969, 1980) has been acclaimed or attacked for the popularity or unpopularity of its conclusions rather than its scientific merit. The fuel that fires this controversy is a volatile mix of strongly held convictions about the way things ought to be and a host of contrary facts. In an egalitarian society, we want all groups to be equal not only with respect to rights and opportunities, but also with respect to outcomes. It offends our sensibilities that some groups, particularly those which have been historical victims of discrimination, do not perform as well as more privileged groups on tests of intelligence and aptitude. It is especially painful to consider that these differences might be more strongly influenced by differences in genetics than by differences in environment. For these and other reasons, the research on the causes of between-group differences in intelligence is emotional, often unpleasant, and voluminous.

In contrast to the fame (infamy?) of nature–nurture research, the psychological study of deafness remains obscure. The few scientists who have attempted to link the study of deafness with larger psychological issues (e.g., Rudolph Pintner, Hans Furth, McKay Vernon, Oliver Sacks, Ursula Bellugi, and Edward Klima) stand in rare company. As a consequence, most psychologists know little of nor understand the psychological significance of research on deaf people.

This book is an attempt to bridge the prominent subject of group differences with the obscure subject of deafness. This bridge is an important link between two fields of investigation that were previously unrelated, yet have so much in common. What constitutes environmental deprivation, and the impact of environmental deprivation on intelligence, has been vigorously studied by scholars interested in the nature–nurture debate, and by scholars interested in deafness. Sadly, these investigations have coexisted in apparent isolation from each other. My purpose in writing this book is to build a bridge between these two lines of inquiry, so that each can learn from the other.

My effort to build such a bridge reflects my own journey into the fields of deafness and psychology. I spent my junior undergraduate year as an "exchange student" at Gallaudet University (then Gallaudet College). During that time, I met a young assistant professor of psychology, Dr. I. King Jordan, who inspired me to change my major and pursue a career in psychology. (Dr. Jordan is now president of Gallaudet University, and the first deaf president in Gallaudet's distinguished history.) Later, I returned to Gallaudet for graduate training in school psychology. After graduating from Gallaudet, I began working as a school psychologist at the California School for the Deaf in Fremont, California.

My interest in deafness was fully developed when I met Dr. Arthur Jensen at the University of California. I entered Berkeley in pursuit of my doctorate in school psychology, and began taking courses with Professor Jensen in part because I wanted so desperately to show him the error of his ways. I had been led to believe that the issue of between-group differences in intelligence had been irrevocably decided in favor of egalitarians, and only dogmatists (or worse) still clung to the antiquated belief that some racial and ethnic groups had lower IQ distributions than other groups.

Although my efforts to dispute Dr. Jensen had little impact on his views, they had a profound effect on mine. In my struggle to understand the nature and causes of between-group differences in intelligence, I reached for research on deafness as a comparison group. As I argue in this book, deaf people suffer profound deprivation as a result of their hearing loss. I was sure that the study of intelligence in deaf people would illustrate the ways in which environmental deprivation caused impoverished intelligence and consequent low IQs. Certain as I was to find this conclusion, I reasoned that I could then proceed to show how environment, not genetics, caused lower IQs among disadvantaged, deprived groups. Sadly, my efforts culminated in a trauma well known to scientific history, namely, my perfectly good theory was ruined by my data. As I show in this book, the issue is far more complicated, and leads to a less comfortable outcome than the one which I anticipated when I began my work.

My hope is that this book will succeed in opening dialogue between previously isolated interests. I do not pretend that the book represents the only, best, or most definitive conclusions to be drawn by linking research on deafness with nature–nurture research in intelligence. I have no doubts that some will object to my conclusions; I, too, did not part lightly with my dearly held beliefs. More important, I hope others will critique my methods and elucidate ways in which these disparate fields of inquiry should, and should not, be linked. If this book prompts those interested in nature–nurture issues to consider a broader range of data, or encourages those interested in deafness to frame their work in terms of larger issues in psychology, it will be a success.

There are many who have contributed to the development of this book. The efforts of Cecil Reynolds and Eliot Werner, who stayed with me through substantial revisions and significant delays, are appreciated. Without my parents, who taught me that honesty is more important than conformity, I would never have found the persistence needed to finish the book. The influence of my teachers, especially Professors Jordan and Jensen, is evident throughout. Finally, I want to acknowledge Jill Serota Braden, my editor, friend, and wife, and my children, Rachel and Daniel, without whose love and support my work would not have been possible.

Contents

1

Deafness as a Natural Experiment

Deafness is a unique experiment of nature. Through the accident of hearing loss, deaf people grow up in a world deprived of sound and speech. Most deaf children are born into a world in which their parents, siblings, relatives, and neighbors converse, argue, joke, and learn in the inaccessible medium of sound. Consequently, deaf children must make their way in the world with little exposure to and limited mastery of language.

The implications of deafness as an unfortunate accident but potentially valuable natural experiment have been developed in two stages. The first stage is philosophical. Historically, philosophers have perceived deafness in terms of its implications for the nature of thought and the definition of reason. The second stage is psychological. Psychologists built on the philosophical perspective by adding the discipline and technology of science to the study of deafness. Each of these perspectives is important to understanding deafness as a natural experiment condition.

Philosophical Perspective

The Relationship between Thought and Language

Language acquisition has been the hallmark of intelligence since the birth of philosophy. Socrates proposed that language and reason are inextricably linked. In fact, Socrates and his followers held that *language*, the set of symbols by which people communicated their ideas, and *reason*, the act of rational thought, were one and the same. Although Socrates and Plato, and later Aristotle, defined Western thought as the distinction of form and content, none of the ancients applied this distinction to separate language from reason (i.e., intelligence). The notion that language and reason were one and the same continued, despite the fact that the works of Plato and Aristotle mention deaf people as a class, and so they were known to these philosophers.

The failure to separate language from reason spawned a number of assumptions that shaped views of the human condition, and views of deafness. Religious, legal, and social perspectives of humanity have been shaped by the juxtaposition of language and the intellect. Christianity embraced the dualistic separation of the mind from the body, and held that the exercise of faith was the ultimate act of the intellect. This meant that salvation was possible only for those who could reason, which was demonstrated solely by their ability to speak. Legally, the possession of property was usually restricted to those with sufficient intellect to understand how to dispose of and use the property. The test of intellect most often employed, and which in some places remains, was the ability of the owner to speak. Socially, those who did not acquire language not only were shut off from normal channels of social intercourse, but were also an embarrassment to families, who often concluded the affliction was a punishment for past sins.

These perspectives are best expressed in the cliché "deaf and dumb," which is derived from the Latin phrase connoting the inability to hear and the inability to reason, or speak. It is not surprising that early laws and social customs made no distinction between deaf people and mentally retarded people. It is singularly unfortunate that such confusion has continued well into the twentieth century, and is even found in current psychological practice (Sullivan & Vernon, 1979; Vernon & Brown, 1964).

Sign language has been known to exist for more than 1,000 years. The first permanent records of signs date to the tenth century c.e. (Siger, 1968). These records commonly show positions of the hand to express letters of the alphabet, although some records also illustrate gestures signifying whole words or units of expression (i.e., signs). These historical data come primarily from the archives of the Catholic Church. There is no record that the clergy appreciated the irony of recording the signs and gestures of a fully formed language in their efforts to teach deaf people Latin, which the clergy felt would provide deaf people the vehicle for reason and salvation. Their efforts were directed toward making pupils recite the creed and commandments of the Church in Latin. It was widely believed that the language of Latin has unique properties for expressing ideas and disciplining rational inquiry, as embodied in the concept of formal discipline. The rejection of formal discipline (i.e., the belief that instruction of Latin improves the general quality, efficiency, and logical character of reasoning in other academic disciplines) is one of the first contributions of educational psychology. However, until the early part of the twentieth century, Latin was believed to be a unique medium for the expression and development of reason, made all the more important by its status as the official language of the Church. Given this context, it is not surprising that clergy failed to recognize sign language as a viable, self-contained language that reflected intellectual activity.

Although the treatment and prevailing understanding of deafness changed little during the first 1,600 years of the common era, records suggest isolated efforts to serve and understand deaf people. In the third century, Alexander of Aphrodisius proposed that deaf people did not speak because they did not hear (and therefore could not imitate and monitor voices). This proposal contradicted the popular belief that deaf people had a permanent disability of the speech mechanism. His insight did not appreciably affect the use of the term deaf and dumb, but it did predate "modern" science in noting that deafness did not carry with it defects of the larynx or other speech organs. The Venerable Bede, writing in 691 C.E., noted that Bishop John of York taught a deaf man to speak. This was regarded as a miracle, again because of the assumption that such speech could lead to salvation.

However, René Descartes was the first philosopher to challenge the conventional wisdom that language and the rational intellect were inextricably one. Descartes recognized that language must be learned, but it was essential to his rationalist position that the process of thought, or rationality, was innate. Descartes came to the conclusion that language was a consequence, not the condition, of rational thought. This distinction allowed for the possibility that deaf people, despite their inability to speak, could possess a rational intellect. In fact, deaf people must possess the ability to think rationally independent of language in order to demonstrate the innate rationality of humans.

It is no accident that Descartes was the first to develop and cite deafness as a natural experiment. To the best of my knowledge, he is the first person to recognize and apply the natural experiment created by deafness for the purpose of examining the relationship between thought and language. Specifically, Descartes argued that deaf people spontaneously created and used signs and gestures to communicate with each other, even though they were never taught such a language system. He went on to note that gorillas, chimpanzees, and other animals in the Paris zoo who could be thought to have the physical ability to produce signs did not do so, nor did they acquire speech (thus presaging the work of Gardner and Gardner [1969] by about 300 years). He concluded that deaf people's spontaneous development and use of a sign system showed their innate ability to think, reason, and develop abstract thoughts even though they could not hear or use spoken language. Despite the power of this insight, few students of philosophy noted or particularly appreciated Descartes's use of deafness as a natural experiment condition.

Efforts to Serve Deaf People

Formal instruction of deaf people in signs and speech predates and continues beyond Descartes's insights. In Spain, Pedro Ponce de León reputedly taught deaf children to speak Spanish, and inculcated a knowledge of other subjects as well. Ponce de León's work during the sixteenth century was spurred by the desires of a Spanish nobleman to have his deaf son inherit the family estate. Laws governing transfer of property specified that the inheritor must be able to speak (i.e., to reason). In France, Charles Michel, the Abbé de L'Epée, taught deaf children through the use of "natural signs." L'Epée is often referred to as the "Father of Deaf Education" because he was the first individual to be clearly identified with attempts to teach deaf people through the combined application of speech and signs. There is no evidence to suggest that L'Epée was aware of Descartes' references to deafness, although they shared the presumption that deaf people could reason via a medium other than speech. Instead, L'Epée's work was based largely on a clinical appreciation that deaf children appeared to be smarter, more alert, and otherwise different from children who would now be considered mentally retarded. On the basis of these observations, L'Epée independently embarked on the formal process of educating deaf children to speak, sign, and write. Meanwhile, in Germany, Samuel Heinicke founded the first public school to teach deaf children. Heinicke's methods stressed speech, also known as the oral method of instruction.

The early history of deaf education (as educators of deaf children refer to their specialty) reflects philosophical imperatives to define the nature of humanity meeting sporadically with the clinical imperative to serve deaf people. These meetings represent two distinct approaches to the study of deafness. Philosophically, deafness is studied as an abnormality that may prove or disprove a philosophical position. Clinically, deafness is studied out of a desire to serve deaf people without concern for philosophical questions.

The current status of deaf education is similarly characterized by a clash between philosophical and clinical approaches to deafness. The primary force behind deaf education is the clinical mandate to serve deaf children, and the mandate and its methods come primarily from contact with deaf people. The impetus to educate deaf children often adapts and reflects contemporary philosophy of education, but these components of the broad philosophical context are often incorporated into deaf education in a sporadic, reactive fashion. In much the same way that Ponce de León, L'Epée, and others forged ahead with little awareness of the broader philosophical perspective of their time, deaf educators are often moved to serve deaf people with little knowledge but great desire. Conversely, philosophers (and later, scientists) are often motivated to study deafness in the service of inquiry, yet they often do so with little appreciation of the complex social and psychological aspects of deafness known to clinicians who serve the deaf community.

Scientific Perspective

The work of Diderot and other rationalist philosophers extended the philosophical perspective of deafness into the realm of scientific inquiry. Diderot's (1875) work, which consisted primarily of obtaining deaf adult's responses to various questions about the nature of religious themes and ideas, extended the introspective methods of philosophy by applying methods of data collection emerging from the new science of psychology. From a clinical perspective, Greenberger's (1889) work is probably the first published use of a psychological "test" to assist in selection and classification of deaf pupils within a residential school setting. These philosophical–scientific approaches to deafness remained largely independent of the clinical imperative to serve deaf people.

The study of deafness might have remained qualitative and introspective in its direction were it not for the introduction of intelligence tests in the early twentieth century by Alfred Binet. A French psychologist, Binet was commissioned to develop a way to discriminate those children who would benefit from formal instruction from those who would be better served by learning a trade or skill. Binet altered the scientific approach to the measurement of individual differences from Galton's psychophysical laboratory (aka "brass instruments psychology") to the measurement of intelligence through a collection of items or problems. The ability to pass these items was known to vary as a function of age.

Binet's approach to testing intelligence quickly became popular, and is still the model used by most contemporary intelligence tests. However, it is important to note that the scientific approach to testing intelligence had its origin in the educational effort to serve children. Binet's approach to measuring intelligence is the method and the foil for the ways in which intelligence has been and is currently studied. Binet's approach is known as *idiographic*, emphasizing the individual differences within a class or category. In the study of intelligence, the idiographic approach measures differences in intelligence within the class of humans. The idiographic approach is the foil for the *nomothetic* approach, which emphasizes the universal characteristics shared by all members of the class. The nomothetic approach measures the characteristics that all humans share, or the "essence" of intelligent behavior in people. The nomothetic approach used introspective, problem-solving methods to study the growth and development of cognition and reason, whereas the idiographic approach led to the development of intelligence tests, whereby individuals may be ranked relative to others with regard to their intellectual abilities.

Each of these methods has been applied to the study of intelligence in deaf children. The nomothetic approach was carried forward in Europe by German and French psychologists. German psychologists were influenced by the neuropsychological work of Broca and others, who first proposed that deafness might lead to neurological abnormalities akin to aphasia. They employed methods such as sorting and classification tasks, whereby subjects would be asked to group objects on the basis of color, shape, function, or some other characteristic. Hofler (1927) applied a sorting task developed by Weigl to the study of deaf children, and concluded that deaf children had severely limited cognitive flexibility. Oleron (1953), and others who were interested in defining the impact that deafness had on thinking and reasoning abilities, extended Hofler's work. Studies of abnormal individuals, such as deaf people, are critical to distilling the nature of intelligence from a nomothetic perspective.

MacMillan and Bruner (1906) were the first psychologists to systematically employ an idiographic approach to the study of deaf people's psychological abilities. They used psychophysical tests such as sensitivity for determining weights, judging size from touch, simple memory tests, and the like. However, Pintner was the first psychologist to apply intelligence tests to the study of deaf people's intelligence. Pintner used Binet's intelligence test to measure deaf children's intelligence (Pintner & Paterson, 1915a). His work, and the work of his colleagues and students at Ohio State University (and later, the Teacher's College of Columbia University in New York), began the formal, systematic measurement of the intellective abilities of deaf people. The primary focus of this work was the application of the idiographic approach to the education of deaf children. For example, Pintner and his students addressed questions such as "How does the intelligence of children in residential schools compare to children in day programs?" Although intellectual tests were valuable from an applied research perspective for practical questions related to deaf education, Pintner was also concerned with the effects of deafness on the development of intelligence. The combination of the clinical imperative to serve deaf people and the idiographic study of intelligence using deaf children as a natural experiment condition is first expressed in Pintner's work, although the blend of these interests continues to the present day in research on deaf people.

Nomothetic and idiographic studies of deafness as a natural experiment assume that a capricious act of nature, namely, deafness, creates a condition whereby language exposure and auditory stimulation are severely limited. The unfortunate fact that individuals were deafened at or shortly after birth creates an experimental condition, in which deaf people could be thought of as subjects who are denied language and auditory stimulation. In contrast, their normal-hearing peers constitute a "control" group, or those who receive normal exposure to language and auditory input. Thus, comparisons between deaf and normal-hearing people illustrate the effects of the "treatment" of deafness on intelligence.

Early researchers of deafness as a natural experiment made a number of assumptions with regard to the "treatment" imposed by deafness. The first assumption made in deafness as a natural experiment was that deaf children fail to acquire language as a result of their deafness. Because they cannot hear the speech used by their parents, siblings, and others in their world, children do not acquire language in the same way that their normal-hearing peers acquire and use language. This assumption was supported by research and clinical experience showing that 4-year-old deaf children have vocabularies of less than 100 words (Vernon, 1967c). In contrast, normal-hearing children of the same age were shown to have vocabularies of 2,000–5,000 words and, more importantly, a fundamental grasp of pragmatic, syntactic, and semantic language skills that eluded deaf children. These observations led researchers to conclude that deaf children could be considered to have no functional language. As Vernon states (1967c, p. 327), "deaf children offer a suitable experimental group for a study in which language is the independent variable."

Auditory deprivation was also proposed as part of the "treatment" associated with deafness. In particular, Myklebust (1964) and his colleagues proposed that the lack of auditory stimulation qualitatively shifted the organization of the intellect within an individual. In other words, because deaf people do not have the ability to receive auditory information, the information-processing structures that they develop are shifted to accommodate to their input channels. Myklebust characterized this structural reorganization of intelligence as an "organismic shift," representing an intraorganismic structural change. Thus, the scientific approach to deafness as a natural experiment characterized the treatment imposed by deafness in terms of deprivation, and in terms of organic alterations in intellectual structure due to auditory deprivation.

It is critical to the understanding of deafness as a natural experiment to recognize that many factors are believed to be independent of deafness. Essentially, it is assumed that other factors associated with intelligence (e.g., genetics, socioeconomic status, parent–child interaction patterns) are the same for deaf and hearing children. Additionally, it is assumed that the families in which deaf children are raised do not use a means of communication accessible to the deaf child. These assumptions are critical to the argument that deafness constitutes a treatment in which auditory deprivation and language exposure are the variables manipulated by deafness. Concomitant factors associated with deafness are minimized or ignored altogether in investigations of intelligence among deaf people. Therefore, deafness is considered to be an accidental manipulation of language exposure and auditory deprivation, and it is not considered to confound other factors that might be important to the development of intelligence. It has been assumed that language and audition are the only critical factors associated with deafness for most of the twentieth century, but it will be shown that this assumption is no longer tenable.

Outcomes of the Natural Experiment

There are at least two ways in which to use the outcomes of the natural experiment of deafness (i.e., the cognitive performance of deaf people) to enhance knowledge of intelligence. The first application, which is the most common in the literature, is to interpret deaf people's cognitive performance as a reflection of the link between intelligence and language. The second application is to examine the IQs of deaf people in the context of between-group differences in IQ. A brief overview of each of these approaches is provided in the following sections.

Implications for Understanding Language and Intelligence

What are the effects of deafness on the development of intelligence? There is no single answer to this question, because different methods yield different results. Early researchers were initially divided on the nature of the question regarding intellectual development (i.e., nomothetic vs. idiographic approaches), and they quickly discovered that markedly different outcomes were achieved between methods that rested primarily on verbal means of investigation versus those methods that employed primarily nonverbal means of investigation. Therefore, verbal and nonverbal approaches offer somewhat different conclusions regarding the effects of deafness on the development of intelligence, as do nomothetic and idiographic approaches.

Nomothetic investigations using classification problems, reasoning tests, and Piagetian tasks report that deafness delays, but does not severely alter, cognitive development in children. Speculation that deafness leads to abnormal or clinically deviant behavior was rejected. Instead, researchers felt that deaf children's performance on classification and reasoning tasks was representative of children younger in age. Deficits in the intellectual flexibility and reasoning capacity of deaf people are noted throughout the nomothetic literature (e.g., Oleron, 1953). However, when tasks are developed to minimize the role of language in the comprehension and completion of the task, deaf children's performance appears to be comparable to normal-hearing children from relatively low-stimulation environments (Furth, 1966). The often-noted delay in the development of Piagetian skills may disappear altogether as deaf people reach adulthood (Stevens & Carlson, 1978; Youniss, 1974). Therefore, results from the nomothetic approach show that deafness affects the performance of intellectual tasks that demand the comprehension of language to understand the task, or demand the use of language to complete the task. When language demands are minimized, but cognitive demands remain stable, deaf people appear to be somewhat delayed but generally similar to their normal-hearing peers.

A similar conclusion is put forth by those using idiographic methods of research. On verbal tests of intelligence, deaf children perform well below their normal-hearing peers (Pintner, Eisenson, & Stanton, 1946). The early application of the predominately verbal Binet scale (Pintner & Paterson, 1915a) denoted severe deficits in intellectual performance relative to normal-hearing children. Measures of academic achievement also show severe deficits in deaf people, particularly for language-related tests (e.g., reading comprehension). In contrast, performance on nonverbal tests of intelligence placed deaf people within the average to low-average range relative to normal-hearing people (Myklebust, 1964; Pintner, et al., 1946; Vernon, 1967c). Furthermore, the overlap between deaf people and normal-hearing people in terms of their nonverbal IQ distributions suggested they are much more similar than they are different with regard to intelligence measured via nonverbal tests.

The similarity of the findings of the nomothetic and idiographic approaches is striking. Essentially, both approaches agree that deafness severely inhibits the development of intellectual skills that depend on language for the comprehension or solution of a task. The approaches also agree that deaf and normal-hearing people perform similarly when the language demands, but not the intellectual demands, of the tasks are reduced. The results of the natural experiment condition generated a consensus among researchers in the field of deafness that intellectual capacity is largely unaffected by deafness; language exposure and auditory deprivation have little effect on intelligence. The lower performance of deaf people on verbal tasks was felt to be a result of confounding the language impairments of deaf people with the cognitive demands of the task. The adcquate performance of deaf people on cognitively complex, but language-reduced, tasks support the hypothesis that intellectual capacity is essentially unaffected by linguistic and auditory factors. This consensus is most forcefully presented in the three conclusions that Vernon (1967c, p. 331) reached after an extensive review of intelligence research with deaf people:

1. *There is no functional relationship between verbal language and cognition or thought process.*
2. *Verbal language is not the mediating symbol system of thought. . . .*
3. *There is no relationship between concept formation and level of verbal language development* (author's italics).

Implications for IQ Differences between Groups

It is remarkable that the results of deafness as a natural experiment in intelligence have not been applied to understanding differences in intelligence between racial or ethnic groups. The nature and causes of between-group differences in intelligence for racial or ethnic groups have been hotly debated in the professional and lay press. Differences are often attributed to environment, genetics, or gene-environment interactions. Unfortunately, the isolation of genetic, environmental, and interaction factors is complicated by the confounding of these factors within society (e.g., North American blacks differ from whites in socioeconomic status, dialect, culture, history, and other characteristics in addition to race). In a sense, racial and ethnic identity provide experimental "treatments" in which genetic and environmental factors are confounded. The cumulative effect of these factors produces between-group differences in intelligence.

Much has been written about the nature and causes of differences between racial and ethnic groups on tests of intelligence. A thorough review of the literature is beyond the scope of this chapter. However, a cursory review of research describing the performance of North American blacks and whites (the two most-studied groups in the literature) on tests of intelligence shows that blacks score consistently below whites (e.g., Jensen, 1969, 1980; Loehlin, Lindzey, & Spuhler, 1975). The magnitude of the between-group difference for whites and blacks on tests of intelligence is typically 0.75–1.0 standard deviation units. In other words, the mean for blacks is approximately one standard deviation below the mean for whites on most tests of intelligence. Although blacks score lower than whites on tests of intelligence, there is no consensus regarding the causes of this difference.

Studies of deaf children as a natural experiment in intelligence may shed light on some of the possible causes and explanations of black–white differences in IQ. For example, IQ test critics (e.g., Mercer, 1979; Williams, 1974) contend that there is no meaningful distinction between tests of intelligence and tests of achievement. The high correlation between verbal and nonverbal intelligence tests, and the similarity of black–white differences on verbal and nonverbal intelligence tests, is used to support the contention of IQ test critics that intelligence tests are essentially tests of cultural experiences. These critics claim that differences between blacks and whites can largely be attributed to the culture-loading of IQ test items. Because such items are drawn from predominately white culture, blacks score lower on those items than do whites.

The argument put forth by these critics may be tested by examining the IQs of deaf people. Deaf people, who are certainly denied access to the verbal item content found in verbal IQ tests, score below normal-hearing white and black groups. This outcome is compatible with the argument that between-group differences in IQ are due to the culture-loading of items. However, as will be shown in detail in Chapter 3, deaf people score well above blacks, and very close to whites, on nonverbal IQ tests. The position that there is no meaningful distinction between verbal and nonverbal IQ tests is incompatible with the substantial difference in IQ found when verbal and nonverbal tests are applied to deaf people.

This is but one example of the possible applications of the study of intelligence among deaf people to the understanding of differences in IQ between racial groups. Results from a natural experiment, in which environmental factors (e.g., language exposure) occur independent of race and ethnicity, could allow isolation of heretofore confounded variables. Deafness as a natural experiment offers the possibility of isolating certain environmental effects independent of race and ethnicity and, conversely, examining the possible effects of race across drastic changes in environment.

Problems with Natural Experiment Conclusions

Despite the promise of deafness as a natural experiment independent of race, and the consistency of IQ research results, the conclusions reached from studies of intelligence have contained flaws in reasoning and precision. These flaws stem from (1) simplistic assumptions regarding the definition of deafness as an experiment condition and (2) the narrative methods historically used to synthesize research results, which have been superceded by recent developments in meta-analytic techniques.

Simplistic Assumptions Regarding Deafness

A critical assumption in the use of deaf people as a natural experiment condition in language exposure and auditory deprivation is that other factors known to affect intelligence are independent of deafness. In other words, it must be assumed that deaf people are a random sample who have accidentally been inducted into the experimental treatment imposed by deafness. Recent research (e.g., Braden, 1989b) has shown that deafness confounds many factors believed to affect intelligence. These factors include the prevalence of medical trauma and associated, often sub-rosa handicaps, genetic endowment, child-rearing experiences, family dynamics, proximal social interactions, and distal social interactions. Furthermore, the central assumption of deafness as a "no language" condition is unwarranted in view of recent research showing deaf people's acquisition and use of nonstandard, non-English language in a variety of receptive and expressive modes. Therefore, the popular characterization of deafness as a natural experiment in language exposure and auditory deprivation must be rejected in favor of a characterization that considers the concomitant conditions associated with deafness.

Problems of Analysis and Synthesis

The second problem with conclusions derived from the natural experiment of deafness relates to the methods used to collect and synthesize research. Previous reviews of research (e.g., Myklebust, 1964; Pintner et al., 1946; Vernon, 1967c) have relied on qualitative, descriptive methods for combining results of disparate studies. Although such qualitative comparisons often provide valuable insights into the nature of the findings, new methods for the identification and synthesis of research have been proposed in the last decade (e.g., Wolf, 1986). These methods offer quantitative tools to combine results across studies and test specific hypotheses by using the results of multiple studies. Likewise, these methods have found previously unrecognized problems with the practice of reviewing research (e.g., the "file drawer problem," in which exclusive use of published results may skew the estimated impact of a given treatment or condition). Reanalysis and synthesis of the literature using meta-analytic techniques could alter some of the conclusions reached by previous reviews of the study of intelligence among deaf people, and is certainly a more powerful approach to the topic than has previously appeared in the literature.

Organization and Overview of the Remaining Chapters

Despite problems with previous research, the study of intelligence among deaf people is unique in its potential to offer valuable insight into the nature of intelligence, intellectual development, and the causes of between-group differences in intelligence. However, the promises offered by studies of intelligence among deaf people must be critically evaluated against the problems inherent in such research. Therefore, Chapter 2 includes a reanalysis of the "treatment" induced by deafness as a natural experiment. Particular attention is given to confounds among variables that are known to affect the development of intelligence. The natural experiment condition of deafness is revised and reframed in Chapter 2 as a natural experiment in which the conditions associated with deafness share many, but not all, of the conditions experienced by disadvantaged minority groups. The assumption that deafness is a condition in which language exposure and auditory deprivation are randomly manipulated is shown to be a simplistic, erroneous view of deafness.

The results of studies investigating intelligence among deaf people are combined and reported in Chapter 3. Quantitative summary of results as well as qualitative compilations are provided to define the results of deafness as a natural experiment condition. Study and subject characteristics are examined to identify experimental factors and subject characteristics that affect outcomes. Whenever possible, these results are presented according to the qualitative and quantitative practices of meta-analysis, to allow for precise estimation of outcomes and rigorous tests of hypotheses regarding variations in results.

Methodological problems and issues associated with the measurement of intelligence among deaf people are considered in Chapter 4. Validity, reliability, test bias, and procedural issues are reviewed to identify potential problems of interpretation associated with the synthesis of outcomes reported in Chapter 3. The primary focus of the chapter is to answer the question "Are the results from studies of deaf people valid for the purpose of understanding between-group differences in IQ?"

In Chapter 5, the conditions and results of deafness as a natural experiment are applied to some popular theories accounting for between-group differences in intelligence. Essentially, factors that may account for differences in IQ between racial and ethnic groups should also account for differences between deaf and normal-hearing groups, to the extent that factors associated with minority groups are also associated with deafness. Chapter 5 therefore explores the implications that studies of deaf people's intelligence have for theories of between-group differences in IQ. Conclusions regarding deafness as a natural experiment condition, and the value such research has for studies of between-group differences in IQ, are presented in Chapter 6.

2

Deafness as a Natural Experiment—Revisited

The compelling appeal of deafness as a natural experiment in language deprivation must be tempered with recent research showing that much more than language is affected by deafness. When deaf children are born to normal-hearing parents, they are deprived of more than language. Although deafness is more complex than philosophers and psychologists have described it, it is still appealing as a natural experiment. In fact, the complexity of factors associated with deafness makes it a richer, more fertile ground for research than a simple experiment in language deprivation.

There are six factors associated with deafness that are of interest to scholars who want to explore environmental effects on intelligence. These factors are listed in Table 2.1. The ways in which each is associated with deafness are described in the rest of this chapter. A brief overview of key concepts accompanies the discussion for those unfamiliar with deafness.

Auditory Deprivation and Hearing Loss

The term *deafness* implies a complete lack of hearing. Although some individuals may, in fact, have no auditory sensation, most deaf individuals have some residual hearing. The degree of hearing associated with people who describe themselves as deaf may vary from no sensation except pain in the ears, which occurs when sounds exceed 110 dB, to essentially normal auditory sensitivity coupled with an inability to discriminate foreground from background noise. The heterogeneous nature of deafness is obscured by terms such as "deafness," or

TABLE 2.1. Conditions in Deafness as a Natural Experiment

Condition	Description
Auditory deprivation	Congenital deafness deprives the child of consistent, coherent auditory stimulation.
Language exposure	Children of hearing parents cannot gain access to the native language of the family during critical language formation years. Language following initiation of signs is nonstandard, inconsistent, and infrequent.
Medical or organic trauma	Medical conditions associated with deafness include additional physical, sensory, and neurological traumata.
Genetic endowment	Major gene syndromes and chromosomal anomalies are often associated with physical and mental disabilities; other genetic effects are unknown.
Family dynamics	Deaf children of hearing parents frequently experience dysfunctional parent–child and family interactions.
Social interactions	Deaf children experience rejection and isolation from normal hearing peers in school and social settings.

worse, references to deaf people in a collective fashion: namely, "the deaf."[1] These terms obscure diverse abilities in auditory perception as well as marked individual differences (such as intelligence) among deaf people.

Definition of Hearing Loss

Hearing loss is described by three characteristics: (1) the organic nature or etiology of the hearing loss, (2) the severity of the hearing loss, and (3) the onset of the hearing loss. Auditory impairment is defined by the application of all three of these factors to a particular individual. Each factor is necessary, but none is sufficient, to describe the nature and extent of hearing loss.

Organic Description

The proximal organic cause of a hearing impairment is interference in the transfer of sound waves to the temporal lobe. There are essentially two points at which problems can occur in the transformation of sound waves to neural impulses. The first point is the conduction of sound waves via the external and middle ear. The passage of sound waves down the external auditory canal, and the agitation of the eardrum and associated bones, conducts the movement of sound

---

[1] I am indebted to Dr. I. King Jordan, President of Galluadet University, for pointing this out to me.

waves in air to a point in the inner ear (the oval window). Problems with the apparatus for conducting sound, such as a blockage of the auditory canal, rupture of the eardrum, or calcification of the bones in the middle ear, result in distortion and decreased sensitivity to sound. Most people have experienced a temporary hearing loss of this type when they have a virus or cold. Fluid in the middle ear builds up as a result of the virus, resulting in difficulty hearing and, in some cases, a sense of disequilibrium. Hearing impairments caused by obstructions in motion transfer are termed "conductive" impairments, and are usually treatable by medical intervention.

The second point at which hearing may be impaired is the transformation of motion to neural impulses. This type of hearing impairment is termed a *sensorineural* impairment. Sensorineural impairments may occur in the cochlea (the organ that transforms impulses in the fluid of the inner ear to electrical, or neural, impulses) or the auditory nerve, which connects the cochlea to the brain. Impairments of this type are generally resistant to intervention, although cochlear implants are being conducted on a limited, experimental basis with selected patients. At present, cochlear implants offer limited improvements for people who become deaf later in life. The technology of cochlear implants will undoubtedly improve, but at present, the primary approach to minimizing sensorineural impairments is to manipulate the input signal (i.e., amplify sound going into the ear to achieve greater response).

These two classifications of organic causes of hearing loss, conductive and sensorineural, are complemented by a third category of hearing impairment called "mixed," literally meaning a mix of conductive and sensorineural impairments. Mixed impairments are typically treated as co-occurring conductive and sensorineural losses, but the presence of a conductive loss typically complicates remediation of the sensorineural impairment via amplification. This is because the conductive component of the loss may vary substantially from one day to the next (e.g., variable fluid buildup in the middle ear), making it extremely difficult to calibrate amplification to a comfortable and effective level.

The final aspect of an organic description of a hearing loss is the specification of whether impairment is unilateral or bilateral (i.e., is present in one or both ears). Therefore, the organic aspects of hearing impairment are described as conductive, sensorineural, or mixed types, and the scope of impairment is either unilateral or bilateral. These terms are presented in Table 2.2.

Severity

The severity of a hearing impairment is defined using two dimensions. The first dimension is frequency. Frequency determines the pitch or tone of the sound, and is measured in cycles per second (denoted by the unit of measure Hertz, or Hz). The second continuum of hearing impairment is the intensity, or loudness, of

TABLE 2.2. Organic Descriptors of Hearing Loss

Type of loss	Definition	Treatment
Conductive	Interference in the transfer of sound through the external auditory canal and/or middle ear.	Medication to control fluid buildup; surgery to remove or reduce blockage.
Sensorineural	Failure to successfully convert motion to neural impulse (cochlea) or conduct neural impulse to brain (auditory nerve).	Amplify incoming sound. Cochlear implant is experimental treatment in a few cases.
Mixed	Combination of conductive and sensorineural loss.	Treat conductive and sensorineural aspects separately (however, conductive loss often complicates amplification).
Unilateral	Loss occurs in only one ear.	
Bilateral	Loss occurs in both ears.	

the sound. Sound intensity is measured on a logarithmic scale denoted by decibels (or dB). Thus, hearing impairment is defined as the intensity needed for an individual to perceive sound at a specific frequency. Thresholds for hearing perception (i.e., the point at which an individual detects the presence of the tone approximately half the time it is present) are measured by repeatedly presenting a tone, while varying the intensity of the tone, until the threshold is identified. The results are charted on a two-dimensional matrix, with frequency displayed on the horizontal axis, and intensity shown down the vertical axis. The two-dimensional matrix is called an audiogram; a sample audiogram is shown in Figure 2.1.

Two features are important to note on the audiogram. The first is that there is a limited range of frequencies (500–2,000 Hz) associated with speech reception. This frequency range comprises the frequencies used to create speech, and so they are of primary concern in the diagnosis and remediation of hearing impairment. The second feature is the degree of sensitivity needed to perceive sounds in this range. Descriptive terms are attached to decibel ranges to provide a qualitative guide to what is normal speech perception. For example, a threshold between 0–20 dB is considered "average," in that most individuals will be able to perceive frequencies at intensities within this range. In contrast, individuals with a threshold above 90 dB have a profound hearing loss relative to the norm.

Several clinical measures of hearing impairment are also generated in an audiological exam. These measures include a pure tone average, speech detection threshold, and speech reception threshold. An individual's pure tone average (PTA) is the average of the decibel threshold ratings at 500, 1,000, and 2,000 Hz. In other words, a PTA of 70 dB means the average threshold of reception across the speech range is 70 dB, which suggests a severe hearing loss. The speech detection threshold (SDT) is the individual's threshold for speech perception. This

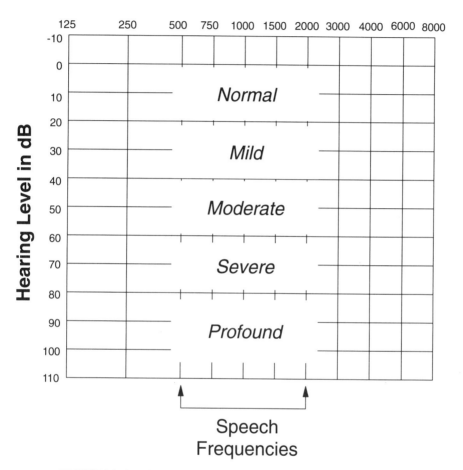

FIGURE 2.1. Sample audiogram and ranges for levels of hearing impairment.

value is usually similar to but not exactly the same as the PTA, because speech is simultaneously broadcast across many frequencies. Consequently, the SDT is often lower than the PTA. Finally, the speech reception threshold (SRT) is the intensity with which speech must be presented in order for the individual to comprehend it. The SRT differs from the SDT in that the SDT is merely the level at which an individual becomes aware that speech is present, whereas the SRT is the level at which speech is loud enough for the individual to understand it. Because of the constraints of the ear (which yields the sensation of pain to sounds nearing 120 dB), it is often impossible to establish SRTs for people with severe to profound hearing impairments (i.e., no amount of amplification results in adequate speech reception). These terms are presented in Table 2.3.

Onset

The final characteristic used to describe hearing impairments is the onset and prognosis of the hearing impairment. Hearing impairments may emerge at any time in an individual's life. Medically, a distinction is drawn between congenital and adventitious onset of hearing impairment. Psychologically, a distinction is drawn between prelingual and postlingual onset of hearing impairment. Because the point at which language emerges varies considerably among normal children, the point at which language is "acquired" cannot be accurately defined. It is therefore difficult to quantify the distinction between prelingual and postlingual onset. Some suggest that 2 years of age be considered the cutting point, because most children begin speaking in one-word utterances by this age. Others suggest 5 years as the age for separating prelingual from postlingual onset, because most children have acquired basic grammar, syntax, and coherent conversational skills by this age. Although it is psychologically relevant to identify the onset of a hearing impairment relative to language acquisition, there is no specific agreement regarding the dividing line between prelingual and postlingual onset.

TABLE 2.3. Terms Used to Describe the Severity of Hearing Impairment

Term	Definition
Normal	Hearing loss of 0–20 dB; normal ability to converse.
Mild	Hearing loss of 20–40 dB, with difficulty discriminating some sounds in normal conversation.
Moderate	Hearing loss of 40–60 dB, with substantial difficulty discriminating sounds in normal conversation.
Severe	Hearing loss of 60–80 dB, resulting in significant and consistent disruption in conversation. May be unable to converse outside significantly limited interchanges.
Profound	Hearing loss greater than 80 dB, resulting in extreme difficulty in conversation; unlikely to understand speech to a useful degree.
Pure tone average (PTA)	Average intensity (in dB) needed for a person to perceive sounds across frequencies associated with speech.
Speech detection threshold (SRT)	Intensity of speech (in dB) needed for a person to be aware that speech is present in the environment.
Speech reception threshold (SRT).	Intensity of speech (in dB) needed for a person to understand speech (may not be attainable for persons with severe and profound hearing losses).

Another problem created by the prelingual versus postlingual distinction is that onset is confounded with cause of hearing impairment. A child who becomes deaf at 4 years of age is likely to be deaf due to severe trauma (e.g., spinal meningitis, scarlet fever), whereas a child who is deaf at birth is likely to be deaf due to other causes (e.g., maternal rubella, genetics). Consequently, the distinction of onset of hearing loss into prelingual versus postlingual is not consistent among all researchers, and may also confound the cause of deafness with its onset.

The prognosis of the hearing impairment is also important in describing its developmental characteristics. Some impairments are chronic, with no change over time, whereas others may vary in a predictable or unpredictable manner. Hearing impairments that do not change over time are considered stable. A hearing impairment that deteriorates, or becomes worse, over time is a progressive hearing loss. A hearing loss that is erratic is an intermittent or variable hearing loss. Changes in hearing are usually a function of the etiology of the impairment. For example, a conductive loss due to otosclerosis is progressive, because it is associated with increased calcification and rigidity of the bones in the middle ear. Chronic ear infections often create variable hearing impairments. Factors associated with changes in hearing include genetics, specific medical conditions, and aging.

Definition of Deafness

Together, the dimensions of organic description, severity, and onset describe the physical parameters of deafness. For the purposes of this book deaf people are defined as individuals with (1) bilateral, mixed, or sensorineural hearing impairments that are (2) severe to profound (i.e., a PTA $\geq$ 60 dB) with high SDTs and SRTs, (3) prelingual onset, and stable and progressive prognosis (i.e., not improving or variable).

Justification of these criteria is in order. Organically, a hearing impairment that is unilateral has limited tangible effect on psychological development. People who have unilateral hearing impairments function much the same as those with normal bilateral hearing. Granted, a unilateral hearing loss is a major inconvenience, but it does not appreciably affect auditory performance from the perspective of developmental psychology. Although the specification of a mixed or sensorineural loss is arbitrary (i.e., a moderate conductive loss is just as problematic as a moderate sensorineural loss), the fact that most conductive losses are correctable via medical intervention or amplification argues against considering most individuals with conductive losses as "deaf."

The severity of the hearing loss included in this definition of deafness is consistent with ANSI (American National Standards Institute) standards, and is consistent with the psycholinguistic relevance of speech detection and comprehension. Most people with severe to profound bilateral losses experience substantial difficulty perceiving sounds and speech, even when equipped with devices to assist auditory perception. Finally, onset criteria include individuals who have not acquired language via oral/auditory means. When coupled with the criteria for severity and type of loss, the definition of deafness used in this book includes individuals who experience significant difficulty in acquiring, understanding, and producing spoken language.

Deaf versus Hard-of-Hearing

The definition of deafness may be compared and contrasted with the definition of hard-of-hearing. Hard-of-hearing people are individuals with (1) bilateral hearing impairments of any type that are (2) in the mild to moderate range (20–60 dB PTA) with moderate to high SDTs and SRTs, (3) prelingual onset, and stable and variable prognosis. The primary distinction between a person who is deaf and one who is hard-of-hearing is the degree to which auditory input is available and useful for the acquisition of speech. Hard-of-hearing people generally develop oral/auditory language skills, albeit with some difficulty, whereas deaf people generally rely to a large degree or entirely on visual means of communication.

Two factors complicate the distinction between deaf and hard-of-hearing. First, amplification of sound, such as with a hearing aid, can alter the impact of the auditory impairment. Some types of hearing losses are amenable to correction through amplification, and others are not. Generally, severity of loss affects the efficacy of amplification as an intervention, with severe to profound losses being resistant to successful correction. The reason for this is simple: as sound is amplified, it is distorted. Significant amplification can result in marked distortion of sound, so that input is perceptible, but garbled. Recent advances in technology now allow systematic amplification of specific frequency bands, which helps reduce garbled input, but the degree to which sound must be amplified for individuals with severe and profound hearing losses still results in distorted input. In many cases, input is so distorted that it annoys more than assists. Consequently, many individuals with severe to profound hearing impairments simply do not wear hearing aids. However, successful amplification can change an individual's receptive abilities, thus complicating the distinction between deaf and hard-of-hearing individuals.

The second factor that complicates discrimination of deaf and hard-of-hearing classifications is the clinical response to amplification. Some individuals with similar hearing losses and identical hearing aids will nonetheless respond differently to sounds and speech. Perhaps the most extreme example is found in the condition termed *auditory agnosia*, in which an individual has normal hearing, but is unable to understand auditory input. Such individuals cannot discriminate sounds or acquire speech. Other factors affect response to amplification, such as recruitment (i.e., a markedly limited range between sound perception threshold and the experience of discomfort), motivation to use a hearing aid, or ability to properly fit an aid to the ear in a comfortable, effective manner. These factors affect the degree to which an individual will profit from amplification, and consequently blur the distinction between deaf and hard-of-hearing.

Given all of the factors that complicate definitions of deafness, it is not surprising that many writers fail to explicitly define what they mean when they refer to deafness, the deaf, or otherwise describe hearing-impaired participants in psychological research. Many writers simply describe subjects' hearing impairment in terms of mean PTAs or median age of onset. These limited descriptions obscure potentially important variations in types of hearing loss, use of amplification, response to amplification, and other factors that could significantly affect individuals' responses to their hearing impairments.

Despite the complexity of defining deafness, there can be little doubt that severe to profound hearing impairments seriously and appreciably affect the ability of an individual to acquire oral/auditory language. Increasing severity of hearing impairment is associated with increased difficultly in language acquisition and use. Likewise, increased severity of hearing impairment is also associated with progressive inability to use nonlinguistic sound in a psychologically meaningful way (e.g., passive monitoring of the environment). On the one hand, the definition of deafness in terms of a bilateral, severe to profound, prelingual hearing loss obscures individual differences in the response to hearing impairment. On the other hand, the definition comprises individuals whose psychological development (e.g., language acquisition, psychosocial interactions) is significantly affected by their hearing impairment.

Lacunae of Hearing Loss and Deafness

When I. King Jordan, the first deaf president of Gallaudet University (the world's first institution of higher education founded specifically to serve deaf people), proclaimed "The only thing deaf people cannot do is hear," he was making a powerful political and social statement. Deaf people certainly have the rights and privileges granted to other members of society, and they must not be constrained by outmoded, paternalistic notions that they are "handicapped" and are to be pitied, not respected. However, is it entirely accurate to assume that the only problem associated with deafness is the inability to hear?

The answer to this question is apparently no. There are indeed other problems associated with deafness. Some of these problems are physical, and stem from a common etiology with deafness (e.g., spinal meningitis often damages other areas of the central nervous system in addition to auditory functioning). Others are psychosocial, resulting from the interaction of being deaf in a normal-hearing world. These related physical and psychosocial problems are the focus of other sections in this chapter. However, it is also possible that deafness, in and of itself, causes additional physical and psychological problems, including neural degeneration and vestibular dysfunction.

Hearing loss may lead to atrophy or degeneration in areas of the brain beyond the pathways conducting sound (Conrad, 1979). For example, cats with cochlear lesions experience degeneration of neural tissue, extending from the cochlea to the auditory lobe of the brain (Cowan, 1970). Early auditory deprivation leads to functional loss of hearing in rats (Batkin, Groth, Watson, & Ansperry, 1970) and atrophy of the auditory cortex (Stein & Schuckman, 1973). These deficits are not reversed when auditory perception is restored. These results concur with other data in suggesting that early auditory loss is associated with organic and functional losses in auditory-based behavior (Kyle, 1978). Because language and the act of thinking are typically described as vocal or subvocal processes, it is an open question whether the early auditory deprivation experienced by deaf and hard-of-hearing children leads to irreversible organic deficits associated with language and thinking (e.g., Conrad, 1979).

The theory that deafness leads to neural degeneration in humans is by no means proven. Although animal studies of auditory deprivation and malfunction suggest deaf people might demonstrate atrophy in the parts of the brain associated with audition (e.g., the temporal lobes), one cannot assume that what happens in animals will necessarily happen in humans. Of course, the most direct way to test the neural degeneration hypothesis is to replicate animal studies with humans (i.e., systematically deprive humans of auditory stimulation and then perform autopsies to determine whether the deprivation led to smaller, less developed temporal lobes). In addition to the problems of recruiting volunteers and getting such research approved by Human Subjects Committees, ethics pose a problem for this line of research. In the absence of an unusual case history (e.g., a child born with normal hearing raised in the absence of sound), it is unlikely that there will be a definitive answer to the question of whether the auditory deprivation imposed by deafness leads to degeneration or retarded development of neural tissue.

It is clear that deafness is often accompanied by vestibular orientation difficulties. The semicircular canals are fluid-filled tubes, inside of which are small cilia. Movement of the fluid past these cilia produce the sensations needed to establish vestibular orientation. One can be made aware of this function simply by spinning about for a few moments and then standing still and closing one's eyes. The sensation of movement, despite the fact one is standing still, attests to the motion of the fluid in the semicircular canals. Another example of the influence of the semicircular canals is seasickness, in which individuals experience nausea because their visual perception of no motion is at odds with the perception of motion generated by the semicircular canals.

The cilia in the semicircular canals can be reduced or destroyed by some of the causes of sensorineural hearing loss. For example, meningitis, scarlet fever, and adverse responses to the mycin family of drugs can damage both the cochlea and the cilia in the semicircular canals. This in turn creates vestibular orientation problems for some deaf people. Although most deaf people adapt to the lack of sensation from the semicircular canals through visual orientation, it is not uncommon for a deaf person to have severely impaired balance when visual information is limited (e.g., at night).

The psychological impact of vestibular orientation problems is not known. There are no published studies linking vestibular sensation to the development of intelligence, socialization, or other aspects of deaf people. This dearth of literature may not, however, be solely due to neglect. A deaf professor at Gallaudet University told me of an effort by a United States Navy research group to study the link between deafness and vestibular orientation, especially as it might relate to one's susceptibility to experience motion sickness. He said that about a dozen deaf people were flown to the Antarctic Sea during the Antarctic winter storm season, so that Navy researchers could observe their reaction to extreme conditions likely to elicit motion sickness. Apparently, the research was never completed, because the researchers were so sick they were quite incapacitated. This professor did tell me that the deaf volunteers had a great time sitting in the hold of the ship playing cards, although they were occasionally troubled by the cards sliding off the table when the ship passed through severe swells.

Summary of Auditory Deprivation and Hearing Loss

For the purposes of this book, deaf people are defined as those people whose hearing impairment is sufficiently severe, and occurred at such an age, that normal language acquisition via speech is severely or altogether impaired. This "functional" definition has its problems, but it emphasizes the psychological factors associated with hearing impairment. The functional definitions proposed for use in this book roughly correspond with the audiological parameters listed in Table 2.4.

Hard-of-hearing people are defined as those people whose hearing impairment is sufficiently severe, and occurred at such an age, that normal language acquisition is attenuated or slowed. However, the primary mode of communication for hard-of-hearing people is still oral/auditory. *Deafened* is a term that describes the auditory limitations associated with deaf people, but onset has been sufficiently postponed so that normal (oral/auditory) language has been acquired prior to the hearing loss. In contrast, "hearing-impaired" is a generic category referring to all individuals with hearing outside normal limits. Although there are shortcomings with these generalizations, and the match between these psychological terms and audiological criteria is not perfect, there is substantial consensus regarding the

TABLE 2.4. Functional Definitions of Hearing Impairment

Term	Definition
Deaf	Person with a prelingual, stable, severe to profound, bilateral hearing impairment that severely or completely impairs the acquisition of vocal/auditory language.
Hard-of-hearing	Person with a prelingual, stable, bilateral hearing impairment (usually mild to severe) that interferes with, but does not prevent, the acquisition of vocal/auditory language.
Deafened	Person whose hearing loss onset is postlingual, and who retains and relies on internalized vocal/auditory language.
Hearing–impaired	Person with any chronic hearing loss outside normal limits (i.e., mild or greater), regardless of severity, onset, etiology, or prognosis.

meanings and applications of these terms across researchers and time (e.g., Furth, 1966; Myklebust, 1964; Pintner et al., 1946; Schildroth & Karchmer, 1986; Vernon, 1967c).

Neurological sequelae of deafness (i.e., atrophy or degeneration in auditory centers of the brain) are suspected, but as yet unproven. It is known that some deaf people experience vestibular orientation problems, but there is no evidence to indicate that such problems have a meaningful impact on their psychological development.

Language Exposure

The raison d'être of deafness as a natural experiment has been the assumption that auditory impairment denies access to and acquisition of language in deaf people. This assumption is generally correct. Severe to profound hearing impairment inhibits or prevents the acquisition of language. Furthermore, more than 90% of deaf children in the Western hemisphere are born into families in which both parents have normal hearing (Conrad, 1979; Schildroth, 1986). Thus, deaf children grow up in homes where the primary means of communication is speech. Consequently, it is reasonable to argue that deafness is a natural experiment in which language exposure is severely limited or altogether excluded from the deaf child's environment.

However, language deprivation is not easily defined. It is not enough to conclude that deaf children are, or are not, exposed to language. Language exposure varies in many important respects, including:

(1) The degree to which deaf children are exposed to language.
(2) The modalities in which language is presented.

(3) The language that is presented to deaf children.

(4) The neurolinguistic aspects of nonstandard language exposure.

Each of these variants must be considered when describing deafness as an experiment in language deprivation.

Degree of Language Exposure

Degree of exposure to language is defined by two features: (1) the duration of language exposure over the individual's childhood and (2) the frequency of the exposure provided. Both of these factors are critical to the acquisition of language.

Duration

The duration of language exposure is essentially determined by exposure onset. Because language exposure is not stopped, the age at which language exposure is initiated determines the duration of language exposure. For normal-hearing children, language exposure may begin before birth (i.e., the fetus may detect the voice of its mother talking), but it certainly begins immediately following birth. Normal-hearing infants are exposed to the sounds of conversation in their environment throughout their development.

Not so for deaf infants. Although deaf infants are exposed to and engage in the paralinguistic aspects of parent–child interactions, they do not have access to the language used in these interactions. In most cases, attempts to expose deaf children to language begin in earnest following the diagnosis of the child's deafness. Once initiated, the frequency of language exposure may vary according to the motivation, skills, and resources available to families with deaf children. Most deaf children are raised in settings in which at least some attempt is made to develop communication and language skills. However, issues of language onset are somewhat different for deaf than for hard-of-hearing children.

Onset of Language Exposure for Deaf Children

The onset of language exposure is usually quite delayed for deaf children. This is due in part to the delayed diagnosis of deafness in infants. The primary characteristic for identifying hearing impairment is delayed onset of speech. Although many children say their first words at or near 12 months of age, many other children are 18 months or even 2 years of age before they begin speaking. Therefore, well-meaning physicians may discourage testing of children with language delays until it is clear that such delays are indeed abnormal. In delaying audiometric testing of infants, physicians unwittingly contribute to delayed onset of systematic language exposure for deaf children. Recent advances in early detection of hearing loss, including the use of auditory-evoked potentials and identification of risk factors in screening programs, have assisted in earlier detection of hearing loss (e.g., Mindel & Vernon, 1987). It is not clear at this time whether early diagnosis is necessarily coupled with early provision of language, but it is logical to assume some connection between diagnosis and attempts to provide language exposure. Deaf children born in the last two decades are therefore more likely to be exposed to language earlier, or for a longer duration, than deaf children born prior to advances in early detection technology.

Although it is unlikely that deaf children will be exposed to language prior to diagnosis of their hearing impairment, the onset of language may be delayed well past the date of diagnosis. Parental uncertainty over the diagnosis, often coupled with the unreliable nature of early auditory tests and intermittent variations in the child's hearing loss, may delay a definitive diagnosis of deafness for many months. Even after a child's hearing loss is established, parents may be psychologically unable or unwilling to take steps to alter the way in which they communicate with their deaf child (Rainer & Altshuler, 1967). Finally, even enthusiastic parents will typically require training to alter their linguistic behavior to conform to the needs of their deaf child. Management of auditory training, careful presentation of oral language, or use of gestural language are skills that require time to learn, further delaying the onset of language exposure for deaf children.

The child's enrollment in an educational program also affects the onset of language exposure. Early identification efforts are often linked with intervention programs that teach the family communication methods, and they may also provide direct intervention with the child in an educational, home, or combined setting. Such early-intervention programs are a relatively new educational development (although the John Tracey clinic in Los Angeles has offered on-site and correspondence programs for more than 40 years). As recently as 20 years ago, it was assumed that the first systematic exposure to language experienced by deaf children was their enrollment in a special educational program (usually at 6–8 years of age; Vernon, 1967c). Fortunately, early intervention programs have increased in the past two decades due to federal legislation (e.g., PL 94-142, PL 99-457) and local efforts to increase family–child interventions for deaf infants.

Defining Onset of Language Exposure for Hard-of-Hearing Children

Defining the onset of language exposure for hard-of-hearing children is more difficult than defining exposure for deaf children. By definition, hard-of-hearing children have some access to speech prior to the diagnosis of their hearing impairment. Additionally, the method of exposing such children to language is typically oral/auditory training, which is easier for parents to learn than other methods of communication (e.g., sign language). Unfortunately, the fact that hard-of-hearing children may have some usable expressive and receptive language skills may contribute to delayed diagnosis and increased parental denial of the child's hearing loss, which could delay deliberate efforts for language exposure. Hard-of-hearing children are consequently exposed to language earlier than deaf children, although deliberate and controlled efforts for language exposure are often delayed due to the linguistic success of hard-of-hearing children.

The sequence of events that typically occurs prior to systematic onset of language exposure is presented in Figure 2.2. In many cases, parents will cycle through certain stages many times before progressing to the next step. For example, the diagnosis of deafness and the parents' acceptance of that diagnosis may require visits to numerous physicians. This has been referred to as "doctor shopping," in which the uncertainty of diagnosis, combined with the parents' desire for a more optimistic prognosis, results in a number of different appointments with a variety of specialists. This process can take months, and in some exceptional cases, years, until a consistent diagnosis is provided by specialists and accepted by parents. The net effect of repetitions of any given cycle in the sequence is to delay the initiation of language onset.

Frequency and Intensity of Exposure

Hearing-impaired children are delayed in their exposure to language, and the frequency and intensity of their language exposure is also limited. Their hearing impairment denies them the accidental, casual, and informal language input that bombards normal-hearing children every day. To communicate with deaf children requires special efforts; therefore, the only language to which they are exposed is language delivered by the deliberate, intentional efforts of others. The overwhelming impact of this limitation on language development has been characterized by the phrase, "The problem with deaf children is not that they can't hear, it's that they can't overhear." A child's deafness consequently shuts out many opportunities to monitor and participate in linguistic interchanges, thus severely restricting the frequency of language exposure.

The intensity of the language stimulation provided to deaf children is also restricted. Children whose primary exposure is oral are exposed to stimuli in which about half of the information needed to discriminate meaningful speech sounds is missing. In other words, less than half of the sounds needed to understand English speech can be discriminated solely from lip movements. The homophonous nature of speech leads to some interesting misunderstandings even among skilled lipreaders. Henry Kisor's autobiography, in which he describes the challenges he confronts as a deaf person who depends exclusively on lipreading, is entitled *What's That Pig Outdoors?* The title comes from a hilarious episode in which Mr. Kisor's flatulence caused his son to burst into the room and ask, "What's that big

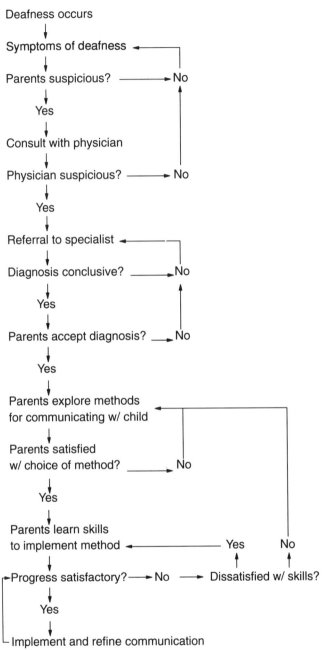

FIGURE 2.2 Sequence of steps leading to language exposure in deaf children.

loud noise?" to which Mr. Kisor replied, "What pig outdoors?" (Kisor, 1990, pp. xv/xvi). Thus, even deliberate efforts to provide language exposure typically lack intensity due to the restricted media through which language can be provided.

Deaf children whose primary exposure to language is some form of gestural communication must bear the brunt of their parents' (and teachers') attempts to master gestural language expression. As a consequence, deaf children are usually exposed to language interchanges in which the sophistication of language presented to them is artificially constrained by the adult's difficulties in manual expression. Likewise, individuals who are not fluent in gestural systems are less likely than fluent peers to initiate and engage in conversation, perhaps because they perceive themselves to be inadequate language models. This is particularly true of parents and others who are just beginning to learn a new system of language expression. The limited competence of novice adults limits the intensity and frequency of language exposure in home and school settings.

The frequency of exposure for hard-of-hearing children is arguably greater, primarily because their hearing loss is less constraining to those who would communicate with them than is true for deaf children. The availability of "normal" communication channels encourages and empowers adults in the hard-of-hearing child's world to initiate and maintain linguistic interchanges. However, the knowledge that the child has a hearing impairment, and the typical advice to gain the child's attention before speaking, face the child squarely, and articulate clearly, may lead adults not directly involved in the child's education to initiate fewer linguistic interchanges with hard-of-hearing children.

The ability of hard-of-hearing children to passively monitor language is severely restricted. In fact, the hard-of-hearing child's ability to overhear, or monitor language not directly confronting the child, is only marginally better than deaf children's ability to overhear. This is because the distorted auditory signals that hard-of-hearing children receive are extremely difficult to decipher without additional cues (e.g., visual monitoring of lip movements), or reduction of competing sounds (e.g., reduced background noise). Thus, hard-of-hearing children find themselves somewhat in between their normal-hearing and deaf peers. With respect to direct, intentional language exposure, they experience a relatively slight disadvantage relative to normal-hearing peers, but a relatively great advantage over deaf peers. However, with respect to passive monitoring of indirect language, they share a severe disadvantage with their deaf peers relative to the frequency of exposure their normal-hearing peers receive.

Intensity of language exposure also favors hard-of-hearing children relative to deaf peers. Because hard-of-hearing children get some useful auditory input, they are more likely than a deaf peer to understand a linguistic interchange. Likewise, hard-of-hearing children place less demand on the speaker, which encourages greater complexity of interchanges. As a consequence, there is a reciprocal system favoring more intense linguistic interchanges with hard-of-hearing children than with deaf children. By getting more from the interchange, and by placing fewer demands on the speaker, hard-of-hearing children are exposed to more intense interactions, which facilitates their own language development, which in turn encourages more complex or intense language exposure than that experienced by their deaf peers.

It is not sufficient simply to note greater or lesser frequency and intensity of language exposure for deaf versus hard-of-hearing versus normal-hearing children. Instead, it must be emphasized that frequency and intensity act in a cumulative, recursive fashion. Because deaf and hard-of-hearing children place more demands on speakers, they experience less frequent linguistic interchanges. Additionally, the intensity of their language experiences are limited. Reduced frequency, coupled with less intense interactions, yields less language development, which in turn places more demands on the speaker. Thus, a cumulative, recursive cycle is initiated, in which deaf and hard-of-hearing children are provided fewer and less intense language opportunities, which in turn limits their ability to respond effectively to language, which in turn further limits the frequency and intensity of linguistic interchanges experienced by deaf and hard-of-hearing children.

Language Modality

There are three modes in which language is presented to deaf children: (1) the oral/auditory mode, (2) the gestural/visual mode, and (3) the combined mode (i.e., oral/gestural and auditory/visual). Each of these media for conveying language affect the degree to which hearing-impaired children are exposed to language.

Oral/Auditory Mode

The presentation of language in the oral/auditory mode (i.e., talking) is a popular method for communicating to deaf children. The simplicity of this statement obscures important advances in oral/auditory language exposure, such as auditory amplification of selected frequencies to enhance input and reduced distortion of amplified sound. However, it captures the general notion behind oral/auditory means for exposing deaf children to language, which is to help the child adapt to the communication norm rather than adapt the communication norm to the child. To the degree that deaf children are able to use auditory and concurrent visual stimuli to decode language, they will have access to a wide range of linguistic interchanges.

Unfortunately, the primary medium for oral language is sound, and deaf people have severe to profound impairments in sound detection and use. In most cases, deaf children are unable to discriminate isolated auditory input to a degree sufficient to comprehend language. Therefore, oral presentation of language also encourages deaf children to use visual cues (i.e., lipreading) for decoding the language presented to them. The fact that visual cues associated with speech are often ambiguous is problematic, and complicates presentation of oral/auditory language. The twofold problems associated with oral/auditory language presentation (i.e., distorted or imperceptible auditory input and ambiguous visual signals) render it a medium of limited value for most deaf children.

In contrast, most hard-of-hearing children rely primarily on oral/auditory means of language exchange. Hard-of-hearing children's ability to detect and discriminate speech sounds aids them in their efforts to decode speech. With better auditory input, ambiguities in visual stimuli can be delimited, thus increasing the value of the conjoint visual movement of lips in speech and the sound produced by speech. However, systematic errors in detection and comprehension still plague most hard-of-hearing children, despite their efforts to comprehend what is said to them.

Although there are some steps that speakers may take to enhance the comprehension of speech (e.g., clearly and naturally enunciating words, reducing visual obstructions around the mouth such as beards), the technology for presenting speech remains limited. There have been some advances in attempts to enhance the reception of auditory input on the part of the hearing-impaired child. These advances include medical interventions, such as management of middle ear fluid accumulation and ossification to reduce conductive impairments, cochlear implants to alter sensorineural impairments, and technological advances in the provision of amplification. By definition, the benefits of these remedies have little impact on the language comprehension of deaf people, although they have undoubtedly assisted hard-of-hearing and deafened people to gain access to the auditory channel.

There is also an effort to enhance the quality of the visual signal that accompanies speech via the supplemental use of hand shapes placed near the mouth. This method, called "cued speech" (Cornett, 1975), attempts to reduce the ambiguity of lip positions associated with multiple phonemes. Preliminary research with a small number of hearing-impaired children suggests this medium may facilitate oral/auditory language exposure, but at present the method is rarely used. In sum, oral/auditory means of language presentation provide relatively little language exposure to deaf people, although the medium remains the primary language channel for hard-of-hearing people.

Gestural/Visual Mode

It is possible to present language in naturalistic settings without relying on oral/auditory means. The most common application of this medium is the use of signs, which are linguistically equivalent to spoken words or phrases. Signs are typically discriminated on the basis of three features: handshape, motion, and spatial location of the sign (Stokoe, 1960). The use of the term gestural in the gestural/visual presentation of language should not be construed as implying a concreteness or universality in creation of signs. Gestures may be defined as movements closely tied to the act or object to which they refer, so that others familiar with the act or object can comprehend the meaning of the gesture without knowing the linguistic signal for the concept. In contrast, signs are physical movements that may have been derived from a movement associated with the referent object or action, but which have, over time, taken on an arbitrary, abstract meaning that can be understood only if the receiver is familiar with the sign system. For example, the North American sign for salt would be unrecognizable to most North Americans because it is derived from the act of dipping a knife into a salt dish and lightly tapping the knife to distribute the salt over the food, a practice unfamiliar to most contemporary Americans. The sign for salt is also quite different in other countries, rendering the sign incomprehensible to signers from other cultures.

A second application of language presentation using the gestural/visual channel is fingerspelling. This is the use of handshapes to represent letters of the alphabet, which are then presented in succession to spell words. This process is akin to writing and reading, except that the medium for expression is manual (handshapes) rather than graphic, and is constrained to serial or successive presentation of letters versus the parallel or whole-word presentation that characterizes words on the printed page. In North America, fingerspelling is typically limited to words that have no common signs (e.g., a person's last name) or situations that require precise English translations, although it has been tried as a primary medium for communication. This method is named the Rochester Method after the school in Rochester, New York, which advocated the use of fingerspelling as a primary medium of instruction and communication. Like cued speech, the Rochester Method is not widely used in contemporary deaf education.

Combined Mode

The combined mode is the third major language modality used with hearing-impaired children. As the name implies, the combined method presents oral/auditory and gestural/visual information simultaneously. This is achieved by concurrently saying and signing, or saying and fingerspelling, a message. This medium assumes that multimodal presentation of language is most beneficial, because hearing-impaired children are provided with the broadest possible band of input, from which they select the information they can use in decoding language. This method is considered appropriate for all hearing-impaired children, in that predominately oral/auditory language receivers (i.e., hard-of-hearing children) can use the oral/auditory input and either ignore or apply the additional gestural/visual information. In contrast, predominately gestural/visual language receivers (i.e., deaf children) can use the gestural/visual input and either ignore or apply the concurrent oral/auditory input. The simultaneous method requires more effort from the speaker than the other two modes, in that speakers must be able to speak clearly, sign or fingerspell clearly, and coordinate these two actions concurrently to produce a coherent language model.

Use of Modalities with Deaf People

These modes are used to varying degrees by families and educational programs in their attempts to teach deaf children language. Fully 64.7% of families in North America do not use signs (i.e., gestural/visual language) with their deaf children (Jordan & Karchmer, 1986). Qualitative accounts of parents who use signs suggest that even in homes in which signing is provided, it is often of poor quality and, even then, is often not adopted until the deaf child is of preschool or school-entry age (Mindel & Vernon, 1987). However, 66% of the educational programs in North America incorporate sign language in their instructional curricula, with the majority of these programs combining signs and speech.

Sign language use also varies as a function of student age (e.g., 50% of children 6–8 years use signs, whereas 85% of children 18–20 use signs as their primary mode of communication). Scholars of mental testing history may be interested to note that the first psychological account of increasing sign language use with advancing age was presented by Binet and Simon (1910), the "inventors" of the modern intelligence test. They noted that most deaf people eventually used sign language as their primary mode of communication and, based on this fact, argued that oral instructional approaches should be abandoned. Subsequent investigations of sign use by age have attributed the increase primarily to the cumulative failure of oral/auditory methods, which becomes more evident with advancing age. As deaf children develop, they begin using sign language (with or without the consent of parents and teachers).

Other factors are also associated with the use of language modalities. Not surprisingly, hearing loss and age of onset are strongly associated with sign use. Severe and profoundly deaf children, and those with onset before 3 years of age, use sign language more often than moderatelyhearing-impaired peers or peers whose hearing impairment began after 3 years of age. Ethnic status covaries in an unusual way with sign language use. Whereas 73% of ethnic minority deaf children use signs in school (compared to 61% of ethnic majority schoolmates), only 27% of ethnic minority deaf children come from homes that use signs (compared to 39% of ethnic majority schoolmates).

These data paint a strange linguistic landscape for deaf children. Hearing-impaired children are most likely to live in homes in which there is no signing, but are most likely to be enrolled in educational programs that use signs. This odd trend is more pronounced for deaf children of ethnic minority (nonwhite) status than for ethnic majority children in North America (Jordan & Karchmer, 1986). Language opportunities at school have more impact on deaf children than familial language models, as evidenced by the fact that the vast majority of adolescents and adults adopt signs as their primary mode of communication. Thus, deaf children move between two linguistic words, one of which uses speech only (typically the home), and one of which uses signs and speech (typically the school). As they grow older, deaf children adopt the world of signs as their preferred linguistic home.

Language versus Modality

Those unfamiliar with deafness and sign language often make one of two erroneous assumptions about the languages conveyed by various modalities: (1) speech is the only way to convey abstract language (signs are "concrete" gestures for primitive communication), or (2) signs and speech are simply two different ways to represent a spoken language (i.e., signs are abstract, but mirror or mimic the dominant spoken language). Neither of these assumptions is correct. As is so often the case, the truth is more complicated. The language conveyed by a given modality must be considered separately from the modality in which it is presented. This is particularly true for sign systems, which are typically used to present three kinds of language:

1. Sign languages (i.e., languages whose ontogeny and existence are tied to signs).
2. Gestural representations of spoken languages (i.e., signs that were developed and are currently used to represent spoken language).
3. Gestural pidgins (i.e., an admixture of one or more sign languages with one or more gestural systems for presenting spoken language).

Each of these language types is elaborated to distinguish signs as a linguistic modality from the language conveyed through the use of signs.

Sign Languages

Languages using gestural signs have been observed for hundreds of years. As noted previously, although the original gesture used to represent an object or action may have been closely tied to the referent in movement or appearance, the gesture gradually loses its close association with context and becomes context-free, or arbitrary, in the meaning it represents. One such naturally occurring gestural language is American Sign Language (ASL), the language used by the North American deaf community. The transition of signs over time conforms to psycholinguistic parameters (Frishberg, 1975), and ASL is as arbitrary and abstract as any spoken language (Stokoe, 1960). However, ASL is not a gestural representation of English or Standard American Speech. Its grammar and prosody are markedly distinct from English, and so ASL is considered a language in its own right. Consequently, hearing-impaired American children that are exposed to ASL differ from their normal-hearing peers not only in the onset, degree, and modality of language, but also in the type of language to which they are exposed.

Gestural Representations of Spoken Languages

Not all gestural/visual languages are natural languages, nor are they always distinct from the spoken language of the society in which the hearing-impaired child lives. There have been many attempts to create artificial sign systems in the last 25 years for the purpose of exposing deaf children to the language used by the society in which they live. These efforts were initiated in North America, where systems were developed to represent spoken English (or more precisely, Standard American Speech) in a gestural medium (e.g., Anthony, 1966). Whereas some of these sign systems use grammatical units as the morphological bases of their signs, others use semantic units borrowed from existing (ASL) signs and add or alter handshapes, movements, or sign location in order to render English words into gestures. The deaf community has resisted such artificial attempts to alter their language, but the fact remains that artificial signing systems enjoy widespread use in educational programs in North America. Because these programs have achieved modest success (cf. Johnson, Liddell, & Erting, 1989), other countries are also creating and adopting gestural renditions of the spoken language for use in educating hearing-impaired children.

Gestural Pidgins

Not surprisingly, the juxtaposition of native sign languages (e.g., ASL) and gestural representations of spoken languages (e.g., English) have bred a pidgin, or an admixture, of the two languages. This pidgin is distinctive from, yet contains many elements of, the parent languages. The North American pidgin of ASL and English signs has been called pidgin sign English, or PSE (Woodward, 1973). It is a blend of ASL and gestural English in which neither language is fully expressed, and in which there are systematic regional variations. This is the language to which the majority of North American deaf children are exposed, even if the speaker-signer's native language is English. There are two reasons why this is so. One is that nearly all popular sign systems borrow signs from ASL, and then teach these ASL signs to individuals using the English translation of the sign to assign meaning. This creates signers who use ASL signs with English word order. The second reason is that ASL is rarely passed on from parents to children. Only 4%

of the deaf children born in North America (Karchmer, Trybus, & Paquin, 1977) and England (Conrad, 1979) are born to two deaf parents, meaning 4% or less are born to homes that use a native sign language.[2] The net effect is that most hearing-impaired children are exposed to ASL signs being used by native English speakers, and consequently are exposed to a pidgin.

The type of language to which hearing-impaired children are exposed is further complicated by two departures from standard PSE. The first departure is due to developmental variations in language development and use among signing peers. Whereas normal-hearing children converse with each other in fairly accurate approximations of their native language, hearing-impaired children who use signs converse with each other in a nonstandard mix of PSE and gestures termed "Childrenese" (Cokely & Gawlick, 1975). This nonstandard mix is affected by children's developmental level, their exposure and mastery of the dominant spoken language, and their exposure to and mastery of a sign pidgin. Therefore, social communication among hearing-impaired children who use signs is distinct from standard PSE, which is already a pidgin formed from two languages.

The second departure from standard PSE occurs when individuals attempt to implement the combined method for communicating with hearing-impaired children. Because the combined method demands that speakers concurrently sign and say their message, the expression of language demands much greater resources than either approach in isolation. Observational studies of normal-hearing teachers who are instructing hearing-impaired children find that teachers systematically delete signs when using the combined method (Kluwin, 1981; Luetke-Stahlman, 1988; cf. Mayer & Lowenbraun, 1990). Furthermore, teachers are unaware of their deletions. They feel that they accurately represent what they say in English with what they sign in gestural English. These findings suggest that most individuals who attempt the combined approach (i.e., teachers and parents of hearing-impaired children) will systematically deviate from PSE standards, and will probably be unaware of the fact that they are providing a nonstandard language model. This is less problematic for hard-of-hearing children (who attend primarily to the auditory signal) than for deaf children (who depend on the visual signal provided by gestures).

Neurological Lacunae of Language Exposure

There are two distinct issues to consider in the discussion of neurological lacunae of language exposure. The first is whether reduced language exposure has

---

[2]In addition, most educators of deaf children are not hearing impaired, and therefore learn gestural communication as an expressive form of their native spoken language. Johnson et al., 1989, have proposed radical alternatives (e.g., allowing only teachers with native competence in ASL to teach in elementary grades) to change this state of affairs.

generalized effects on neurological development (i.e., whether language deprivation leads to atrophy or less complex development of the brain). The second issue is whether exposure to language in modes other than the oral/auditory mode presents neurological processing demands on the observer that differ from those placed on the listener, thus causing changes in neurological development. These issues may be framed in two ways: (1) Does language deprivation lead to stunted or incomplete neurological development? or (2) Does exposure to nonstandard language media change or shift neurological development? Each of these issues is discussed in the following sections.

Neurological Lacunae of Language Deprivation

There are few cases in which normal-hearing children have been raised without exposure to speech or other language. The Wild Boy of Aveyron (Lane, 1977) and the case of Genie (Fromkin, Krashen, Curtiss, Rigler, & Rigler, 1974) are two case studies in which children experienced severe linguistic deprivation at early ages. Both cases reported mental retardation and a generalized reduction of sensory acuity. Although rapid gains were made following initiation of normal language stimulation in the case of Genie, her cognitive functioning remained below the average range. However, both cases, and others like them, cannot rule out the possibility of congenital anomalies in the children (i.e., preexisting organic deficits). In fact, it is even possible that the children were abandoned or isolated because of congenital deficits. The evidence that humans suffer irreversible organic or functional deficits as a consequence of early language deprivation is simply inconclusive, and is likely to remain so due to the unethical nature of any "experiments" that could adequately test the issue.

Neurological Constraints on Attention

At a sensory level, the neurological demands of sign language limit the amount of language an individual can observe over a given period of time relative to a listener. The sign language observer must visually attend to a series of movements in space and time. Foveal vision is narrowly focused and requires frequent refreshment of an image (i.e., moving the eye so that the image changes location on the retina) to maintain a signal. In contrast, audition is a relatively passive enterprise, in which sound is received without vigilance. The environment must be actively monitored to receive visual information; in contrast, the auditory aspects of the environment are continually monitored in either an active or passive fashion. Consequently, the neurological demands signs place on the receiver make it virtually impossible to monitor in a passive sense, and (because of the vigilance required to maintain focused visual activity) make long-term attention to a visual signal more difficult than long-term attention to auditory speech.

In part because of the processing demands sign language places on receivers, and in part because of the demands placed on the sender, ASL has evolved in a manner that streamlines sending and receiving efforts to conform to the gestural/visual channel (Frishberg, 1975). However, artificial sign systems developed to represent English often, albeit unwittingly, violate these gestural/visual processing constraints. In fact, the fundamental assumption that simultaneous presentation of speech and signs will benefit the receiver is questionable (Parnasis & Samar, 1982). Increases in the information in a communication channel result in increasing comprehension up to a point, after which additional increases in information result in a loss of information below peak levels. It is possible that the simultaneous presentation of speech and signs may place excessive demands on the receiver's processing resources, resulting in a greater loss of information than the presentation of either mode in isolation. However, there are few empirical studies of this topic, and so it is not known to what degree gestural representations of English resist comprehension due to their violation of visual processing constraints, or to what degree hearing-impaired individuals are assisted by multimodal presentation of language.

Information Processing Demands

Despite the fact that deaf people process language in a gestural/visual modality, they store and retrieve language in a manner similar to that of normal-hearing people. Studies of verbal (not vocal) memory in deaf people show that they tend to make semantic errors on recognition tasks (Siple, Fischer, & Bellugi, 1977) and spontaneously group words into semantic categories (Liben, Nowell, & Posnansky, 1978) in a manner similar to their normal-hearing peers. These studies suggest encoding and recall processes similar to those by which normal-hearing people encode and recall oral/auditory language. Furthermore, deaf stroke victims show neuropsychological localization of language storage, processing, and production that is remarkably similar to neuropsychological organization in normal-hearing individuals (Poizner, Klima, & Bellugi, 1987). Experimental studies and trauma research suggest that, despite the fact deaf people rely on gestural/visual language modalities, neuropsychological processing of language is similar (though not identical in all respects) for deaf and normal-hearing peers.

Thus, the primary effect of deafness on neurolinguistic processing is restricted linguistic input. This restriction is due to the demanding nature of the visual channel (e.g., inability to passively monitor the environment, severely restricted field of focus). Secondary neurological lacunae may occur when gestural/visual language systems (of the type commonly used in educational programs and by families who adopt signs for use in the home) are incompatible with neuropsychological processing demands, thus resulting in lost information. There is no compelling evidence to suggest that deafness radically alters the way in which language is encoded, processed, stored, or retrieved, although there is some evidence that neurological organization differs in some subtle ways that enhance visual language processing.

Summary of Language Exposure

Deaf and hard-of-hearing children are exposed to nonstandard language models less frequently, less intensively, for shorter durations, and later in life than their normal-hearing peers. Additionally, language presented to them is often nonstandard in its linguistic form and sensory modality. Although some minor changes in neurological structure may occur as a result of the unusual language exposure experienced by deaf children, it appears that there are neither major nor generalized neurological lacunae as a consequence of reduced, nonstandard language exposure.

Many researchers halt their investigations at this point and conclude that deaf children simply do not acquire language. For example, Furth (1966, p. 13) stated that "the vast majority of people, born deaf, *do not acquire functional language competence*" (author's italics). Vernon (1967c, p. 327) echoes this sentiment by asserting that "deaf children offer a suitable experimental group for a study in which language is the independent variable." These conclusions are based on the observations that deaf children are often deprived of language throughout childhood, and that deaf children perform quite poorly on tests of language and reading skills.

However, Conrad (1979) points out that, although "a substantial body of research has come to accept that deaf people represent a perfect control for the study of the role of language in oral thinking" (p. 12), there is no evidence that those doing research have attempted to directly measure the internalized language skills of the deaf people studied. Conrad notes that deprivation and reduced exposure may not necessarily lead to a failure to internalize and use language. Conrad finds that many deaf children internalize some language, although the likelihood that they will internalize language is inversely related to degree of hearing impairment (i.e., profoundly deaf children are less likely than moderately deaf children to internalize language). Internalized language facilitates vocal, cognitive, and academic skills in the deaf children studied by Conrad.

The distinction between language deprivation, which is an external condition, and internal language, which mediates cognitive, academic, and linguistic tasks, is often overlooked in studies of deaf children. However, the assumption that most deaf children fail to develop an effective internal language is not necessarily inaccurate. Less than half of all deaf children acquire a functional means for internal language representation by the age of 16 years (Conrad, 1979). Therefore, it is reasonable to conclude that many deaf children do not acquire internal language, and that even those who do acquire internal language do not achieve the levels of fluency demonstrated by their normal-hearing peers.

Medical Trauma

Hearing-impaired people experience higher rates of medical trauma than normal-hearing peers. This is because deaf children often lose their hearing due to medical trauma. A recent survey by Brown (1986) of over 55,000 hearing-impaired, school-aged children describes the prevalence and incidence of medical trauma associated with deafness. Approximately 60% of the school-aged deaf population has a known or reported cause of deafness, of which 49% is reportedly due to some form of medical trauma. Commonly reported classes of medical trauma causing deafness include maternal rubella (12%), meningitis (7%), premature birth (4%), pregnancy complications (3%), otitis media (3%), and other at-birth or adventitious causes. A large proportion of children (40%) report an unknown cause of deafness. These and other data point to the conclusion that at least half of all deaf people are deaf due to some form of medical trauma.

Moreover, in many cases, deafness is not the only physical sequelae of the trauma. Fully 30.4% of those deaf children whose etiology is known have a handicap in addition to deafness. The proportion of those with an additional handicap varies according to the reported cause of deafness. The percentage with an additional handicap among hereditarily deaf children (17.8%) is less than the proportion for meningitic deafness (25%), maternal rubella (38.6%), and otitis media (42%). Physical handicaps (e.g., visual impairment, brain damage, orthopedic impairment) are found in 15.2% of the hearing-impaired population, whereas 21.3% have a cognitive-behavioral disability in addition to deafness. The most prevalent cognitive-behavioral disabilities are mental retardation (8.5%), specific learning disabilities (8.1%), visual problems (6.1%), and emotional/behavioral problems (5.6%). These data are in agreement with previous studies of deaf children (e.g., Vernon, 1967a, 1967b, 1967d) that show marked prevalence of additional physical and cognitive-behavioral disabilities among children who are deaf due to medical trauma.

It is likely that the prevalence of cognitive-behavioral disabilities is under-reported among deaf populations. The primary argument in favor of underreporting lies in the limitations of differential diagnosis with deaf children. It is often difficult, and in some cases impossible, to discriminate the effects of a cognitive-behavioral disability (e.g., learning disability) from the effects of deafness. Therefore, some researchers in the field (e.g., Conrad & Weiskrantz, 1981) argue that research conducted on deaf children with no reported additional handicaps is still likely to include a significant number of deaf children with additional sub-rosa handicaps.

My own work as a psychologist with deaf children supports the argument that additional handicaps, especially cognitive-behavioral impairments, are underreported among hearing-impaired children. One case may serve to illustrate this point. I saw a 15-year-old female as part of a psychoeducational evaluation. She worked with me for approximately 15 minutes before "introducing" me to her imaginary friend. During the 3-hour psychological evaluation, she frequently signed to this friend, pulled out a chair for the friend to sit on, and otherwise engaged in inappropriate references to a fictitious person. It was not possible for me to clearly establish that her interaction with the "friend" was a willful (albeit grossly immature) fantasy, or a hallucination. Psychological test data also suggested significant emotional difficulties. When I questioned the psychologist from the referring school district (who had evaluated the child a few months before the referral) about the abnormal behavior exhibited by the girl, the psychologist reported that he was aware of the behavior, but thought it might be relatively normal for a lonely, isolated deaf child to create an imaginary friend. In short, competent professionals were aware of the child's bizarre behavior, but were inclined to see this as "normal for a deaf child." Anecdotal experiences, and problems associated with surveys of deaf populations, suggest that the rates of additional handicapping conditions are underreported among school-aged deaf children.

Surveys of etiology and physical sequelae associated with deafness suggest a high prevalence of significant medical trauma among deaf people. Furthermore, many of those experiencing trauma have medical sequelae in addition to deafness. Problems with differential diagnosis, and ignorance of the psychological development of deaf children among professionals, may underestimate the prevalence of additional handicaps among hearing-impaired children.

Genetic Endowment

Approximately 12% of the hearing-impaired children in North America (Brown, 1986) and England (Conrad, 1979) are diagnosed as having an hereditary cause of deafness. However, population genetics estimates suggest a much higher rate of genetic deafness than is reported (Nance & Sweeny, 1975; Rose, Conneally, & Nance, 1977). Specifically, it is estimated that nearly half (52%) of all deaf children are deaf due to genetic causes. The wide discrepancy between the estimated prevalence of genetic deafness (52%) and its reported prevalence (12%) is attributed to inadequate methods for medical diagnosis of genetic deafness. For example, parents may pass on autosomal recessive genes that produce deafness in their child, without having any previous cases of deafness in either family. Reconciliation of reported and estimated prevalence figures for hereditary deafness is possible if one is willing to assign an undiagnosed hereditary etiology to the majority of "unknown" causes (which constitute approximately 40% of the population). Current researchers (e.g., Brown, 1986) have generally accepted the notion that about half of the deaf population is deaf due to genetic causes.

Factors Associated with Genetic Deafness

There are a number of important factors that covary with genetic deafness. Perhaps the most important is the relatively low prevalence of additional handicapping disorders among hereditarily deaf children (about half the rate that is reported for other causes of deafness, or 17%). Additionally, the proportion of children who are white and female are higher among hereditarily deaf children than other deaf children (Karchmer et al., 1977; Wolff & Harkins, 1986). There have also been proposals of a genetic link between intelligence and hereditary deafness (e.g., Kusche, Greenberg, & Garfield, 1983; Pintner, 1928), which will be reviewed in detail in Chapter 3. For the purposes of identifying factors confounded with the natural experiment imposed by deafness, it is important to highlight that approximately half of all deaf children are believed to have abnormal genetic endowments (i.e., they are hereditarily deaf), and that those who have been diagnosed as genetically deaf have a lower prevalence of additional handicaps.

Family Dynamics

Hearing impairment is associated with changes in family dynamics. Deafness alters the parent–child relationship and the structure of the family system. The impact of deafness on parent–child interactions and the family system are described in the following sections.

Parent–Child Relationships

Parental Responses to Diagnosis

The finding that a child has a hearing loss elicits a powerful emotional response from the child's parents. In addition to the expected feelings of grief and sadness associated with the discovery that one's child has a physical impairment, it has been hypothesized that the parents of deaf children also exhibit maladaptive responses to deafness. Specifically, parents of deaf children often deny the initial diagnosis, in many cases despite the certainty of the diagnosis and the certainty of prognosis. Such parents may engage in "doctor shopping"—seeking advice and contact with many different professionals—in their search to substantiate their denial of the child's deafness. When such efforts are unsuccessful, they respond with unconscious feelings of rage at the child (e.g., "Why aren't you normal?") and concurrent feelings of guilt (e.g., "What did I do to cause this?"). These feelings may unconsciously affect the relationship between parent and child throughout the child's developmental years (Altshuler, 1974).

Dependency

In addition to the psychological impact that the diagnosis of a handicap may have on parents, the fact that deafness severely constrains communication interferes with the deaf child's resolution of developmental milestones. For example, deaf children's inability to passively monitor their environment may lead them to be excessively dependent on their parents. Periods of dependent behavior are often followed by periods of unrealistic independence. Behavioral swings from dependence to independence characterize the period of autonomy development in normal-hearing children (known to most parents as the "terrible twos"). However, the limitations on the communication channel imposed by deafness interact with parental feelings of guilt and anger to inhibit normal emotional development in deaf children (Schlesinger & Meadow, 1972). Consequently, the relationship between deaf children and their parents is often characterized by dramatic swings between overprotective, dependent interactions and parental attempts to control the child's rebellious search for independence.

Observational studies of parents interacting with deaf children support theoretical predictions and clinical impressions of abnormal parent–child relationships. Mothers of deaf children tend to express more disagreement, tension and antagonism, and control (via suggestions) in their interactions with their deaf children than mothers of hearing children (Goss, 1970). In contrast, mothers of normal-hearing children ask questions, solicit opinions, and use language to support their children more often than mothers of deaf children. Studies of mothers with a deaf son and a normal-hearing son show mothers interacting differently with each child, in a way that encourages social competence and motivation among the normal-hearing boys while eroding independent, motive-oriented behavior among the deaf boys (Stinson, 1974). Clinical observations also point to a tendency among parents of deaf children to rely on nonverbal, controlling, and punitive forms of communication with their hearing-impaired children (e.g., Schlesinger & Meadow, 1972; Mindel & Vernon, 1987).

Family Systems

A handicapped child places an added stressor on the family system. As such, the hearing-impaired child may select, or come to adopt, a role within the family that alters the family system in a maladaptive way. "The presence of a handi-capped child disrupts the typical patterns of family interaction and role relation-ships" (Hannah & Midlarsky, 1985, p. 512). The child may be singled-out for excessive attention and support in order to mask other problems within the family system, or may be the proverbial scapegoat on whom the problems of the family system are blamed. In either case, the limited ability of the deaf child to com-municate with other family members leads to an abnormal interaction pattern, which is exaggerated by the differential interest and ability that family members express in learning to communicate with the deaf child. It is relatively common for a sibling or parent to become a buffer between the child and the rest of the family, because it is this person who is best able to communicate with the deaf child. This leads to an abnormal pattern of family interactions, which may inhibit the social-emotional development of the deaf child.

Social Interactions

Deaf children are likely to be born into low socioeconomic status (SES) homes. The prevalence of deafness is somewhat more common among low-SES families than high-SES families. Two reasons have been offered to explain this phenomenon: (1) unhealthy environmental factors and poor medical care are associated with low SES, thus resulting in higher prevalence and more severe incidence rates of medical trauma among low-SES families, and (2) genetic anomalies are more common among low-SES individuals. Therefore, hearing-impaired children are more likely to come from low-SES homes than their normal-hearing peers, and to start the socialization process at a relative disadvantage. However, it is important to note that deafness is found among all SES groups. In fact, the SES of deaf children in most representative surveys more closely ap-proximates the distribution of SES in dominant majority groups than the SES distribution of minority groups.

Interactions between Deaf People and Society

As deaf children come in contact with society, they discover that their hearing impairments affect interactions between themselves and individuals outside the family. In fact, the communication barriers present in deafness have led to the development of deaf subcultures in most countries. In North America, 95% of married deaf adults are married to a deaf spouse (Vernon, 1969). There are social organizations serving deaf people, institutions of higher learning serving deaf people, and a language unique to deaf individuals (ASL). Like other members of minority groups, deaf people typically work in settings along with members of other social groups (i.e., normal-hearing people), but choose to spend their after-work time with members of their own social group (i.e., hearing-impaired people). Consequently, deafness has been recognized for many years as constituting a distinct social subculture within the dominant culture of normal-hearing people. In fact, the lowersocial status of deaf people has also been recognized for many years:

> For the most part the deaf [sic] live as members of a minority group within a social world in which the majority of people hear, and the frustrations and difficulties involved in deafness are largely those created by the adjustment between the majority who has more and the minority which has less. (Heider & Heider, 1941, p. 120)

Despite the fact that deaf individuals may form a collective subculture, they must still interact with members of the majority culture. These social interactions may be divided into two distinct classes of interaction: (1) proximal interactions, in which a deaf person is in direct contact with a hearing individual, and (2) distal interactions, in which a deaf person observes or is observed without direct contact. People with hearing impairment fare quite differently in each of these types of interactions.

Proximal Interactions

From a sociological perspective, deaf children are unusual in that they are a minority within their own families. Typically, neither parent is a member of the group to which the deaf child belongs. In this sense, the child is somewhat like a mixed-racial offspring, in that the child cannot identify with, nor be clearly identified as, a member of the predominate social group to which the parents belong. The socialization process of the deaf child is therefore abnormal. An example of the abnormal socialization process is a common belief among young deaf children that they will die before reaching adulthood, or become hearing when they become older, because they have never seen nor met a deaf adult (Mindel & Vernon, 1987). Typically, deaf children are raised by normal-hearing parents, live in a home with normal-hearing siblings, are taught by normal-hearing teachers, and live in a neighborhood with normal-hearing children. The only contact with other deaf people experienced by most deaf children comes from sharing a classroom with other hearing-impaired children, who themselves live in a similarly isolated world. Thus, the primary unit for inducting deaf children into the subculture of the hearing-impaired is not the family, and it may or may not be the school. This means that deaf children are a minority within their own families, and in their communities.

Proximal interactions with peers at school may also be isolating and debilitating for the deaf child. Normal-hearing peers are not only limited in their ability to communicate with hearing-impaired peers, but they often go out of their way to ostracize hearing-impaired classmates. Ostracism of all types of disabilities is common in elementary schools (Levitt & Cohen, 1976). However, negative attributions toward hearing-impaired children are also common among school teachers (Blood & Blood, 1982). Attempts to reduce resistance toward hearing-impaired children among normal-hearing peers not only lack demonstrated effectiveness; such attempts may even increase ostracism by calling attention to the hearing-impaired child's disability (e.g., Vandell, Anderson, Ehrhart, & Wilson, 1982). Therefore, deaf children receive little support from their normal-hearing peers, and are often subject to distinctly negative proximal social interactions.

Recent changes in North American education emphasize "least restrictive environment," or placement as near to a regular classroom as possible. This emphasis has reduced the number of contacts among hearing-impaired children and deaf adults. Most deaf children today are served in mainstreamed programs, in which they attend regular classes along with normal-hearing children, with part-time support from a resource teacher, interpreter, or aide. Staff members of the regular school have normal hearing virtually without exception. In contrast, staff members of large residential schools created specifically to serve deaf children typically employ a relatively large proportion of deaf staff members (Schildroth, 1986). Recent shifts in educational programming have decreased the number of children who attend full-time and residential educational placements, which means hearing-impaired children are spending less time with their hearing-impaired peers and deaf adults (Schildroth, 1986). Therefore, deaf children often lack the support of friendly proximal interactions with members of their social group, and are actively ostracized or ignored by normal-hearing peers.

The isolation and persecution suffered by deaf people extend into adulthood. The effects of societal discrimination have been presented in fiction (e.g., Greenberg, 1970), in qualitative accounts of the socialization of deaf people (e.g., Jacobs, 1974), and are documented in employment and income data collected for deaf adults (e.g., Schein & Delk, 1974). Despite their ability to work in many occupations, deaf adults are severely underemployed relative to normal-hearing peers of similar educational status. However, unemployment rates for deaf adults are similar to those of normal-hearing adults, a fact that is attributed to a strong work ethic within the deaf community. The primary causes of severe underemployment among deaf adults are the negative social stereotypes held by majority culture (normal-hearing) people about deaf and hearing-impaired people, and deaf people's inadequate educational achievement in literacy and language (which will be described in greater detail in Chapter 3). Recent changes in employment patterns, as manifested by the large growth of the human services sector, bodes ill for deaf people. Because they have difficulty communicating with normal-hearing people, and because they typically have significantly delayed educational achievement, the proportion of unemployed and underemployed deaf people seems likely to increase in the coming years.

Despite the fact that deaf people are rejected and discriminated against, or in part because of it, deaf people have banded together to form an active, vibrant subculture. The deaf subculture of North America has been studied more than deaf subcultures in other countries, but deaf communities have been identified internationally. The subculture is defined by customs, shared experiences, folklore, and the anthropological hallmarks associated with a long-standing community (e.g., Humphries & Padden, 1988). The socializing institutions of the deaf community have traditionally been residential schools for deaf children, in which children come in contact with other deaf children and deaf adults. In these settings, deaf adults inculcate children into the deaf community via social organizations (e.g., the Junior National Association of the Deaf), folk history, and other interactions. The opportunity for an academic and professionally elite cadre within the deaf community has been provided by Gallaudet University, an institution of higher learning specifically founded in the middle 1800s to serve deaf students.

The role of Gallaudet University as a pillar of the deaf community was underscored in March, 1988, when students protested the appointment of a normal-hearing person as president of the institution. The fact that Gallaudet had never had a hearing-impaired president, coupled with the fact that there were qualified deaf applicants for the position, prompted the students, faculty, and greater deaf community to protest. The protesters effectively forced a change of presidents, resulting in the appointment of Dr. I. King Jordan, Jr., as the first deaf president of Gallaudet University. The national media coverage of this event captured the intense frustrations of deaf people in dealing with the neglect and discrimination imposed on them by normal-hearing people and documented their long-standing struggle to assume some degree of control over their educational and social institutions.

It is important to note that the struggle for identity and autonomy will always challenge the deaf community, because the intergenerational transmission of deaf culture is diminished by birth trends. More than 90% of deaf community members have normal-hearing parents and family members. The inculcation of deaf individuals into the deaf community, and the transmission of deaf culture to new members, is further threatened by continued efforts toward mainstreaming deaf people. By placing deaf children in classes with normal-hearing peers and normal-hearing teachers, and concomitantly reducing enrollments at large, residential schools, the traditional means for socializing deaf children into the deaf community are eroding. Whether this situation is good or bad is irrelevant to the concerns of deafness as a natural experiment condition. However, it is clear that deaf people are socially disadvantaged when they come in direct contact with the dominant, normal-hearing culture, and that deaf people have responded to ostracism and disadvantage by creating a strong minority subculture, complete with its own customs, folklore, and language.

Distal Interactions

Although deaf people are at a serious disadvantage in proximal, face-to-face interactions with normal-hearing people, they are not quite as disadvantaged in distal interactions. In fact, deafness has often been called the invisible handicap, because there are no overt manifestations of the disability. Hearing aids worn by a deaf person may suggest a hearing loss, but aids are becoming less obtrusive as technological advances shrink the size of aids. In distal interactions, such as passing by another person, or being viewed at a distance, deaf people have no special status other than that granted by their race or physical characteristics unrelated to deafness. Deaf people who are members of a majority or dominant racial group therefore enjoy the same status as normal-hearing members of the same group, whereas deaf people who are members of racial minorities may be thought of as sharing whatever distal impressions or expectations are assigned to normal-hearing members of their group.

Another form of distal interaction between deaf people and the normal-hearing culture is the portrayals of deaf people in popular media. Television programs, books, and other media provide an image of deaf people for the general public, and such media provide (or fail to provide) role models for deaf people. The treatment of deaf people in literature has not been favorable (Batson & Bergman, 1973). Most deaf characters are portrayed as pitiful, fearsome, or otherwise bizarre. Fictional images of deaf people are often unrealistic (e.g., a deaf character will be puzzled by a telephone, yet the same character will be able to read lips at a distance of 50 yards). Furthermore, plots often end in a "cure" for the deafness, implying that deaf people are "broken" and need to be "fixed" to be complete. Nonfiction material, which might be thought of as "deaf history" or "deaf culture," is virtually nonexistent in the public arena. In contrast to increased sensitivity in schools and the media toward the role of minorities in history, the role of deaf people remains virtually ignored. This is due in part to the fact that most famous hearing-impaired people (e.g., Thomas Edison) cannot be identified as members of the deaf community despite their hearing impairment. Histories of deafness and accurate portrayals of deaf culture (e.g., Humphries & Padden, 1988) are available, but they have not been disseminated to the majority of normal-hearing people via popular media, school curricula, or other means.

In recent years, the popular media have increased their accuracy in portrayals of deafness. For example, *Children of a Lesser God* is a play (also produced as a movie) about a deaf woman who insists on maintaining her deaf identity despite the pleas of a normal-hearing teacher. Other examples of increased sensitivity to deafness in the popular media include children's books (e.g., *Jamie's Tiger* [1978], by J. Wahl and T. de Paola), use of deaf actors and actresses to play deaf characters, increased visibility of the National Theatre of the Deaf, and the media attention devoted to Gallaudet University's student protests of March 1988. However, this sensitivity is quite recent, and its long-term impact on stereotypes held about deaf people is as yet unknown. The fact that normal-hearing people still use the expression "deaf and dumb" or "deaf mute" to describe hearing-impaired people suggests there are still many inaccurate stereotypes of deafness. Gains made by other minorities (e.g., African-Americans are now depicted on television in a variety of roles) have promoted sensitivity to human diversity, but as yet, deafness enjoys neither the attention nor the role models granted to other minorities in popular media.*

Summary

Hearing-impaired people experience extreme disadvantage in proximal interactions with normal-hearing people, and are at a disadvantage in distal interactions. Although negative stereotypes and expectancies about deaf people appear to be widely held by normal-hearing people, the fact that deaf people do not exhibit overt physical characteristics identifying them as deaf may prevent normal-hearing people from automatically assigning such stereotypical expectations to them. However, in proximal contact, the deaf person's impairment becomes evident in the inability of the deaf person to understand what is said, and in the often incomprehensible speech produced by the deaf person. These factors may lead normal-hearing people to inaccurately diagnose a deaf person's handicap (e.g., difficulties in comprehension and speech problems are commonly associated with mental retardation and emotional disturbance). Psychologists occasionally make mistakes in differential diagnosis of deafness and mental retardation (Sullivan & Vernon, 1979); it is not surprising that uneducated lay people make similar misdiagnoses. Thus, deaf people appear to enjoy a degree of anonymity in distal social interactions not afforded to other minorities (e.g., orthopedically impaired, racial minorities), but such an advantage is lost in proximal interactions. In proximal interactions, normal-hearing people may stereotype the deaf person according to inaccurate expectancies associated with deafness, mental retardation, or other indiscriminate stereotypes reserved for people who may have physical or mental disorders.

Summary of Factors Confounded with Deafness

Deafness as a natural experiment confounds much more than language deprivation. Deafness is characterized by auditory deprivation, inconsistent exposure to a nonstandard language presented via nonstandard physical modalities, medical

---

*Since this was written, the television program "Reasonable Doubts" aired on a major North American network. The program starred a deaf actress (Marlee Matlin) playing a deaf lawyer, a step toward visibility and recognition of deaf people. But appearances of deaf actors and portrayals of deaf characters are still rare in the major media.

trauma and a concomitant high prevalence of additional handicapping conditions, abnormal genetic endowments, abnormal and often pathological family dynamics, and negative proximal and distal social interactions. However, deaf people also form an active, vibrant subculture, and deaf people are beginning to enjoy some changes in how they are treated and understood by society at large. Furthermore, there is no compelling evidence to show that deaf people are radically "different" from normal-hearing people in a qualitative sense (e.g., deaf people have similar neuropsychological structures for linguistic processing). Thus, the cumulative effects of deafness appear to be incremental, and include physiological, neurological, genetic, epidemiological, and sociological factors that should be considered in defining deafness. A final caveat is also in order: the variation within the population of hearing-impaired or deaf individuals is not adequately defined, but is likely to be considerable. It may not be assumed that all deaf people are equally subject to all of the conditions associated with deafness.

Exceptions to the Natural Experiment of Deafness

There are some important exceptions to the natural experiment of deafness. These exceptions are created by the hearing status of one or more of the deaf child's siblings, or by the hearing status of the deaf child's parents. These factors are associated with changes in the conditions of deafness as a natural experiment, and they have been recognized as distinct conditions in the psychological literature. The combination of these conditions creates distinct variations of the natural experiment of deafness.

Deaf Children with a Deaf Sibling

Deaf children with normal-hearing parents and one or more deaf siblings (HP/DS) differ from deaf children who live in families where all other members of the family have normal hearing. They differ with respect to other deaf children of normal-hearing parents on five critical dimensions:

1. Language exposure
2. Medical trauma
3. Genetic endowment
4. Family dynamics
5. Social interactions

However, HP/DS are similar to deaf children whose parents and siblings have normal hearing (HP) with respect to the dimension of hearing loss severity and type, as the degree and type of hearing loss does not appear to be related to the presence of a deaf sibling.

Language Exposure. Because HP/DS have a deaf sibling, they have more frequent opportunities to communicate with family members. The logic of this statement rests on two assumptions: (1) the other hearing-impaired sibling will probably adopt similar communication methods (e.g., sign language), thus providing a "fluent" family member with whom to communicate, and (2) the presence of two or more hearing-impaired children in a family increases the incentive for normal-hearing family members to learn alternative modes of communication.

This argument implies that HP/DS are exposed to language in a different manner than HP peers. Specifically, it is assumed that linguistic interactions would be more frequent, and of longer duration, than interactions experienced by HP because the communication proficiency of family members (the deaf sibling and the parents) would be better than the communication proficiency held by family members of HP. However, the frequency and duration of linguistic interactions experienced by HP/DS is believed to be less than those experienced by normal-hearing peers, because the children's deafness demands more effort from (and thus restricts communication with) normal-hearing family members.

The type of language to which HP/DS are exposed is also different from the language to which HP are exposed. HP/DS spend more time than HP or normal-hearing peers communicating with insufficiently skilled communicators, because the major person with whom HP/DS will communicate is their hearing-impaired sibling. Thus, HP/DS are exposed to nonstandard sign language or idiomatic gestural systems (e.g., "Childrenese" described by Cokely & Gawlick, 1975) more than HP or normal-hearing peers.

The argument that HP/DS differ from HP with respect to duration, frequency, and type of language exposure is at this time rationally derived. To the best of my knowledge, there are no empirical studies comparing the linguistic environments provided in HP/DS homes to language exposure provided in HP homes. The rationale is, at this time, logically sound but empirically unsupported. This should caution against strong conclusions with respect to linguistic differences between HP/DS and HP.

Medical Trauma and Genetic Endowment. HP/DS are assumed to be deaf due to recessive genetic causes, because the likelihood that nongenetic deafness would occur two times in a family is infinitesimal (Nance & Sweeny, 1975; Rose et al., 1977). Therefore, HP/DS are assumed to be genetically deaf, although exact diagnosis of the genetic syndrome associated with such deafness is rarely possible due to the recessive nature of the genetic transmission and the lack of associated physical anomalies.

How likely is the assumption that HP/DS are genetically deaf? On the one hand, the genetic etiology of HP/DS rests on the statistical premise that nongenetic deafness (i.e., deafness due to medical trauma) would be very unlikely to occur twice in one family. On the other hand, if the parents carried recessive genes for deafness, the probability of two deaf siblings in a family is much greater (approximately 10,000 times greater than the probability of two nongenetic cases of deafness). However, these probabilities have been developed assuming statistical independence of nongenetic deafness within families. The odds may be considerably less if one assumes that families who suffer medical trauma with the first child might be more likely to suffer medical trauma with the second (e.g., complications of pregnancy over successive pregnancies, poor postnatal medical care leading to high rates of infection). Unfortunately, these odds cannot be quantified, and so the safest conclusion is that most HP/DS are genetically deaf due to recessive autosomal genetic traits.

The complementary assumption made regarding HP/DS is that they do not have additional handicapping conditions that are commonly associated with medical trauma (Conrad & Weiskrantz, 1981; Kusche et al., 1983). Thus, HP/DS may be assumed to have similar rates of additional handicapping conditions to those found in the general population, because these children have not been known to suffer any medical trauma. In contrast, approximately 50% of HP are assumed to be deaf due to medical trauma, and therefore have high incidence rates of observable and sub-rosa handicaps in addition deafness.

A caveat to the assumption that genetically deaf children have a lower prevalence of additional handicaps must be stated at this time. Single-gene and chromosomal syndromes can bring about severe physical anomalies in addition to deafness. For example, some recessive genetic disorders include a host of physical and mental sequelae in addition to hearing impairment (Konigsmark & Gorlin, 1976). Such cases are typically excluded from samples of HP/DS (and HP) by psychological researchers because of concomitant physical anomalies. Because at least some recessive genetic conditions associated with hearing impairment also carry additional handicaps, and because HP/DS are deaf due to genetic causes, the assumption that HP/DS have no additional handicaps because they are not subject to high rates of medical trauma presupposes that any additional handicaps associated with genetic deafness are observable and may be excluded from samples of HP/DS.

It appears paradoxical to assume that medical trauma induces high rates of sub-rosa additional handicapping conditions, but that the recessive genetic anomalies giving rise to HP/DS are free from sub-rosa conditions. However, the assumption that HP/DS are genetically deaf, and consequently do not have additional handicapping conditions, is common in the literature (e.g., Conrad & Weiskrantz, 1981). Surveys also show that genetically deaf children have lower rates of additional handicapping conditions than nongenetically deaf children, but the reported rates for observable additional handicaps among genetically deaf children (17%) are well above rates reported for normal-hearing children (Brown, 1986). Therefore, it is best to conceive of HP/DS as a variation on deafness as a natural experiment in which the prevalence of additional disabling conditions is lower than in HP, but still well above the prevalence rates associated with normal-hearing peers.

Family Dynamics. It is assumed that the presence of more than one deaf child in a family may alter the family dynamics in ways that are different from families in which no child is hearing-impaired, or only one child is hearing-impaired. For example, a second deaf child might reduce the tendency for parental denial and increase parental acceptance and coping of deafness in parent–child relationships. However, it could also be hypothesized that an additional deaf child would add additional stress on the family unit, and further distort patterns of family interactions. Because there are no empirical studies of this issue, it is not possible to draw firm conclusions regarding in what ways, and the degree to which, family dynamics might differ between HP/DS, HP, and normal-hearing children.

Social Interactions. Because HP/DS have a deaf sibling, they may be assumed to have more frequent opportunities for positive social interaction. Not only do HP/DS have a sibling with whom to interact, but it could be assumed that the deaf siblings could support each other in coping with an often hostile social environment. Also, the presence of two deaf siblings within the family may act as a greater incentive for parents to establish contacts with other hearing-impaired children to provide playmates for the HP/DS in the family. It would not be expected that the availability of a deaf sibling would radically alter the way in which society responded to or treated the deaf child, but it could be argued that the availability of a supportive deaf sibling could help alleviate some of the adverse psychological consequences of social interactions. Once again, this is a rational argument that is, as yet, unsupported by empirical data.

Summary. HP/DS offer a variation of deafness as a natural experiment in which auditory deprivation is assumed to be similar to HP peers. The variations created by HP/DS status are believed to include changes in language exposure (frequency, duration, and type), low prevalence of medical trauma, and high prevalence of hereditary deafness. In addition, it is suspected that the presence of two or more deaf children in a family alters the family dynamics and mediates the impact of social interactions for HP/DS. From a psychological perspective, the critical feature attributed to HP/DS as a natural experiment is the ability to isolate genetic endowment from environmental features. Psychologists who have studied HP/DS (e.g., Conrad & Weiskrantz, 1981; Kusche et al, 1983) argue that HP/DS have essentially the same environment as HP, but because they may be assumed to be genetically deaf, HP/DS provide the means to isolate the potential effects of genetic endowment from the environmental impact of deafness.

Deaf Children of Deaf Parents

The differences between deaf children of deaf parents (DP) and other hearing impaired children have led DP to become the most frequently studied subgroup of deaf children. DP are distinguished from other hearing-impaired, and normal-hearing, children on six primary factors:

1. Auditory deprivation
2. Language exposure
3. Medical trauma
4. Genetic endowment
5. Family dynamics
6. Social interactions

The conditions shared by DP on these factors make them the most widely studied, and arguably the most important, variation in the natural experiment imposed by deafness.

Auditory Deprivation. Surveys of educational programs for hearing-impaired children report that DP have more severe hearing losses than HP counterparts (Karchmer et al., 1977). Furthermore, they are less likely to use hearing aids in a consistent manner than HP peers, and virtually all DP have congenital hearing losses. Therefore, DP may be assumed to receive less auditory stimulation than HP or normal-hearing peers, and are less consistent and efficacious in mitigating the effects of hearing impairment.

Language Exposure. Perhaps the most widely recognized distinction between DP and HP peers is the consistent, early exposure to language provided to DP. In families with two deaf parents, sign language is likely to be the primary mode of communication for all family members (Brill, 1969; Karchmer et al., 1977; Meadow, 1968; Sisco & Anderson, 1980; Stevenson, 1964). Therefore, DP are exposed to language in an accessible medium from the time they are born. The fact that all members of the family (even normal-hearing siblings) use signs as their primary mode of communication means that DP are afforded linguistic interactions similar to those experienced by normal-hearing peers in terms of duration, frequency, and consistency.

It should be recognized, however, that the content and modality of DP linguistic interaction differ significantly from that of normal-hearing peers. It is widely assumed that deaf parents use American Sign Language, and that deaf parents are fully proficient in ASL. It is further assumed that DP therefore acquire ASL early in life, in the same way that normal-hearing children acquire English. However, this assumption may not be warranted. The research showing that ASL is a sophisticated, flexible, and abstract language (e.g., Bellugi, 1972) has typically been conducted on third-generation deaf adults (i.e., deaf adults whose parents and grandparents were native deaf signers). It is not known what proportion of the parents of DP have deaf ancestors, or what proportion might be native signers of ASL (i.e., were born into a family using ASL where they naturally acquired it).

Because 90% or more of deaf people have two hearing parents, and because most hearing parent families do not use sign language as their primary means of communication, it is dangerous to make the assumption that all of the deaf parents of deaf children are fully proficient in the use of ASL. Some may be, but others may use a sign pidgin or other nonstandard mix of gestures, English signs, and ASL.

The medium in which language is presented to DP is certainly different than the medium in which language is presented to normal-hearing peers. The gestural/visual aspect of sign language may affect the process of language acquisition. Observational studies of DP suggest that they start signing at earlier ages than is common for normal-hearing peers to start talking (McIntire, 1977). It may be that gestural sign production, which requires gross motor coordination, develops faster than the oral-muscular coordination required for speech production. In any event, reciprocal communication is initiated earlier in the lives of DP than normal-hearing peers, and begins much earlier than for HP or HP/DS peers. Also, DP are likely to be exposed to ASL or sign pidgins with strong ASL components, and may therefore be exposed to signs that have evolved to conform to receptive and expressive information-processing demands. In contrast, those few HP and HP/DS who are exposed to sign systems in the home may be assumed to be exposed to predominately English-based signs or speech. These English-based systems often fail to conform to gestural/visual channels as effectively as ASL. DP share a constraint similar to HP and HP/DS peers, in that they cannot passively monitor language in the environment the way that normal-hearing children can monitor language via passive listening, but their language environments are far more similar to normal-hearing peers than those of any of their deaf counterparts.

Medical Trauma and Genetic Endowment. DP are assumed to be relatively free from medical trauma. The logic of the argument in favor of this position is the same as for HP/DS, namely, that DP are genetically deaf, and the odds that a child would be deaf due to nongenetic causes are much smaller than the odds favoring genetic causes when one or more family members are also deaf. However, a critical difference between HP/DS and DP is the type of genetic deafness. Whereas the genetic deafness in HP/DS must, by definition, be recessive (i.e., both parents have normal hearing), the genetic deafness in DP is assumed to be a dominant form of genetic transmission.

Dominant forms of genetic deafness have been identified on the basis of associated physical anomalies. For example, Waardenburg's syndrome is a dominant form of deafness often associated with prematurely gray hair, heterochromia (i.e., eyes of two different colors), the appearance of eyes being spaced far apart (an effect due to joining of the skin below the eye directly to the nose), and, in some cases, mental retardation (Konigsmark & Gorlin, 1976). Most dominant forms of deafness, however, are not associated with other physical characteristics.

Therefore, the genetic status of DP as children who have inherited a dominant form of deafness is largely inferred from the hearing status of the parents, rather than any direct diagnosis per se. Surveys suggest low rates of additional handicapping conditions for DP, and those who conduct research in deafness typically select DP as a comparison group that is free from additional disabilities.

Family Dynamics. A number of researchers have proposed that the family systems and parent–child interactions of DP are essentially comparable to the experiences of normal-hearing children. This argument is based on the proposition that the parents are deaf, and therefore deafness is not likely to constitute a serious shock or threat to the parents. The fact that DP have lower rates of social-emotional problems than HP peers is often explained by this proposition (e.g., Meadow, 1968).

However, the argument that family dynamics are sound in DP is actually offered as a post hoc explanation of the relative social success of DP. Observations of family dynamics and parent–child interactions between deaf parents and their children do not necessarily support this argument. For example, Galenson et al. (1979) found that deaf parents were less nurturing, interacted less, and were less supportive than a control group of normal-hearing parents. It is therefore an open question as to whether the family dynamics and parent–child interactions of DP are similar to normal-hearing siblings, although they are assumed to be superior to interactions experienced by HP and HP/DS peers because the family uses a linguistic medium that allows access for all family members.

Many DP also have deaf siblings (Karchmer et al., 1977). It is assumed that the higher rate of deaf siblings among DP is due to the dominant genetic deafness within the family. It is not known in what ways, if any, family dynamics are affected by multiple deaf children, but it has generally been assumed that it exerts no strong effect. However, research on the normal-hearing siblings of deaf children suggests that mixtures of normal-hearing and deaf children within a family headed by deaf parents may provide unusual or abnormal patterns of family dynamics (Evans, 1984).

Social Interactions. DP are much more likely to come from low-SES homes than HP, HP/DS, or normal-hearing peers. In fact, surveys of adult deaf people (e.g., Schein & Delk, 1974) suggest that deaf parents experience high rates of low SES in comparison to the general population. This fact is attributed to the severe underemployment of deaf people due to poor educational attainment and job discrimination. Therefore, DP are typically raised in homes with low SES, in that their parents typically have limited educational attainment, limited incomes, and otherwise fare poorly on measures of SES. The distribution of SES among DP is therefore similar to, yet somewhat lower than, economically disadvantaged minority groups. DP also differ from HP and normal-hearing peers in ethnic status.

Although the ethnic proportions found among HP are comparable to the ethnic composition of normal-hearing society, DP are rarely members of ethnic minorities. For example, a survey of North American hearing-impaired children (Karchmer et al., 1977) found that 71.9% of HP were white, 13.8% were black, and 14.3% were Hispanic. In contrast, 96% of DP were white, 4% were Hispanic, and none were black. This phenomenon appears to be robust over time, because recent surveys (e.g., Brown, 1986) find similarly low rates of minority racial status among hereditarily deaf children. Unfortunately, such research does not typically isolate HP/DS from DP, and so it is not clear whether the low proportion of minority group members noted for genetically deaf people also applies to HP/DS.

Interactions between DP and normal-hearing individuals would be assumed to be comparable to the interactions experienced by HP and HP/DS. However, DP differ from HP and HP/DS in that it is assumed that the parents of DP inculcate DP into the deaf community. Support for this assumption is found in school enrollment patterns. Most DP are enrolled in residential schools for deaf children, despite their unusually low rates of additional handicapping conditions (Karchmer et al., 1977). Furthermore, it is assumed that deaf parents maintain social contacts with other families headed by deaf parents, and so would provide opportunities for their children to associate with other deaf children. Such contact would be likely to increase supportive peer contacts for DP, as well as provide opportunities for nonfamilial deaf role models. Therefore, DP probably spend less time in the company of normal-hearing people, and more time in the company of hearing-impaired people, than HP or HP/DS peers. These propositions are based on the assumptions that deaf parents are members of the deaf community and would actively encourage their children to participate in the deaf community.

Unfortunately, there are no data that bear directly on these assumptions. Qualitative accounts suggest deaf parents do indeed inculcate their children into the deaf community. On the one hand, the significant number of normal-hearing people with deaf parents who have chosen careers in deafness (e.g., sign language interpreters, teachers) also suggests that deaf parents inculcate all their children, not just hearing-impaired offspring, into the deaf community. On the other hand, most parents of DP are probably offspring of normal-hearing parents. This means that the grandparents may not be active members of the deaf community, or may have limited or distorted awareness of deaf culture. This is suggested in accounts of DP being raised by normal-hearing grandparents (e.g., Rayson, 1987). The fact that deaf culture is not directly transmitted across generations suggests that even DP will often be deprived of consistent exposure to deaf culture. The poor educational attainment and low SES of the parents of DP may also inhibit their desire and ability to initiate deaf children into deaf culture. These circumstances are similar to circumstances experienced by normal-hearing members of minority cultures, who are often ignorant of their own minority culture and are discouraged from celebrating their culture by the dominant majority. Conversely, DP are at a significant advantage relative to HP and HP/DS, in that they share the same minority status as their parents (i.e., hearing-impaired), whereas HP and HP/DS are literally a minority within their own families.

Summary. DP are an important variant of deafness as a natural experiment condition, because they differ from HP and HP/DS on nearly all dimensions associated with deafness. Although DP are at a relative disadvantage with reference to auditory deprivation, DP enjoy advantages over HP and HP/DS peers on constructs related to language exposure, prevalence of medical trauma, and some sociological constructs. It has been proposed, albeit without evidence, that DP also experience healthier family dynamics than HP and HP/DS. Although they are much more likely to be from low-SES homes, DP are also assumed to have social advantages not afforded to other hearing-impaired people. In many ways, DP are similar to normal-hearing children who are members of ethnic minority groups. They share linguistic and cultural differences, low SES, and generally negative stereotypes held about them by the dominant culture. However, DP are much less likely to be members of ethnic minority groups, which may provide an advantage in distal social interactions. DP also differ from some minority groups in that they have no history of slavery, nor can they trace their cultural origins to a time or place where they represented a majority culture. Clearly, early characterizations of DP as identical to HP with the exception of early language exposure (e.g., Brill, 1969; Stevenson, 1964) are simplistic and unrealistic, and distort some intriguing characteristics associated with DP.

Conclusions: Deaf Children as a Natural Experiment

The perspective held by philosophers, and later by psychologists, that deafness is a rare and powerful natural experiment is certainly true. The perspective that deafness represents an experiment solely with respect to language deprivation is certainly false. Language exposure is reduced and altered by auditory impairment. Deaf children raised by normal-hearing parents (who also have nohearing-impaired siblings) undoubtedly receive less exposure to language than their normal-hearing cohorts. Additionally, the restrictions placed on their receptive abilities bring about concomitant changes in the type of language, and the linguistic media, to which deaf children are exposed. Therefore, the primary characteristic manipulated by deafness as a natural experiment condition is language exposure.

However, language exposure is not the only condition associated with deafness that may affect the development of intelligence. Deafness also confounds reduced, inconsistent, and garbled auditory stimulation, medical trauma and associated physical and cognitive-behavioral handicaps, genetic anomalies, altered and dysfunctional family dynamics, and sociological factors that generally place deaf children at a disadvantage relative to their normal-hearing cohorts. Some of these factors may be presumed to influence the development of intelligence among deaf children in much the same way that they are presumed to influence intelligence among normal-hearing children (e.g., SES). Conversely, the effect of some factors may not be estimated because they are unique to deaf children (e.g., being a minority member within one's own family).

The conditions of deafness as a natural experiment are further complicated by subgroups of deaf children. Specifically, deaf children of hearing parents with no deaf siblings (HP) differ from deaf children of hearing parents with one or more deaf siblings (HP/DS), and these groups in turn differ from deaf children of deaf parents (DP). These groups vary with respect to auditory deprivation, language exposure, medical and genetic factors, family dynamics, and sociological parameters. Consequently, contrasts and comparisons between these subgroups may provide insight into how these factors associated with deafness affect the development of intelligence.

Despite the ability to define multiple domains associated with deafness, and to distinguish between subgroups of deaf people, there is still a considerable gap between what is known about deafness in general and what any particular deaf person experiences in the course of intellectual development. For example, most congenitally, profoundly deaf people will use sign language as their primary means of communication, but it cannot be inferred that all of them do so. Likewise, variability on key criteria in any one domain (e.g., onset, type, severity, and use of a hearing aid in auditory impairment) cannot be systematically measured or controlled. The conceptualization of deafness as a natural experiment mandates an emphasis on aggregate distinctions between groups, but it should be remembered that there is considerable variability within groups. If the natural experiment of deafness appears complex, then I have done a good job of identifying the factors confounded with deafness.

If this natural experiment appears so hopelessly confounded that it cannot be seen as potentially valuable, then I have erred. The fact that deafness is a complex web of tangled factors in no way invalidates its value as a natural experiment. Deafness, and associated environmental and genetic factors, provides a rare opportunity to study the effects of environment and genes that is not possible in controlled experimentation. It is clear that intentional, systematic manipulation of factors associated with deafness would be unethical. Therefore, the only way to study the impact these factors have on the development of intelligence in humans is to study naturally occurring phenomena that change genetic and environmental factors (e.g., adoption, deafness).

The critical feature that the natural experiment of deafness provides to the study of intellectual differences between racial and ethnic groups is the separation of race from the host of variables associated with deafness. In many social settings, race is confounded with language exposure, prevalence of medical trauma, non-standard family constellations and dynamics, and a wide array of sociological parameters. The fact that race is essentially a biological, and therefore genetic, condition also confounds genetic factors. Consequently, determining the relative contributions of genetic and environmental factors to the well-documented differences in IQ between racial groups is difficult, if not impossible. I have argued elsewhere (Braden, 1988) that the attempts to isolate environmental from genetic effects using currently existing conditions has obfuscated the important study of between-group differences in IQ. Because the most desirable course of action (i.e., direct experimentation by manipulation of environmental and genetic influences) is not available, natural experiment conditions in which the confounding effects of genetic endowment (specifically, race) and environment are manipulated provide potentially fertile ground for research. Deafness is one such natural experiment, which should be considered along with other quasi-experiments (e.g., adoption) in the attempt to study the relative impacts of genetic and environmental effects on intelligence.

Two metaphors for the natural experiment of deafness could tie the study of intelligence in deaf people to a broader psychological and scientific base. The first metaphor would be that of minority group status. Deaf people clearly constitute a cultural minority group. They share a common (nonstandard) language, are held in low esteem by dominant majority groups, are often discriminated against in social and economic interactions, and suffer the economic and political effects of impoverishment and powerlessness. However, deafness is dissimilar from minority group status in a number of ways. Deaf people experience many disabilities not normally experienced by racial or ethnic minorities, including drastically reduced exposure to language presented in nonstandard media, auditory deprivation, high rates of organic traumata, reduced or nonexistent exposure to the content and members of their minority culture, abnormal genetic endowment, and dysfunctional family interactions. Deaf people are at a relative advantage compared to other minority groups in distal social interactions, and (in most cases) in their apparent membership in dominant racial or ethnic groups. Deaf people differ from ethnic and racial minority groups in that they are born into families that do not share their minority status, they are not members of a minority group that is in the majority in another time or place, nor do they often have a history of the deliberate economic exploitation that is often associated with ethnic and racial minorities (e.g., deaf people have never been imported into a country to provide inexpensive labor to advance the dominant majority).

The second metaphor for deafness as a natural experiment is provided by adoption studies. Adoption studies disrupt the confound between genetics and environment by placing a child into a family with whom the child presumably has little genetic relationship. Oddly enough, deafness complements adoption as a quasi-experimental condition. Whereas adopted children are different genetically from family members, but share a common familial environment, deaf children are genetically similar to family members, but experience a radically different within-family environment due to their deafness. The analogy between adoption and deafness must be tempered by the fact that deaf children with normal-hearing parents and siblings have recessive genetic deafness, and therefore a genotype that may differ from the genotypes shared by their siblings. Thus, in much the same way that adopted children are studied to determine the degree to which genetics and environment influence the development of intelligence, I believe that deaf people may be studied to discriminate the effects of environment and intelligence. The outcomes of this "natural experiment" created by deafness can therefore be explored to enhance our understanding of the ways in which genetics and environment act to affect the distribution of intelligence between groups.

3

The Study of Deaf People's Intelligence

Deaf people provide a compelling natural experiment in the study of intelligence. The outcomes of this natural experiment are summarized in this chapter. Published and unpublished studies of deaf people deliberately, and in some cases unwittingly, describe the consequences of language deprivation, high rates of organic trauma, and the many other factors associated with deafness. Many studies intended to draw a parallel between the conditions experienced by deaf people and their consequent intelligence; many other studies simply reported intelligence test scores as part of research unrelated to deafness as a natural experiment. Regardless of the intent of the study, research reporting deaf people's performance on tests of intelligence was examined and included in this review.

One of the great challenges in this effort is locating relevant material As I have argued elsewhere (Braden, 1989a, 1992), research on deafness is widely scattered between traditional research media (e.g., refereed publications, books, scholarly presentations), educational resources (e.g., Educational Resource Information Center [ERIC]), and the media focusing on deafness (e.g., newsletters, journals, unpublished manuscripts). The studies were acquired over years of searching published articles and reviewing unpublished sources (such as dissertations, ERIC manuscripts, and extensive personal solicitation of writers and researchers in the field for unpublished works). Although there are undoubtedly some studies that were inadvertently overlooked in this search, the 208 studies included in this review, which capture data from 171,517 hearing-impaired people in 234 independent samples, provide the largest single compilation of data describing deaf people's intelligence to date.

In this chapter, I will set the stage for the results obtained from this analysis by describing the methods used to obtain and review the influence of deafness on intelligence. The research will then be analyzed to show in what ways deafness,

65

and the factors associated with deafness, influences the development of intelligence. These results will lay the foundation for understanding environmental and genetic effects on intelligence, and how such factors may affect differences in IQ between groups of people.

Methods of Obtaining and Reviewing Studies

Studies were obtained over a multiyear search of the literature. At various times during the search, computerized data bases (e.g., ERIC, Psychological Abstracts) were reviewed for studies reporting intelligence data from samples of deaf people. Identified studies were obtained, and the reference lists within these studies was used to identify and obtain other studies. In this manner, a large body of studies reporting the IQs of deaf people were identified and collected for analysis. The second phase of the search constituted a volume-by-volume review of the most productive sources of published studies (viz. *American Annals of the Deaf* and *Volta Review*) for articles that included intelligence data, but may not have appeared in the computerized searches or other reference lists because the article's focus was not the intelligence of deaf people (e.g., an article describing instructional outcomes of a program might report the mean IQ of the sample as descriptive data). The third phase of the search identified books, proceedings of conferences and conventions, and other booklike material from three university library systems (including Gallaudet University's Deafness Collection). Finally, major contributors in the field, and those responsible for control of dissemination channels (e.g., editors of major journals), were contacted by letter and by telephone to solicit unpublished works, technical reports, and other resources not identified by other search strategies.

Throughout the search for studies, the following criteria were used to include or exclude studies from the pool for analysis:

1. The study must use some identifiable test of intelligence, of which the primary focus is individual differences (e.g., experimental tests of individual differences in intellect were included, but studies using Piagetian measures or other methods eschewing individual differences were excluded).
2. The study must describe the performance of the sample in either quantitative (e.g., M IQ = 99.92) or qualitative (e.g., "two-years delayed") fashion. (Studies merely reporting that intelligence tests were used, or those reporting correlations without levels of performance, were excluded from the analysis.)
3. The study must report data for hearing-impaired individuals separately from normal-hearing or other groups of individuals in the study, and must

provide a direct (e.g., control group mean) or indirect (e.g., standard score based on a normative group) bench mark for comparison with normal-hearing people.

4. Studies reporting data from tests of achievement or adaptive behavior may be included if scores are provided in an age-ratio, standard score, or other norm-referenced form. (Studies reporting achievement data by grade equivalent, that is, criterion-referenced metrics, were excluded from the analysis.)

5. Studies must be written in English, or have an English-language abstract describing major results.

The application of these criteria to the studies identified in the search yielded a final count of 208 studies. Studies using more than one sample were listed as independent sources, whereas studies using more than one test on the same sample were listed as redundant sources. The sample size, means, and other relevant data (e.g., name and type of test) were compiled into a single data base. IQs or qualitative descriptions of performance on intelligence tests were recorded from each study. Studies reporting IQs from a test with a normative mean other than 100 and a normative standard deviation other than 15 were converted to a scale equal to a standard IQ scale (e.g., British Ability Scale subtest scores, with a $M = 50$ and $SD = 10$, were transformed to scores with $M = 100$ and $SD = 15$). Studies reporting raw scores for hearing-impaired people were converted to standard scores based on the normal-hearing control group means and standard deviations. If control group data were not reported (e.g., only significance outcomes were reported), the outcome was treated as qualitative data. Meta-analytic techniques for analyzing the data base (e.g., Bangert-Drowns, Kulik, & Kulik, 1984; Light & Pillemer, 1984; Wolf, 1986) were used to collapse information across all studies to provide a comprehensive view of deaf people's intelligence.

Bibliometric Analyses

The bibliometric characteristics of the resulting data base were examined to determine the nature and characteristics of the bibliometric sample. There are a few key questions that must be asked before analyses can be conducted on a large data base. The first question is, Can each study be thought of as a unique, independent data point, or should some studies be excluded or treated differently than other studies? Generally, one hopes to answer this question in the affirmative, because it will provide the largest and most powerful data base for subsequent analyses. The question of integrity can be divided into two empirical questions: (1) Is there evidence of publication bias?, and (2) Are different results achieved if redundant sources (i.e., multiple scores from the same sample) are treated as independent sources (i.e., separate scores) in the analyses? (See Wolf, 1986, for a discussion of this issue.)

In this case, the answer to both of these questions is no. There is no evidence of publication bias ($t_{(178)}$ = 0.85, NS), which allows published and unpublished studies to be combined into a single data base. Likewise, there is no difference between the outcomes of independent sources and redundant sources ($t_{(178)}$ = 0.45, NS), which allowed repeated measures taken on a single sample to be coded and treated as independent reports. Thus, the final data base consisted of 324 reports of mean IQ, and 52 qualitative reports of intelligence from samples of hearing-impaired people, which were derived from 208 distinct studies containing 234 distinct samples.

This data base of published and unpublished research can be thought of as a mine, from which nuggets of information can be extracted, or mined. The primary tool needed to mine the data base is a question, which is then answered by applying a statistical procedure to the data base. The first questions to be asked of this data base are: (1) Is the year in which the study was disseminated related to the IQ reported in the study? and (2) What kinds of samples were obtained in the studies within this data base?

Year of Dissemination and Reported IQ

The 324 reports of mean IQ were correlated with their year of dissemination. The result was positive (r = .25) and statistically significant ($p < .001$). This means that there is a tendency for earlier studies to yield lower mean IQs than later studies. The relationship between year of dissemination and mean IQ is illustrated in Figure 3.1.

Examination of Figure 3.1 suggests that a few extremely low values, published fairly early in the history of research, lead to the correlation between year of dissemination and mean IQ. There are at least two accounts of the relationship between mean IQ and year of dissemination. The first is that deaf children are "catching up" relative to their normal-hearing peers. The second is that methods used in early studies depress IQs, and that more recent studies use methods less likely to depress IQs. Each of these possibilities is considered in later sections of this chapter. The point I am making at this time is that the "mine" of studies can provide one with the ability to answer a question that no single study could answer. Given that any individual study is released in a particular year, it is not possible for the study itself to note the drift or trend relating low IQs with early research, and relatively higher IQs with later research. The relationship between publication date and IQ will be discussed later in this chapter; for now, let it suffice to say that this analysis provides a good illustration of the kinds of "nuggets" buried in this mine of information regarding deaf people's intelligence.

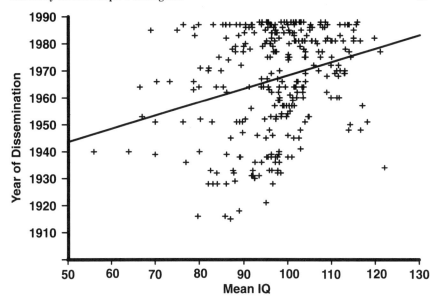

FIGURE 3.1. Year of dissemination and mean IQ reported by studies of deaf people.

Sample Descriptions

The studies contained samples ranging in size from 4 to 21,307 in number (median sample size = 60.5). There is no linear relationship between sample size and the IQ reported from the sample. However, the distribution of IQ is clearly related to sample size, as shown in Figure 3.2.

Visual inspection of Figure 3.2 shows that as sample size increases, the IQs tend to converge on a value near 100. This forms a distribution of findings similar to an inverted funnel, or normal distribution. The shape of this distribution conforms closely to a distribution that is created by the relationship between the standard error of the sample mean and the size of the sample. In other words, larger samples have smaller standard errors, and therefore exhibit less variation, than smaller samples, which have larger standard errors and therefore more variation. This outcome is reassuring, because it indicates that there is a central value on which the data points tend to converge. The issue of normality is important, because if data points are normally distributed around a single point, this suggests that a common source of variation underlies all studies.

There are also quantitative tests to determine whether studies tend to form a symmetrical distribution around a single value. One method used to determine whether the distribution of studies is normal is a test for homogeneity (Wolf, 1986), which requires means and standard deviations of the study to calculate

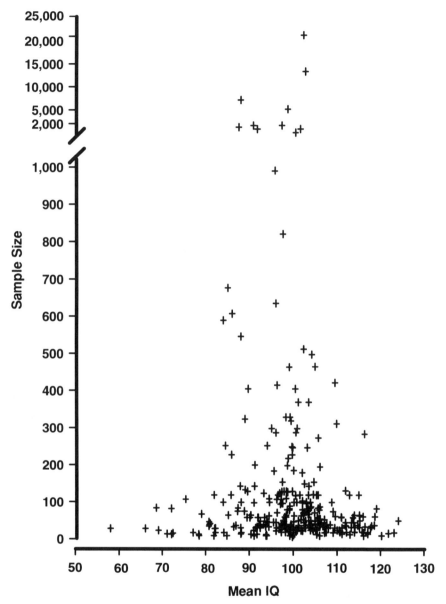

FIGURE 3.2. Distribution of mean IQ by sample size for studies of deaf people.

excessive variation. The 193 studies in the data base with both means and standard deviations were extracted for examination. These 193 studies are normally distributed, in that the test for departure from normality was nonsignificant ($X^2_{(192)}$ = 129.40, NS).

Visual inspection of the data points and the quantitative test of normality concur in suggesting that the studies in this data base are normally distributed about a common mean. However, visual inspection of the distribution of data points suggests a slight negative skew, or leftward drift, in the distribution of studies by sample size. This negative skew is noticeable for all sample sizes. Large sample sizes may have a slight negative skew because many large samples use survey techniques to collect data. Consequently, experimental procedures (which will be shown to affect IQ) are uncontrolled and likely to skew IQs in a negative direction. Comparison of the results of Figure 3.2 to those in Figure 3.1 also suggests that a few studies report substantially lower IQs than the IQs reported by the majority of studies. Causes for the negative skew in reported IQs are considered in later sections of this chapter, and in Chapter 4.

Unfortunately, a large proportion of studies (46%) failed to report hearing loss data for the samples of deaf people included in the studies. However, the studies that reported data generally sampled people with severe to profound hearing losses (44%). Analyses of the methods and sample characteristics, and how these characteristics affect outcome of IQ, are provided in the following sections.

The bibliometric analyses contained in this section describe a large and varied data base of research. The data base contains published and unpublished studies, redundant and independent data points, and it spans a wide range of years, and includes a wide range of sample sizes. Two consistencies or patterns are important to note as precursors to the results contained in other sections: (1) year of dissemination is related to outcome, with earlier studies reporting lower IQs than later, or more recent, studies; and (2) although a large proportion of studies fail to describe the hearing loss of the subjects included in the research, the majority of studies investigated the intellectual performance of severely to profoundly deaf people. These findings set the stage for the critical questions of this book, which are: (1) Does deafness affect IQ? and (2) Can factors associated with deafness be isolated to determine their relative influence on deaf people's IQs?

The Distribution of Deaf People's IQs

The outcomes of the natural experiment of deafness have been reported in quantitative (i.e., mean IQ) and qualitative forms. There are many statistical advantages to working with quantitative outcomes. For this reason, qualitative reports have often been overlooked in meta-analytic investigations (Light &

Pillemer, 1984). To give them their due attention, and to note their place as the foundation for many subsequent quantitative efforts, this review will begin by summarizing qualitative outcomes reported in the literature.

Qualitative Outcomes

The qualitative reports of deaf people's intelligence suggest that deaf people exhibit delayed or retarded intellectual development, but still fall within the low-average range in comparison with normal-hearing peers. The 52 reports of qualitative outcomes were grouped according to accepted labels for IQ ranges in 48 of the cases. The outcomes of this qualitative grouping are presented in Table 3.1

Inspection of Table 3.1 shows that the performance of deaf people on IQ tests is usually within the average to low-average range. Consequently, qualitative reports of the intelligence of hearing-impaired people suggest a distribution of IQs with a center in the lower portion of the average range. However, due to methodological factors, these results may misrepresent the actual distribution of deaf people's intelligence. Studies reporting qualitative outcomes tend to be dated (i.e., published earlier than quantitative studies), use oral methods of test administration, use verbal tests of intelligence, and calculate IQs in a ratio (rather than normative) metric. As will be shown, each of these factors is related to low IQ among samples of hearing-impaired people. Despite the probability that qualitative outcomes are depressed by methods used in the data collection, the outcomes nonetheless suggest that the intelligence of deaf people is within the average to low-average range in comparison with normal-hearing peers.

TABLE 3.1. Qualitative Reports of Deaf Persons' Intelligence

Category (IQ interval)	N studies	Qualitative descriptors in the study
Borderline (65–79)	5	Three year delay; EMR/Borderline; Borderline.
Low Average (80–89)	15	Two to three-year delay; Two-year delay; Low average; Lower; Delayed; Lag in development.
Average (90–109)	24	Average; About 95; Average to low average; Normal; All IQs greater than 90.
Above Average (110–119)	3	Above average; High average.
Superior (120 and above)	1	Superior.
Unclassified	4	10–12% mentally retarded; Fifth grade; Ninth grade; Not pathological.

Quantitative Outcomes

When quantitative reports of IQ are available, it is possible to consider two aspects of the distribution of those IQs: (1) the mean, or the measure of central tendency, and (2) the standard deviation, or the measure of variability. Each of these aspects can be used to describe the outcome of deafness as a natural experiment.

Means

The 324 reports of mean IQ for hearing-impaired subjects were combined to yield a grand mean of 97.14 (SD_m = 10.79), on a scale where the mean is 100 and the standard deviation is 15. Mean IQs from all studies ranged from a minimum of 56.00 to a maximum of 122.00. The median IQ for the data base is 97.79. Although IQ was not related to sample size (r = .05, NS), an unbiased effect size was calculated (Wolf, 1986). The unbiased effect size (M = 97.20) is quite similar to the grand mean. These findings are illustrated in Figure 3.3, which shows the expected mean for normal-hearing peers, the grand (unweighted) mean for deaf people, the median for samples of deaf people, and the unbiased effect size expressed as mean IQ.

The unbiased effect size, the grand mean, and the median are quite consistent

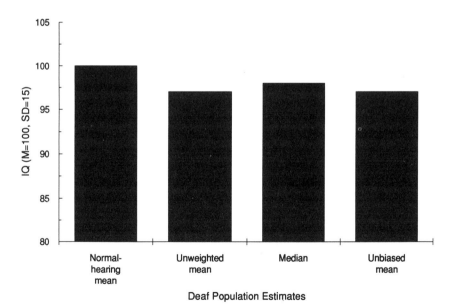

FIGURE 3.3. The expected mean IQ for normal-hearing people and the grand (unweighted) mean, median IQ, and unbiased mean across studies of deaf people.

in describing the mean for hearing-impaired subjects as being well within the average range. However, the grand mean of 97.14 is significantly lower than the normal-hearing mean of 100 ($t_{(323)}$ = 3.27, p < .001). Because the many studies in the data base provide strong statistical power, the difference between the expected mean of 100 and the obtained mean of 97.14 is statistically significant. However, the practical significance is marginal when the magnitude of the difference is expressed as a function of the variability found in the normal sample. The difference between the grand mean for deaf people and the expected mean of 100 is only 0.19 *SD* units. Thus, the practical significance of the difference between deaf and normal-hearing samples is questionable. The mean of 97.14 is quite similar to the normal-hearing population mean of 100.

Standard Deviations

There were 199 reports of standard deviations in the literature. The grand average of standard deviations reported in the literature (M_{sd} = 15.33, SD_{sd} = 3.38) is quite similar to the normal-hearing normative value of 15 ($t_{(198)}$ = 1.36, NS). These results suggest that deaf people not only have a similar average IQ, but also exhibit similar variation on IQ tests relative to normal-hearing cohorts.

The qualitative and quantitative data describing global outcomes suggest that the distributions of IQ in deaf and in normal-hearing populations are quite similar. The qualitative data suggest that the distribution of IQ for hearing-impaired people falls within the average to low-average range. The quantitative data yield a higher estimate, because the grand IQ mean is very close to the mean of normal-hearing people. In addition, the average standard deviation suggests that hearing-impaired and normal-hearing people exhibit a similar spread in their IQ distributions. Thus, at first blush, it would appear that the natural experiment created by deafness has relatively little impact on IQ. This is consistent with other reviews (e.g., Vernon, 1967c) that conclude that deafness has little impact on deaf people's intelligence.

However, there are two caveats to consider. The first is that the distribution of study outcomes is negatively skewed, suggesting that some study features are likely to result in low estimates of IQ. The second caveat is that there are many factors involved in deafness, and perhaps different factors have different influences on IQ. Before the latter issue can be considered, it is imperative to understand the influences of research methods on outcomes. The search for study features related to IQ outcomes will focus on the methodological characteristics of the study, and on the characteristics of the samples used in the study.

The Impact of Methods on Reported IQ

Before a scientist can draw conclusions from a set of data, she must establish whether the ways in which she collected the data influence her outcomes. For example, blood pressure and pulse rate are quite different if taken at rest and during strenuous exercise. The length of a rabbit measured tail to nose is quite different than the length measured ears to toes. Likewise, the methods used in the studies in this review may have affected the IQs reported in those studies. The type of intelligence test used in research, the metric in which IQs are reported, and the procedures used for administration of IQ tests all may affect IQ independently of the individuals who are included in the study. The nature and influence of these methods are discussed in the following sections with respect to how they shape the results of deafness as a natural experiment.

Types of Intelligence Tests

Intelligence tests vary considerably in item content, item structure, the presence and organization of subtests, and other factors that may affect scores. Most individual tests of intelligence used in clinical and research efforts are battery, or general, tests of intelligence. These tests typically assume that any single method for estimating a person's intellectual ability is less accurate than the sum total of a number of distinct, independent estimates. Therefore, battery IQ tests typically employ multiple tests, each of which is termed a subtest, and use procedures for combining the results of multiple subtests into an overall estimate of IQ.

The influence of test type on IQ is illustrated in Figure 3.4, which presents the average IQs derived from four types of intelligence tests. The types of tests are (1) verbal, (2) performance, (3) motor-free nonverbal, and (4) unknown test types. Visual inspection of the results strongly suggests that verbal tests of intelligence and, to a lesser degree, motor-free nonverbal tests of intelligence yield substantially lower estimates of intelligence than do performance and unknown types of intelligence tests. This impression is supported by statistical analyses. However, there are important distinctions to be made between test types in the number of studies, the variability within test type, the ways in which data are collected, and the interpretations derived from the results. These issues are considered in the following sections.

Verbal versus Nonverbal Scales

The distinction between verbal and nonverbal scales is important, because subtests within each scale are based on quite different assumptions about an individual's background prior to testing. Subtests within verbal scales are based on the assumption that the individual being tested has been exposed to the verbal content of the items in the verbal subtests approximately as often as the subjects in the normative sample. In this way, an individual's score on the verbal scale may be assumed to reflect the aptitude or intelligence of the individual, and not merely reflect an individual's past exposure to verbal information. This means that chil-

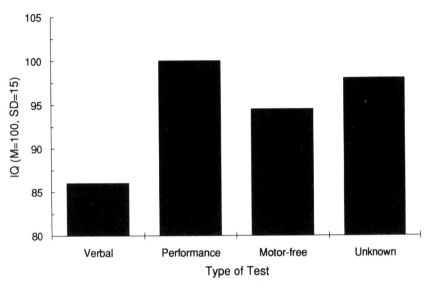

FIGURE 3.4. Mean IQ for studies of deaf people by test type.

dren who score below age-mates on a verbal test are inferred to have lower than average ability, or aptitude, for verbal reasoning. Conversely, individuals who score above age-mates are considered to have above-average aptitude for verbal reasoning. The assumption that children receive approximately equal exposure to vocabulary words, social settings and customs, relationships among word classes, general information, and other content sampled in verbal scales has been hotly debated (e.g., Jensen, 1980; Jensen & Reynolds, 1982; cf. Mercer, 1979; Williams, 1974). However, there is uniform agreement that systematic deprivation of exposure to verbal, socially specific knowledge impairs performance on verbal scales independent of an individual's underlying aptitude (e.g., a monolingual, French-speaking scholar would do poorly on an English-language version of an intelligence test).

The distinction between verbal and nonverbal scales is important when scales are used to assess hearing-impaired people. The assumption that hearing-impaired individuals receive prior exposure to verbal content equal to a normal-hearing normative sample is simply unwarranted. The most commonly identified concomitant of hearing loss is language deprivation and the related social isolation that accompanies deafness. Therefore, the low score of a deaf person on a verbal intelligence scale could imply that the individual has limited verbal aptitude, or it could merely reflect the fact that the deaf person has been denied the opportunity to acquire verbal and social knowledge due to the person's hearing loss. For this reason, verbal scales and intelligence tests with verbal content are strongly discouraged for use with deaf people (e.g., Sullivan & Vernon, 1979; Vernon & Brown, 1964). Consequently, it is essential to separate the results of studies using verbal tests and scales from those using nonverbal tests and scales.

Verbal IQs of Hearing-Impaired People. There are 32 verbal IQ means within the meta-analytic data base. The average of these 32 reports ($M = 85.54$, $SD = 9.54$) is significantly lower than IQs reported for other types of tests ($F_{(3,323)} = 21.79$, $p < .0001$). The standard deviations reported for verbal IQs were also smaller than the global standard deviation estimates ($M_{SD} = 12.84$, $SD_{SD} = 3.26$)($F_{(3,198)} = 5.71$, $p < .001$). Consequently, deaf people do not perform as well on verbal tests of intelligence as they do on other types of intelligence tests, and they have a more restricted range of performance on verbal intelligence tests than on other types of intelligence tests.

The mean verbal IQ for deaf people ($M = 85.54$) is well below the mean for normal-hearing people ($t_{(31)} = -8.78$, $p < .0001$). When expressed as a function of variation in the normal-hearing population, the mean verbal IQ for deaf people is -0.97 SDs below the expected mean—a substantial difference by any account. Also, deaf people exhibit significantly smaller variation in verbal IQ than normal-hearing peers ($t_{(21)} = -3.04$, $p < .01$). The low verbal IQs reported for deaf people are hardly surprising, given the fact that reduced exposure to verbal content depresses scores on tests that sample verbal content. The restricted distribution of verbal IQs may be due to "floor effects," in which the tests simply do not have enough easy items to differentiate among deaf people. The restricted distribution of verbal IQs may could also be caused by the severely constrained linguistic environments of deaf children, which in turn reduce variability between high- and low-scoring people. In either case, the difference between deaf people and their normal-hearing peers is significant from statistical *and* practical perspectives.

The somewhat surprising outcome is that there are so few reports of verbal IQ for hearing-impaired people. Research on intelligence with normal-hearing people uses verbal tests quite frequently, because they are less expensive to purchase and administer, are often more reliable, and are better predictors of academic success than nonverbal tests. However, verbal IQ tests have been recognized as inappropriate for deaf populations since their introduction to the United States at the beginning of the twentieth century. Pintner and Patterson (1917, p. 665) stated, "In 1914 we investigated the possibility of testing the deaf child by means of the Binet-Simon scale [a verbal test of intelligence], finding the scale absolutely impracticable for . . . adequate measure of the deaf child's intelligence." Consequently, researchers and clinicians working with deaf people have avoided the use of verbal tests of intelligence, preferring instead nonverbal scales and tests.

From a research perspective, the avoidance of verbal scales is unfortunate. For example, there is no research to show whether verbal IQ tests are statistically biased measures of deaf person's verbal reasoning performance. It is not known whether verbal IQ tests predict criterion performance (e.g., scholastic achievement) with the same accuracy and precision for deaf children as found for normal-hearing children. However, there are some data reported in the literature that shed light, however dim, on the question of verbal aptitude in deaf people. These data are derived primarily from tests of academic achievement, which is closely related to verbal reasoning and aptitude.

Academic Achievement of Hearing-Impaired People. A substantial research effort has been aimed at defining deaf children's performance on measures of academic achievement. For more than 20 years, the Office of Demographic Studies at Gallaudet University has conducted annual surveys of deaf children's performance on the Stanford Achievement Test (SAT). The Office has also developed national norms of the SAT for hearing-impaired people. The national surveys have complemented smaller-scale efforts to define the academic achievement of hearing-impaired children enrolled in North American schools.

The results of these studies show that the achievement of hearing-impaired children is well below levels reported for their normal-hearing peers. This is true at every age level, and becomes more pronounced over time (e.g., Allen, 1986; Trybus & Karchmer, 1977). The mathematics achievement scores of hearing-impaired children are closer to normal-hearing levels than reading achievement scores, but hearing-impaired children show significant delay in all academic domains. The levels reported for achievement tests on national surveys are similar to verbal IQs reported in the research (i.e., the mean achievement score of hearing-impaired children is one or more standard deviations below normal-hearing norms). Therefore, there is evidence on a larger scale to corroborate poor acquisition of verbal skills and verbal information among hearing-impaired children.

Close inspection of the verbal IQ and achievement data shows that the two measures are substantially correlated (Davis et al., 1986; Maller & Braden, 1993) among hearing-impaired children. However, it is also true that both measures are substantially correlated with the degree of hearing loss of the individual (e.g., Moores et al., 1987). Verbal intelligence tests and achievement tests could tap underlying verbal aptitude, as in normal-hearing populations, or they could merely be related because they are sensitive to hearing loss. In other words, one account of the finding would argue that the underlying aptitude of the individual gives rise to the close relationship of verbal IQ and scholastic achievement tests, whereas another explanation would describe the close relationship between verbal IQ and achievement as an artifact of exposure to verbal content, which is directly mediated by the degree of hearing loss experienced by the individual.

Data reported by Reynolds (1976) suggest that the latter model is the best explanation of the data. When variation in reading comprehension scores due to hearing loss is statistically removed from a regression equation, IQ does not enter as a significant predictor of hearing-impaired children's reading performance. In other words, the effect of exposure to verbal items, as mediated by hearing loss, appears to account for more of the variation in reading comprehension than measures of aptitude, or intellectual ability.

These findings raise the question of whether verbal tests of intelligence are actually biased when used with deaf people. On the one hand, the data reported by Reynolds suggest that verbal IQ tests may demonstrate construct bias for hearing-impaired populations, because they correlate substantially with a measure that is not believed to be related to verbal aptitude (i.e., hearing loss). On the other hand, it is possible that early and consistent deprivation of auditory and linguistic input may stunt the development of verbal abilities in hearing-impaired children, and that the correlations among hearing impairment, achievement, and verbal IQ merely reflect a common base of impoverished verbal aptitude. The distinction between these positions is critical to an appropriate interpretation of the data, for in the first scenario, the low verbal IQs of deaf people are a function of test bias, and in the second scenario, the low verbal IQs of deaf people accurately reflect delayed or impoverished verbal reasoning ability. Clearly these competing hypotheses must be resolved if one is to make any sense of the data.

At least two investigators have attempted to measure the verbal aptitude of hearing-impaired people that underlies performance on psychometric tests. In one study (Miller, 1984), deaf children were administered the Verbal Scale of the Wechsler Intelligence Scale for Children-Revised (WISC-R). Miller first presented an item in signed English, and if the item was failed, she repeated the item up to three additional trials, with each successive rendition departing from English and approaching American Sign Language. The WISC-R verbal IQ of deaf children obtained from this procedure (which deleted the Vocabulary subtest of the WISC-R) placed within the average range ($M = 96.43$). Miller interpreted these results to imply that deaf children, when assessed in their native language, have verbal aptitude within the average range.

Other research suggests that some children experience intellectual deficits regardless of the language used for testing. Conrad (1979) found that deaf children who used some form of subvocal, or subgestural, language for mediating behavior had significantly better performance on tests of achievement and intelligence (verbal and nonverbal) than deaf children with no internal language for mediating behavior. Even when children were matched on severity of hearing loss, those children who had acquired and used an internal language system performed better than those that did not use an internal system. Therefore, Conrad's work suggests that acquisition and use of a language facilitates development of verbal as well as nonverbal aptitude, whereas failure to use an internal language may stunt intellectual development.

The question of whether the effects of language deprivation merely suppress acquisition of verbal knowledge, or whether such deprivation has long-lasting or permanent effects on the development of verbal aptitude, has also been approached from theorists interested in critical stage theories of language acquisition. To date, the evidence has been divided, with some studies showing severe, pervasive, and apparently immutable deficits among hearing-impaired children. For example, Moores (1970) found that deaf children's performance on verbal reasoning tasks was significantly below that of normal-hearing peers, even when the deaf and normal-hearing subjects were matched for academic achievement levels. In other words, academic achievement tests and verbal IQ measures may *over*estimate deaf children's skills. Such findings indirectly support the possibility that early and consistent language deprivation leads to impoverished aptitude for verbal skills. However, neuropsychological studies of deaf adults show that the organization of language and language-related cognitive activities is not severely constrained by congenital, profound deafness (Poizner et al., 1987).

The current state of research does not answer the question, Do deaf children have permanent deficits in verbal aptitude as a result of early linguistic deprivation? Methods to operationally separate acquisition of verbal knowledge from direct assessment of underlying verbal ability have not yet been developed. However, the results from studies of verbal IQ and academic achievement among hearing-impaired people clearly show that hearing loss depresses acquisition of verbal knowledge and skills. Degree of hearing loss is directly and significantly related to verbal IQ and achievement, which supports the conclusion that environmental exposure to verbal knowledge significantly affects performance on verbally loaded tests. Experimental research (Moores, 1970) suggests that the estimate of verbal IQ for hearing-impaired people (about one standard deviation below normal-hearing norms) may overestimate their actual verbal reasoning skills. The question of whether this depressed performance is due to enduring deficits in the development of verbal aptitude or merely reflects a failure to acquire verbal and scholastic knowledge remains unanswered.

Nonverbal Intelligence Tests. The majority of studies investigating the intelligence of deaf people use nonverbal intelligence tests, of which there are two types: (1) performance tests, which require an individual to manipulate materials (e.g., blocks, puzzles) to solve tasks, and (2) motor-free nonverbal tests, which use nonverbal stimuli but do not require manipulation of materials. The most commonly used performance tests of intelligence with deaf people are the Wechsler Performance Scales, whereas the most commonly used motor-free test is Raven's Progressive Matrices. Both types of nonverbal tests minimize or eliminate verbal content in test items, and also attempt to reduce the verbal knowledge needed to understand directions.

Although with deaf people performance tests have been found to yield higher IQs than motor-free tests (e.g., Goetzinger & Rousey, 1957), most recommendations to use nonverbal tests with deaf people do not discriminate between performance and motor-free nonverbal IQ tests. Because test type may affect outcome, the nonverbal IQs included in this meta-analysis were classified according to the type of test used to obtain the IQ (performance or motor-free).

The mean IQ of deaf people from 195 reports using performance tests of intelligence is well within average limits (M = 99.95, SD = 10.52). Furthermore, this mean performance IQ (PIQ) does not differ significantly from the mean of 100 for normal-hearing people ($t_{(194)}$ = −0.07, NS). The average standard deviation from the 119 studies reporting PIQs among deaf people (M_{SD} = 15.36, SD_{SD} = 3.11) is also quite similar to the expected value (M = 15) for normal-hearing people ($t_{(118)}$ = 1.28, NS). Therefore, the mean and standard deviation of deaf people's PIQs are virtually identical to the distribution of PIQs in normal-hearing people.

The results from the motor-free nonverbal tests offer a slightly different conclusion. The 77 studies using motor-free nonverbal tests report a lower mean IQ (M = 94.57, SD = 7.97) than the mean of 100 for normal-hearing people ($t_{(76)}$ = −5.98, p < .0001). This difference is also large enough to have practical meaning (i.e., the average for deaf people is 0.36 SD units below the normal-hearing mean). However, the mean standard deviation (M_{SD} = 15.95, SD_{SD} = 3.64), based on 51 reports of standard deviations, is similar to the standard deviation of 15 reported for normal-hearing people ($t_{(50)}$ = 1.85, NS). These results suggest that the distribution of nonverbal IQ among deaf people, as measured by motor-free tests, is lower than the distribution of nonverbal IQ among normal-hearing people measured by motor-free tests, but the spread of nonverbal IQs is similar for both groups.

The current results also support previous findings that there is a difference between motor-intensive (i.e., performance) nonverbal tests and motor-free nonverbal tests. The average IQ derived from performance tests was higher than the mean IQ of the motor-free nonverbal tests ($F_{(3,320)}$ = 21.79, p < .0001). This finding suggests that performance tests and motor-free nonverbal intelligence tests are not equivalent.

There are at least four explanations why IQs from performance tests of intelligence are higher than IQs from motor-free nonverbal tests of intelligence for deaf people. The first explanation cites communication of task demands. Items on performance tests of intelligence may be readily demonstrated, whereas the processes required for motor-free tests of intelligence are not easily demonstrated. The second explanation cites manual manipulation and dexterity skills. Manual dexterity, perhaps acquired through extensive use of hands for communication, may boost performance on motor-bound tasks relative to performance on motor-free tasks (e.g., Braden, 1985a, 1987). The third explanation is that the solution of motor-free items is facilitated with verbal mediation, whereas the process of solving performance tasks is not particularly enhanced by verbal mediation strategies. Support for the influence of verbal mediation on nonverbal IQ is provided by Conrad (1979), who showed that deaf people with some form of internal language performed better on nonverbal, motor-free IQ tests than deaf people without internal language skills. Finally, it has been suggested that performance tests yield greater feedback than motor-free tasks, and consequently provide impulsive individuals with cues to let them know when their problem-solving strategies are unsuccessful. This in turn allows them the opportunity to correct their responses, leading to higher scores on motor-intensive tests than on motor-free tests (Kostrubala, Reed, & Braden, 1993).

These explanations are not mutually exclusive. For example, both hypotheses two and three could be true, in which case nonverbal intelligence would be depressed among deaf people because they lack internal mediation strategies, but the motor manipulation skills of deaf people boosts performance IQ to average levels. The data needed to test these hypotheses, and possible permutations of multiple hypotheses, are not yet available.

Unknown Types of Intelligence Tests. A minority of the studies reporting IQs for deaf people failed to specify the name or type of intelligence test used to obtain the data. Failure to specify the type of test used to obtain IQ was common for large-scale surveys of IQ (e.g., Ries & Voneiff, 1974; Schildroth, 1976) and for reports of IQ appearing prior to 1940. The mean of the 20 reports using unknown methods for estimating intelligence is well within the average range (M = 98.17, SD = 10.47), and does not differ from the mean of 100 ($t_{(19)}$ = 0.78, NS). Only 8 of these reports also listed standard deviations for the hearing-impaired people in the sample (M_{SD} = 17.35, SD_{SD} = 3.01). Although the larger variation of IQ is not significantly different from the normal-hearing value of 15 ($t_{(7)}$ = 2.20, NS), it approaches significance (p = .06). Coupled with the finding that the mean for unknown tests is between the mean for performance tests and the mean for motor-free tests of nonverbal intelligence, the substantial variability in IQ suggests that the unreported methods used for obtaining IQ mixed verbal, performance and motor-free nonverbal tests. Such a mix would increase the variability of reports, yet not substantially affect the average IQ if the proportions of test types included in the "unknown" category were similar to the proportions of test type reported in the literature. The results from unknown or unreported types of intelligence tests are well within the range of results reported for nonverbal tests, and similarly suggest that the distribution of IQ in deaf people is quite similar to the distribution of IQ in their normal-hearing peers.

Summary of Test-Type Findings. The comparisons among the types of test used to study deaf people's intelligence suggest that substantial and meaningful differences are associated with the type of test employed by the researcher. The use of verbal tests of intelligence yields much lower, and more tightly bunched, IQs than the IQs derived from performance intelligence tests. Likewise, not all nonverbal tests yield similar results. Motor-intensive nonverbal tests of intelligence yield higher IQs than motor-free tests of intelligence. Although the causes for these differences are hotly debated, the important conclusion is that test type must be considered when examining the effects of deafness on IQ.

Methods of Administration

The method by which an examiner administers a test also influences IQ. The method of communication used to administer tests to deaf people can be classified into oral speech, written, combined (speech and signs simultaneously presented), total communication (speech, signs, and other methods needed to convey meaning presented concurrently or in sequence), gestured, and unknown/unreported communication methods. A distinction was drawn between total communication and combined methods, because those studies adopting a total communication approach generally noted a rigid adherence to transliterating (i.e., translating English to signs in a word-for-word correspondence), whereas studies using the combined method adopted a more natural approach (i.e., using speech to supplement signs, but emphasizing comprehension rather than transliteration of directions). The average IQs reported by studies using these methods are presented in Figure 3.5. The results show that the method of test administration affects IQ ($F_{(5,318)}$ = 2.54, $p < .05$). The means and standard deviations of IQs reported for samples of hearing impaired students have been grouped by the method used for intelligence test administration, and are presented in Table 3.2

Meta-analytic findings are supported by the few experimental studies that have directly investigated how varying modes of test administration affect the IQs obtained from the tests. Goetzinger and Rousey (1957) administered the Wechsler Performance Scale to deaf and normal-hearing children using oral and gestural administrations. Although deaf children, who were administered the test in a gestural format, performed less well than normal-hearing peers who were given the test following standard administration in speech, there were no differences in performance between deaf children and normal-hearing children who were both given the test with gestural administration. On the basis of these results, Goetzinger and Rousey concluded that the slightly lower PIQs of deaf children were due to test administration factors, and not to any underlying difference in the distribution of PIQ among hearing-impaired people.

Sullivan's (1982) research likewise suggests that gestural or oral administrations yield lower PIQs than signed or combined administration methods. She assessed a group of hearing-impaired children on the Wechsler Performance Scale numerous times, each time changing the method of test administration. Her use of a counterbalanced design allowed her to conclude that total communication presented directly by the examiner, and total communication provided through an interpreter, produced higher PIQs than gestural or oral administration methods.

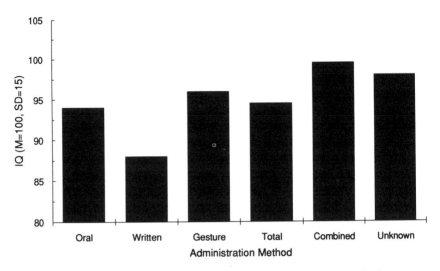

FIGURE 3.5. Mean IQ for studies of deaf people by administration method.

The consistency of experimental findings, clinical recommendations, and meta-analytic results demonstrates that variations in test administration procedures affect IQs reported for deaf people. From the vantage point of understanding how administration methods affect IQ, it is important to note that methods approximating the modes of communication used by the deaf community (i.e., signs, signs with speech) yield IQs closer to the normal-hearing group norm, whereas methods that employ modes of communication less commonly used by the deaf community (i.e., speech, writing) yield IQs lower than the normal-hearing group norm.

IQ Scales

At least four IQ scales, or methods for calculating IQs, are reported in the literature. The first method, which is the most common in the literature and the

TABLE 3.2. IQ Means and Standard Deviations by Method of Test Administration

Type of administration	N Studies	M	SD
Oral/speech	36	93.60	10.70
Written	5	88.25	11.69
Gestural/pantomime	35	96.04	9.18
Total communication	19	94.41	10.49
Combined (speech and signs)	54	99.56	9.13
Unknown/unreported	175	97.88	11.33

most familiar to contemporary psychologists, uses normative data to assign a deviation IQ to a raw score. Assignments are typically based on age, and the common method for assigning deviation IQs is to use published tables to translate a person's raw score, within the person's age group, to assign an IQ.

The second method for deriving IQ is the comparison sample method, in which deaf people's IQs are calculated as standard scores relative to the comparison sample. Fortunately, the comparison samples included in this meta-analysis comprised normal-hearing people with no additional disabilities. This method is similar to normative IQ calculations, with the exception that experimental samples are typically smaller than, and not as carefully selected as, the normative samples used to create IQ test tables.

The third method for calculating IQs is the now-outmoded ratio method. Research conducted 50 years ago or more frequently reports IQ as the ratio of mental age (obtained from an intelligence test) to chronological age, with the resulting number multiplied by 100. This metric, first proposed by Wilhelm Stern but popularized by Louis Terman, still exists in some tests (e.g., the Hiskey-Nebraska Test of Learning Aptitude Learning Quotient), but is rarely used today because of problems associated with equality of ratio IQ distributions across ages. Finally, some studies fail to provide information regarding how IQs were derived. Therefore, the fourth type of scaling method is "unknown," in that insufficient information was available to assign it to one of the other three methods.

Different methods for deriving IQ produce different mean IQs ($F_{(3,179)}$ = 2.99, $p < .05$). The mean for normative methods (i.e., deviation IQs based on normative, rather than experimental, samples) is higher ($M = 97.36$) than IQs derived from experimental samples ($M = 93.42$), ratio IQs ($M = 93.34$) and IQs derived from unknown methods ($M = 91.99$). In other words, researchers who compared deaf people's IQs to normal-hearing, normative samples were likely to yield estimates closer to "average" levels. This finding strengthens the confidence in the conclusion that the distribution of nonverbal IQ among deaf people is quite similar to the distribution of IQ for normal-hearing people, because the normative comparison method is considered to be superior to the other alternatives. As researchers depart from recommended procedures, they are more likely to find differences in mean IQ between groups of hearing-impaired and normal-hearing people. Figure 3.6 illustrates the effect of IQ scale on the mean IQ reported by researchers.

Deaf Norms versus Normal-Hearing Norms

Practitioners and researchers in the field of deafness have the option of using norms obtained from hearing-impaired individuals on at least five tests of intelligence, namely:

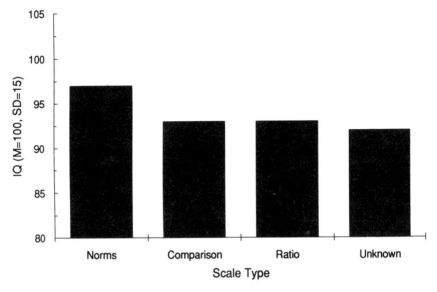

FIGURE 3.6. Mean IQ for studies of deaf people by IQ scale.

1. Wechsler Intelligence Scale for Children-Revised
2. Hiskey-Nebraska Test of Learning Aptitude
3. Snijders-Ooman Nonverbal Intelligence Test
4. Pintner Nonlanguage Test
5. Raven's Progressive Matrices

Although the use of deaf norms is questionable for statistical and clinical reasons (Braden, 1985c, 1990b, 1992), some researchers feel that the use of norms based on hearing-impaired people is preferable to the application of norms based on normal-hearing people for deriving deaf people's IQs. Regardless of the debate over the recommended use of such norms, there is an empirical question to be asked of the literature: Does the use of norms based on deaf people yield IQs that are different than norms based on hearing people?

The answer to this question appears to be no. The mean obtained from 161 studies using norms from normal-hearing people ($M = 95.12$, $SD = 9.57$) is similar ($t_{(178)} = 1.86$, NS) to the mean obtained from 19 studies using norms from hearing-impaired people ($M = 99.43$, $SD = 9.11$). The fact that these means do not differ significantly lends support to the conclusion that the distribution of IQ is quite similar for hearing-impaired and normal-hearing people. However, it is not possible to prove the null hypothesis (i.e., that there are no differences in the distributions of IQ in deaf and normal-hearing people). The comparison of means suggests that there are no statistically significant differences relative to the type of norms assigned, although the probability level associated with this statistic approaches the level needed for critical significance (i.e., the p value of the t statistic = .07, which is only slightly beyond the commonly accepted critical value of .05). Assuming that the means and variances remained constant, it would require about 10 additional studies using deaf norms to achieve statistical significance. Therefore, it is possible that norms based on deaf people may yield slightly higher IQs than norms based on normal-hearing people.

There are three explanations why IQs derived from norms based on deaf people should be higher than IQs based on normal-hearing people. The first possibility is that the slightly lower distribution of IQ among deaf people is sufficiently different from the IQ distribution of normal-hearing people that norms on the slightly lower group yield slightly higher IQs. The second possibility is the age of the samples used to calculate deaf norms. For example, norms for the Hiskey-Nebraska Test of Learning Aptitude (HNTLA), which are based on deaf children in residential schools, appear to be at least 25 years old (an may have been collected in the 1920s). The fact that the population mean of IQ improves over time (Flynn, 1986) means the higher IQs for deaf people obtained on the HNTLA could be due to the fact that deaf people are being compared to cohorts of four generations ago. Such comparisons consistently lead to higher IQs than comparisons to more recent normative samples.

A third possibility is that sampling methods employed in the development of deaf norms systematically skew the normative samples toward lower IQs, which in turn results in higher IQs when the normative samples are used. This seems contradictory at first glance, but a quick analogy may clarify the situation. If one's height were compared to a normative sample, one's normative height score increases as the average of the normative sample decreases (i.e., an individual has a high normative height, or "HQ," relative to midgets, but the same individual has a much lower HQ when the normative sample is professional basketball players). Normative samples of deaf children are neither randomly selected nor stratified, and most samples are taken exclusively from residential schools for the deaf. These factors (as will be shown) are likely to lead to lower scores among the normative group, thus creating artificially high IQs when deaf norms are used.

Therefore, the slight difference in IQ distribution between deaf and normal-hearing people, the dated nature of samples, and/or sampling bias might yield higher IQs when norms based on hearing-impaired people are used than when norms based on normal-hearing people are used to compute IQs. However, it should be remembered that, at the present time, the most conservative interpretation of the results is that use of norms based on hearing status make no difference in the IQs obtained for deaf people.

Summary of Methodological Factors

The results of the meta-analysis are congruent with experimental research, and recommendations for clinical practice, in showing that methods of assessing deaf people affect IQs. Linguistic demands in the content of the test items, and in the comprehension of test directions, affect the obtained IQs. Tests that minimize language loading in item content and that are administered in ways that promote deaf people's comprehension of test and task demand, result in IQ estimates very close to those obtained from normative samples of normal-hearing people. These conclusions do not readily account for the slightly lower IQs obtained on motor-free tests of nonverbal intelligence. However, nonverbal intelligence tests, and the use of gestures, signs, and other forms of manual communication, clearly produce IQs that are close to IQs found for normal-hearing people. When appropriate methods of investigation are used, the findings clearly and consistently point to the conclusion that deaf people's nonverbal intellectual skills are well within average limits and do not differ substantially from the intelligence of normal-hearing peers.

Conclusions regarding verbal intelligence in deaf people are not as clear. It is impossible to separately assess the effects of an impoverished linguistic knowledge base and underlying verbal ability (i.e., do the low verbal IQs of deaf people merely reflect a lack of exposure to spoken language or a deficit in the ability to reason with any form of language?). Perhaps the safest conclusion to draw is that the low verbal IQs of deaf people document the deleterious effects of language deprivation on verbal IQ and achievement, even if the interpretation of these low verbal IQs remains ambiguous.

Demographic Variables Affecting IQ

If it can be shown that how something is studied influences what is found, then it can certainly be argued that what—or whom—is studied is also of importance. There are undoubtedly many ways in which variations in samples can be studied, but the most common approach is to describe samples according to demographic characteristics. By comparing outcomes grouped by demographic characteristics, it becomes possible to determine what kinds of demographic factors could influence the IQs reported for samples of deaf people.

Demographic characteristics can be conceptually organized into two major divisions. The first division is those demographic characteristics associated with IQ differences in normal-hearing people. These general demographic factors include age, gender, and race. Thus, the first set of demographic analyses poses the question, Is the pattern of IQ differences and similarities among demographic groups of deaf people similar to the patterns found in normal-hearing demographic groups? The second division of demographic factors comprises those factors that are of unique interest in the study of deaf people. These deafness-related factors include: (1) age at onset of hearing loss, (2) degree or severity of hearing loss, (3) school placement (residential versus day), (4) additional disabilities, and (5) parental hearing status. The question posed in this second group of analysis is, To what degree do demographic conditions associated with deafness affect IQ? Analyses using both divisions of demographic factors are critical for understanding the relationship between demographics and intelligence in hearing-impaired people.

General Demographic Factors Associated with Intelligence

Age

Because samples in the meta-analysis routinely used groups of hearing-impaired people varying widely in age, it is impossible to correlate reported IQ with the mean age of the sample. However, a number of studies reported IQs for cross sections of hearing-impaired people, usually by ages commonly found in schools (i.e., 6–20 years of age). Some longitudinal research has also been conducted on deaf children enrolled in schools. Consequently, it is possible to examine age as a factor in the IQs and achievement of deaf children, using cross-sectional and longitudinal methods.

Cross-sectional results for achievement tests routinely show deaf people being below the mean of normal-hearing peers at the youngest ages, but the achievement scores of older deaf children and adolescents are much further below their normal-hearing peers than the achievement scores of younger deaf children (e.g., Allen, 1986; Reamer, 1921; Trybus & Karchmer, 1977). This pattern of performance produces a growth curve that decelerates with increasing age, which is comparable to a cumulative deficit phenomenon (Jensen, 1977). The finding of a cumulative deficit in IQ suggests that deafness imposes a form of environmental deprivation in which individuals fail to acquire information and other experiences that facilitate development. Because deaf people are denied opportunities to learn and practice skills early, they approach subsequent experiences with less developed skills and knowledge base than peers raised in enriched environments. This means that they fall further behind as age increases, as has been noted for some groups raised in impoverished environments. The possibility of cumulative deficit, with regard to achievement in deaf people, is quite compatible with the factors associated with deafness (i.e., deaf people do not acquire language easily, and thus begin learning achievement tasks with an impoverished knowledge base and underdeveloped skills for acquiring information).

The cumulative deficit is much more pronounced in cross-sectional analyses of academic achievement than in cross-sectional analyses of nonverbal intelligence. Cross-sectional analyses of IQs obtained on performance and motor-free tests suggest that deaf people are near or somewhat below normal-hearing peers at all ages, but the pattern of lags does not conform to a cumulative deficit curve. Deaf people lag further behind normal-hearing peers between the ages of 10 to 15 years, but then show significant gains relative to normal-hearing peers in the late teens. This pattern of nonverbal IQ gains suggests that developmental factors may influence longitudinal changes in intelligence much more than the environmental factors associated with a cumulative deficit.

Although cross-sectional comparisons are popular psychological research (i.e., few investigators have the means and the patience to follow a group of individuals over the life span), there are some significant drawbacks in cross-sectional designs for investigating longitudinal phenomena. Most important, cross-sectional comparisons confound historical effects with age. For example, if deaf education programs began using markedly improved techniques of instruction and intervention, cross-sectional designs would mimic a cumulative deficit phenomenon, because older people in the study would represent the consequences of inadequate instructional methods. Therefore, longitudinal comparisons to detect changes in intelligence are important to confirm cross-sectional comparisons of changes in IQ and achievement over time.

Longitudinal studies of deaf children's academic achievement show that deaf children gain at faster rates than would be expected from cross-sectional results (Allen, 1986; Trybus & Karchmer, 1977). This finding supports the notion that children educated with current methods derive more benefit from instruction than children who were enrolled in schools years ago. Other factors related to environmental enrichment, or perhaps medical interventions aimed at correcting and managing hearing impairments, may also account for the relatively better progress noted in longitudinal studies in comparison to cross-sectional studies. The cause of greater gains in longitudinal studies is unknown, but it may be that advances made in working with deaf people have begun to reduce the cumulative effects of environmental deprivation experienced. An alternative and equally compelling hypothesis is that less talented deaf people drop out of school at higher rates than brighter, more successful deaf people. This could account for the relative gains noted for deaf people in the late teens.

Unfortunately, there are no large-scale longitudinal studies of intelligence in the literature. Only five studies could be identified that assessed deaf people at two or more points in their lives (Braden, Maller, & Paquin, 1993; Lavos, 1950; Paquin & Braden, 1990; Pintner, 1925; Pintner & Patterson, 1916a). Three of these studies present their results in the form of test–retest stability investigations, whereas the other two studies are primarily interested in the potential effects of residential placement on PIQ. Four studies report gains in IQ over time; the exception is Pintner (1925), who found that deaf people did not improve as much as normal-hearing peers on group tests of intelligence from one age to another. The fact that none of the longitudinal investigations used a control group of normal-hearing people, and all used fairly small samples, limits the power of the results. Therefore, it is questionable whether deaf people experience cumulative deficits in nonverbal IQ relative to normal-hearing people, or whether their apparent lag is due primarily to the cross-sectional nature of the research designs employed in comparisons between ages.

In addition to quantitative changes in IQ over time, qualitative changes in intelligence as a function of age are also of interest. Changes in intellectual structure, or how intelligence is organized, occur as a function of age in normal-hearing children. These changes are typified by increasing diversity in cognitive organization as children approach maturity. Quantitative similarities or differences in IQ may fail to show qualitative differences in the way that normal-hearing and hearing-impaired people approach cognitive tasks. Therefore, comparisons of factor structure on intelligence test batteries between hearing-impaired and normal-hearing people, across ages, may yield insight into how changes in cognitive development occur over time.

The results of factor-analytic studies are mixed. Early reports (e.g., Bolton, 1978; Farrant, 1964) suggested that deaf and normal-hearing people of similar ages have different factor structures. However, I have argued (Braden, 1984, 1985b) that early factor comparisons have two flaws: (1) they fail to use factor analytic methods consistent with intellectual theory and contemporary statistical procedures, and (2) they often include verbal tests, which are attenuated by degree of hearing loss. Reanalyses of earlier factor studies, which use only nonverbal tests and contemporary, theoretically driven factor-analytic methods, suggest that the factor structure for deaf children is similar to that found in normal-hearing children on performance tests of intelligence (Braden, 1985b).

However, not all contemporary factor analyses agree that deaf and normal-hearing children exhibit similar factor structures on nonverbal intelligence test batteries. Research that separates children into relatively homogeneous age groups (e.g., groups children into age strata of 2–4 years) reaches a different conclusion than research that uses relatively heterogenous age groups (e.g., combines children 6-16 years of age). Comparison of factor structures between deaf and normal-hearing age peers in relatively homogeneous age-groups suggest that deaf children eventually develop nonverbal intellective structures that are similar to normal-hearing peers, but that deaf children lag behind normal-hearing peers in the differentiation of intellective abilities over the age span (Braden & Zwiebel, 1992; Zwiebel, 1988; Zwiebel & Mertens, 1985). In other words, longitudinal differences in nonverbal intellectual structures exist between deaf and normal-hearing children at early ages, but these differences disappear over time. Recent research suggests that the age at which deaf children begin to exhibit nonverbal intellectual structures similar to those of their normal hearing peers is about 11 years of age.

The question of whether young deaf children lag behind their normal-hearing peers in the development and differentiation of nonverbal intelligence, or just follow a different path, is unanswered. Deaf children at older ages (e.g., 14–18 years of age) have a markedly different factor structure than normal-hearing children at younger ages (e.g., 6–9 years of age), suggesting that their development is not one of "lagging behind" normal-hearing children. However, the gaps in age between these samples are probably too large to adequately test the "lag" hypothesis. The best interpretation of the available evidence is that young deaf children have a different factor structure (i.e., they organize and approach nonverbal cognitive tasks differently) than normal-hearing peers. These differences apparently disappear as children become older, suggesting that nonverbal intellective structures become more similar over time. Once again, these results suggest that the impact of deafness on the development of nonverbal intelligence is evident, but that the similarities between hearing-impaired and normal-hearing people are far more remarkable than their differences.

Gender

It is impossible to segregate studies in the data base by gender, because all but six studies reported data for samples combining males and females. A review of studies comparing hearing-impaired males to hearing-impaired females suggests few consistent differences between genders within hearing-impaired populations. Studies using younger children (between the ages of 6 and 12 years) suggest that females perform slightly better than males on nonverbal, untimed tests of intelligence (e.g., Draw-a-Person), whereas males tend to perform better on spatial–analytic tasks (e.g., mechanical aptitude tests). Differences between genders with adolescents and adults suggest that males and females are similar with respect to nonverbal IQ, but that females tend to perform better than males on speeded, clerical-type tasks (e.g., the Coding/Digit Symbol subtest of the Wechsler scales). Male–female differences are small and inconsistent, although large samples (e.g., Sisco, 1982) yield statistically significant results. Therefore, it does not appear that there are major IQ differences between genders, although small differences are noted on some subtests. The differences between males and females are not sufficient to alter the factor structure found on tests of intelligence (Sisco, 1982), nor are they of sufficient magnitude to produce differences between gender with respect to IQ. In this respect, the differences between gender noted in deaf samples is quite similar to the small and inconsistent difference found in normal-hearing populations.

Race

The data regarding racial differences within hearing-impaired populations are quite limited. Only 11 studies report data by racial group. Furthermore, large-scale investigations of deaf people (e.g., Anderson & Sisco, 1977; Ries & Voneiff, 1974; Schildroth, 1976) do not report IQs by race. The only racial group comparisons that are reported in the literature compare North American blacks to North American whites. Therefore, the study of IQ within hearing-impaired samples categorized by race is quite limited. This state of affairs is particularly unfortunate in light of the scientific, social, and political importance of race and IQ.

Despite the fact that few studies draw comparisons between groups by race, the results are quite consistent in showing that black, deaf children perform about one-half to two standard deviations below comparison groups. In some studies, the comparison groups are white, deaf children; in other studies, normal-hearing normative data are used for comparisons. Smaller differences are noted on tests of achievement (e.g., Allen, 1986) than on tests of intelligence (e.g., Clegg & White, 1966; Georgia Department of Public Health, 1967). In other words, the differences between black, deaf children and white, deaf children are similar to findings in normal-hearing samples, which show a difference of about one standard deviation between the groups on tests of intelligence. Also, the finding that black–white differences are smaller on achievement tests than on intelligence tests is consistent with findings from normal-hearing samples. Because the implications of these findings warrant extensive discussion from the perspective of understanding differences between racial groups on tests of intelligence, further discussion of these results is reserved for Chapter 5.

Demographic Factors Unique to Deafness

Age at Onset of Hearing Loss

The age at which children acquire a hearing loss is likely to affect their language acquisition and academic achievement. The classic conceptualization of deafness as a natural experiment proposes that congenital deafness prevents the acquisition of language. Subsequent research has suggested that onset prior to the time children normally begin to acquire and use language may be equivalent to congenital deafness in its impact on language acquisition. Therefore, much of the research on intelligence and deafness is limited to children who acquired deafness congenitally or prelingually. It was possible to code some studies with regard to the mean age of deafness onset for the sample. Studies were assigned to categories representing postlingually deaf, prelingually deaf, mixed, or unknown (i.e., insufficient data to make a reliable classification) onset. There were no differences in IQ between these four groups defined by onset of deafness ($F_{(3,309)} = 0.31$, NS).

Unfortunately, most of the studies that are included in the meta-analysis did not maintain consistent standards with respect to age at onset of hearing loss in sample selection (e.g., few studies used only congenitally deaf or only post-lingually deaf subjects). However, a number of studies (e.g., Pintner, 1928; Pintner & Paterson, 1915b; Reamer, 1921; Upshall, 1929) report IQs for people who acquired deafness at various ages. The results are quite consistent in showing that onset of deafness at about 5 years of age or earlier has a substantial impact on verbal IQ and scholastic achievement scores. People who acquire deafness after age 5 years typically have much higher verbal IQ and achievement scores than people who acquire deafness prior to age 5 years. Therefore, it is believed that age of onset significantly affects the acquisition of verbal and scholastic knowledge.

The most common interpretation of these findings is the hypothesis that people who have normal hearing prior to age 5 naturally acquire and use language. Subsequent loss of hearing may restrict or diminish the access these deafened people may have to vocally transmitted information, but because their native language base is intact, they continue to acquire and apply knowledge in a manner quite similar to normal-hearing peers. In contrast, the onset of deafness prior to age 5 years significantly impedes the acquisition of a native language, and therefore severely disrupts the acquisition of reading skills. This interpretation is consistent with what is known regarding language acquisition, although recent research on the process of language learning in childhood and adolescence suggests there may be some features of language that postlingually deaf people may not acquire without significant effort. However, it is clear that prelingual deafness severely inhibits development of language-dependent skills, such as academic achievement and verbal reasoning.

Age of deafness onset has little or no relationship to nonverbal IQ. The results are striking, in that age of onset has no discernable impact on nonverbal intelligence. The lack of relationship between age of onset and nonverbal IQ accounts for the fact that there is no relationship between age of onset and nonverbal IQ across studies, because nearly all of the studies in the meta-analysis used measures of nonverbal IQ.

Degree of Hearing Loss

The nature and extent of hearing loss have also been investigated with regard to intelligence. Each study in the analysis was coded with respect to the severity of hearing loss represented within the sample. Quantitative reports of pure tone averages and qualitative descriptions of hearing loss were classified according to American National Standards Institute standards into the ordinal categories of hard-of-hearing, and moderate, severe, profound, or unknown (i.e., insufficient description to classify the sample) hearing loss. The results of the analysis show that degree of hearing loss is not associated with IQ ($F_{(4,309)} = 1.79$, NS).

There are problems with a meta-analytic approach to testing the relationship between severity of hearing loss and intelligence. The biggest problem is that within-sample variation in hearing loss is considerable, and therefore means or a single classification of hearing loss for each study often obscure significant variation within the sample. Therefore, it is necessary to examine within-sample associations between severity of hearing loss and IQ.

A number of studies (e.g., Bond, 1987; Evans, 1980; Murphy, 1957; Pintner, 1928; Roach & Rosecrans, 1972) show no association between severity of hearing loss and nonverbal IQ. In contrast, there is a strong and reliable association between verbal IQ, scholastic achievement, and hearing loss (Davis et al., 1986; Roach & Rosecrans, 1972). In fact, some studies (e.g., Reynolds, 1976) have found that IQ has no relationship to reading achievement after variation due to hearing loss has been statistically removed from reading achievement scores. Similarly, factor analyses of deaf people's intellectual performance on a variety of intellective tests consistently show verbal IQ and academic achievement tests loading with hearing loss on a common "verbal" factor (e.g., Farrant, 1964; Hine, 1970). In contrast, hearing loss does not load on nonverbal intelligence factors. These findings show that there is no consistent relationship between degree of hearing loss and nonverbal intelligence, although there is a moderate to strong association between degree of hearing loss and language-dependent measures, such as verbal IQ and academic achievement.

Type of School

The question of whether intelligence is related to the type of school that deaf children attend is one that has dogged the field for more than 60 years (e.g., Day, Fusfeld, & Pintner, 1928). Studies included in the meta-analysis were classified according to the source of their samples of deaf subjects. There were seven categories of sources:

1. Residential programs serving deaf children
2. Day schools (i.e., a school exclusively for deaf children from and to which students commute daily)
3. Mixed (i.e., samples that combined children from residential and day programs)
4. Universities
5. Clinics
6. Public schools (with no special programs)
7. Unknown settings (i.e., insufficient data to classify the sample)

The comparison of outcomes across studies suggests no relationship between the source of samples used in research and IQ ($F_{(6,316)} = 1.76$, NS).

Although there is no consistent pattern of between-study variation with respect to institutions from which deaf students are recruited, some studies have specifically compared deaf children enrolled in residential programs to deaf children enrolled in day programs with regard to IQ. There have been consistent reports of differences between groups sampled from residential versus day programs (e.g., Braden et al., 1993; Day et al., 1928; Madden, 1931; Upshall, 1929). In all cases, residential students have a lower mean IQ than students enrolled in day programs. The consistency of direct comparisons between students from residential versus day programs suggests the finding is robust. Interestingly, comparisons in England and Israel also find deaf children in residential schools performing less well than peers in day programs (e.g., Conrad, 1979; Raviv, Sharan, & Strauss, 1973), although there are no comparisons from non-Western nations.

Different researchers have assigned different meanings to the finding of lower IQs among children at residential schools. Early research (e.g., Day et al., 1928; Pintner et al., 1946; Madden, 1931; Upshall, 1929) suggested that sampling characteristics create the difference in the two groups. This argument notes that deaf children who are academically successful, who have no additional disabilities, and who are otherwise performing well are likely to be more intelligent than peers who are unsuccessful, who have additional disabilities, or who are otherwise performing poorly. Successful children are likely to be served in day programs, whereas their less successful peers are more likely to be referred to residential schools. Serving students in a program close to home (e.g., a day program) is generally preferred to sending students away from home to attend school.

This predisposition in educational practice has been codified into law (PL 94-142) and special education regulations in the United States. Similar legislation has been passed in Canada, the United Kingdom, and Israel, among other Western countries. Therefore, the tendency to retain successful, and therefore intelligent, children in day programs is official educational policy; it is only those students who "fail" in day programs that are referred to residential schools. Undoubtedly, some students still attend residential schools primarily on the basis of characteristics unrelated to intelligence (e.g., rural location), but most students entering residential schools are likely to have conditions associated with lower than average intelligence.

Circumstantial evidence favors a selection hypothesis. Residential schools enroll a higher percentage of students with additional disabilities than day programs (Schildroth, 1986). Also, children in residential schools are less academically successful and more likely to be from low socioeconomic homes than their peers enrolled in day programs. These factors have led most researchers to conclude that differences in mean IQs between samples selected from day versus residential programs are primarily due to selection factors.

However, not all researchers have concluded that selection factors account for lower IQs among deaf children in residential programs. It has been argued that the cause of the difference in IQs noted between the two types of programs is due to environmental differences in the programs themselves. In other words, residential schools provide less stimulating environments than day programs (which naturally involve the child returning home after school), and therefore decrease IQ among deaf children (Raviv et al., 1973). Unfortunately, it is impossible to use cross-sectional comparisons to test these hypotheses, because cross-sectional comparisons between samples recruited from residential and day programs confound selection factors with differences in environment. Longitudinal studies, which tap changes in IQ over time for a set of individuals, are needed to determine whether residential schools in fact exert a debilitating influence on IQ.

Longitudinal studies of deaf people are rare. Only five studies were located that provided repeated measures of deaf children over a longitudinal span of more than a few months (Braden et al., 1993; Lavos, 1950; Paquin & Braden, 1990; Pintner, 1925; Pintner & Patterson, 1916a), and all of the studies sampled children from residential programs. The results of three of the five studies show gains in IQ over time, which is inconsistent with the notion that residential programs lower IQs of children. One recent study (Braden et al., 1993) compares changes in performance IQs for deaf children in a commuter program to those in residential settings. The findings offer strong support for the selection hypothesis, in that residentially placed deaf children have lower IQs when first tested than deaf peers in day programs. However, deaf children in residential programs show significant increases in IQ over time, whereas children placed in day programs do not. Interestingly, this study also shows that changes in PIQ are not solely accounted for by regression to the mean (i.e., the tendency for a lower-scoring group to score higher when retested simply because of measurement error).

Far from finding that residential placement *decreases* IQ in deaf children, the only direct longitudinal comparison between deaf children in residential versus day programs shows that residential placement *increases* IQ. This finding suggests that the pejorative stereotype (i.e., that residential programs are barren "holding tanks") should be reconsidered, because the available evidence suggests that residential programs actually enhance nonverbal intellectual development.

Presence of an Additional Disability (AD)

One of the effects confounded with deafness is the presence of an additional disability (AD). As was noted in Chapter 2, the prevalence of ADs among the population of deaf individuals is considerably higher than the prevalence of disabilities among normal-hearing people. Estimates derived from surveys of deaf children enrolled in schools suggest that 23–32% of the deaf population has a diagnosed AD, and difficulties with differential diagnosis of ADs may lead to underestimation of AD prevalence among deaf people.

As shown by the data in Figure 3.7, ADs are associated with low IQ. Studies were classified according to sample characteristics into one of the following

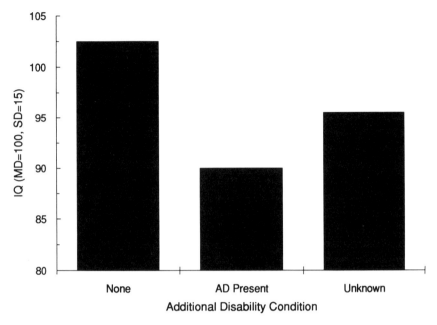

FIGURE 3.7. Mean IQ for studies of deaf people with additional disabilities, without additional disabilities, and those with unknown additional disability status.

categories: no additional disabilities in the sample, presence of ADs in the sample, or unknown (i.e., insufficient data to make a reliable assignment). The differences between groups were in the expected direction, in that samples that systematically eliminated deaf children with ADs had a higher mean ($M = 102.16$, $SD = 9.84$) than samples in unknown ($M = 95.69$, $SD = 9.86$) and AD categories ($M = 89.80$, $SD = 12.37$)($F_{(2,320)} = 16.10$, $p < .0001$).

These results are consistent with studies that evaluate the impact of ADs on deaf children's intelligence (e.g., Conrad, 1979; Ries & Voneiff, 1974; Vernon, 1967a, 1967b, 1967d). These studies consistently report means for deaf children with ADs to be approximately one standard deviation below deaf children without ADs. The presence of ADs is clearly associated with low IQ within samples of deaf children.

Parental Hearing Status

Deaf children who have deaf parents (DP), and those who have normal-hearing parents and deaf siblings (HP/DS), offer some important variations on deafness as a natural experiment. DP and HP/DS are assumed to be genetically deaf, and differ from other deaf people in their exposure to sign language during critical language-learning years. For these reasons, DP and HP/DS have been segregated in some studies of intelligence and deafness.

Studies in the meta-analytic pool were classified according to the parental hearing status of study samples. The status was classified as DP, HP, HP/DS, or unknown (i.e., parental hearing status was not reported for the sample). The means for each of these types of samples differed significantly ($F_{(3,323)} = 20.19, p < .0001$), as shown in Figure 3.8.

Reported IQs for deaf children with unidentified parental status ($M = 94.89$, $SD = 10.16$) were lower than IQs for HP ($M = 99.21$, $SD = 9.44$), HP/DS ($M = 103.63$, $SD = 10.20$), and DP ($M = 108.00$, $SD = 8.34$). The mean IQ from DP samples is significantly above the mean IQ for normal-hearing people ($t_{(35)} = 5.76$, $p < .0001$). In contrast, the mean IQ for samples of HP/DS and HP are not different from the normal-hearing mean of 100 ($ts \leq 1.28$, NS). The mean IQ for samples comprising deaf people whose parental hearing status is unreported or unknown is lower than the normal-hearing IQ mean ($t_{(241)} = -7.82, p < .0001$). Therefore, the factors associated with variations in parental hearing status affect IQ. These results concur with studies that compare DP and HP/DS samples to HP samples (e.g., Braden, 1987; Brill, 1969; Kusche et al., 1983; Sisco & Anderson, 1980; Vernon & Koh, 1970) in finding the DP and HP/DS mean IQs to be above the mean IQ for HP samples.

The study of the intelligence of deaf people by hearing status is one of the few consistently and coherently investigated phenomena in the field of deafness

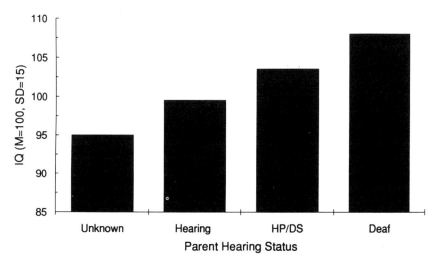

FIGURE 3.8. Mean IQ for studies of deaf children by patental hearing status.

and intelligence. Originally, DP were believed to experience the sequelae and lacunae of deafness, with the important exception that DP are assumed to naturally acquire language from their parents. It has been routinely assumed (but never directly investigated) that the deaf parents of deaf children use American Sign Language (ASL) in the home in much the same way as normal-hearing parents use speech. Studies of language acquisition and use among DP (e.g., McIntire, 1977) have found that deaf parents use ASL to provide their children a language environment similar to that provided by normal-hearing parents, with the exceptions that the language is gestural/visual (as opposed to oral/auditory), and the language is not used by the dominant group in the region (i.e., it is not the language spoken by normal-hearing people). Deaf children of deaf parents also acquire the language in a fashion similar to that of their normal-hearing peers (McIntire, 1977), although DP typically begin to use ASL earlier than normal-hearing children use speech (i.e., at about 9 months of age).

It is important to note that the parents of DP included in studies of intelligence are assumed to provide ASL acquisition experiences similar to spoken-language experiences provided by normal-hearing parents. However, this assumption has not been tested by research. The rigorous selection procedures used in language acquisition studies (e.g., use of adults who are third-generation users of ASL), are vastly different from the standards used by researchers who investigate intelligence in deaf people. In fact, none of the researchers studying intelligence actually interviewed parents of DP to find if they used ASL, sign English, or speech at home; they simply assumed that the parents used ASL.

This creates the possibility that the language environment described by one branch of research is not the same as that inferred by another branch of research. Because they use only third-generation ASL users, language researchers do not study a representative sample of deaf parents. In contrast, studies of IQ among DP typically sample DP without respect to the number of generations that prior ancestors have used signs. Therefore, the assumption that the language provided by deaf parents in studies of DP IQ is similar to the language provided by deaf parents in language acquisition studies is tenuous, but at present, it is the "best guess" regarding the linguistic environment experienced by DP.

The debate regarding the differences in IQ between DP, HP, HP/DS, and normal-hearing peers has permeated literature on deafness for the past 20 years. Originally, it was proposed that DP outperformed HP because of early exposure to and use of ASL. In studies prior to 1979, DP and HP were usually compared with regard to intelligence, academic achievement, speech acquisition and use, and other variables of educational interest. The finding that DP had IQs consistently above the normal-hearing norm was not emphasized until the publication of an article by Sisco and Anderson in 1980, in which they noted that the mean IQ for a sample of DP was well above the average for normal-hearing people. They attributed this finding to the parenting behaviors of deaf parents, arguing that deaf parents provided superior parenting and thus fostered higher IQs among their offspring.

Conrad and Weiskrantz (1981) challenged Sisco and Anderson by reporting data that showed DP did not differ from HP/DS in IQ. Thus, the environment provided by deaf parents could not account for the above-average IQs of DP, because HP/DS also had above-average IQs. Conrad and Weiskrantz argued that additional disabilities (ADs) were the cause of different mean IQs for HP, DP, and HP/DS. They proposed a three-step argument in defense of their interpretation: (1) DP and HP/DS are genetically deaf, (2) DP and HP/DS are therefore free from ADs that are often found among HP (who are often deaf due to medical trauma), and thus (3) DP and HP/DS have higher IQs than HP.

There is one problem with this argument: it cannot account for the fact that DP and HP/DS have mean IQs above the normal-hearing mean. Conrad and Weiskrantz recognized that it would be implausible to assume that the rate of ADs among genetically deaf children would be lower than AD rates for unimpaired, normative samples, which would in turn result in higher IQs than normal-hearing peers. Consequently, Conrad and Weiskrantz attributed the above-average IQs of DP and HP/DS to selection bias of the normative subjects in the British Ability Scales (i.e., the BAS systematically underestimates IQ in British children). The evidence Conrad and Weiskrantz offer in support of their hypothesis is remarkably implausible (see Braden, 1987, and Kusche et al., 1983, for a discussion of this issue).

The debate continued when Kusche et al. (1983) published their research showing that DP and HP/DS had IQs above HP matched on a host of variables, including hearing loss, additional disability, race, gender, socioeconomic status, and other variables. The fact that the DP and HP/DS samples in Kusche et al.'s study also had mean IQs above normal-hearing normative samples was construed as consistent with a link between genetic deafness and intelligence. In other words, Kusche et al. interpreted the reports of above-average IQs for genetically deaf children (i.e., DP and HP/DS) as evidence that is consistent with a link between genes associated with genetic deafness and genes associated with high IQ.

Support for the genetic hypothesis is mixed. I have shown (Braden, 1987) that DP are faster at nonverbal information-processing tasks than either HP or normal-hearing peers. Also, Paquin (1992) found both DP and their parents to have above-average nonverbal IQs. These findings are congruent with a genetic hypothesis, in that assortative mating may lead to higher IQs among DP. However, Zwiebel (1987) reports no differences between genetically deaf and normal-hearing people on the Snidjers-Ooman Nonverbal Intelligence Test. Zwiebel interpreted the similarity of genetically deaf and normal-hearing samples as evidence in support of Conrad and Weiskrantz's claim that DP and HP/DS do not differ significantly in IQ from normal-hearing peers.

It should be noted that, although the total mean IQ for samples of DP and

HP/DS is above average relative to normal-hearing peers, not all studies report statistically significant findings. I believe that the reason Zwiebel failed to show DP were superior to normal-hearing children is because he used a motor-reduced test of intelligence (Braden, 1989b). This hypothesis was investigated in the meta-analytic sample by jointly classifying studies according to parental hearing status of the sample (DP, HP/DS, HP, unknown) and type of intelligence test used to collect data (performance, motor-reduced nonverbal, verbal, unknown). The interaction between parental hearing status and type of IQ test is significant ($F_{(8,323)}$ = 2.10, $p < .05$). Post hoc inspection of the data suggests that DP and HP/DS are above norms for normal-hearing peers on performance and unknown types of IQ tests. They were similar to or slightly below the normal-hearing norm on motor-reduced nonverbal tests of intelligence, and are well below average on verbal IQ tests. Consequently, the type of intelligence test used by a researcher makes it more or less likely for genetically deaf children to achieve above-average IQs.

One way to explain the interaction between genetic deafness and IQ test type is to propose that DP and HP/DS have well-developed motor skills but essentially average nonverbal cognitive skills. This hypothesis is consistent with the findings that DP and HP/DS have above-average PIQs but average or slightly below-average IQs on motor-free nonverbal tests. This proposal would also explain why some researchers find above-average IQs for DP and HP/DS, and why other researchers (who use motor-reduced nonverbal tests) fail to find above-average IQs for DP and HP/DS (Braden, 1987, 1989a). The proposition that DP have better-than-average motor execution skills is supported by experimental research showing superior motor speed for DP groups (Braden, 1985a, 1987). DP and HP/DS may acquire above-average motor dexterity because dexterity and speed are practiced via the repeated, consistent use of sign language. The motor skills acquired through consistent use of signs could then be transferred to performance tests of intelligence, which typically reward the rapid, dexterous manipulation of materials. This explanation is a post hoc account of the data, and has yet to be adequately tested.

The below-average verbal IQs reported for DP are readily explained by noting that DP do not have the opportunity to acquire the English language in a manner similar to their normal-hearing peers, consequently lowering their verbal IQs. There are no IQ tests that have been developed and standardized using ASL or other sign systems. Therefore, DP and other deaf children share a limited knowledge of spoken language, but DP are believed to be more fluent than other deaf peers in nonstandard language (i.e., ASL).

However, DP have consistently higher academic achievement scores than other deaf children. There are two reasons why this may be the case. The most widely cited explanation is that DP have an internal language base, which facilitates their acquisition, storage, and application of academic knowledge. A less commonly but equally tenable explanation is that DP do better because they are more intelligent than their deaf peers, and therefore perform better on achievement-related tasks.

In summary, it is clear that DP and HP/DS, who are assumed to be genetically deaf, have mean PIQs *above* the normal-hearing average. The consistency of findings across studies, and the fact that studies represent North American, British, and Israeli samples, is a provocative finding. However, it is impossible to conclude whether above-average PIQs are due to genetic causes (such as assortative mating or pleiotropic linkage) or to environmental causes (such as early and consistent use of sign language). Such research would be most helpful in shedding light on the interesting and unexpected finding that genetically deaf children have above-average PIQs.

Conclusions

The intelligence of deaf people has been studied by many researchers, either with the intent of understanding the effects of deafness on intelligence, or simply as part of other research. The intent of the research is secondary to the purpose of this review, however. By thoroughly searching the literature, and by statistically combining outcomes across studies, this meta-analysis provides a comprehensive foundation for identifying the effects of deafness on the development of intelligence. By using technologies for bibliographic analysis of research, the review in this chapter goes beyond previous narrative reviews of deaf people's intelligence, and allows the direct investigation of factors believed to affect deaf people's IQs.

At first blush, it would appear that deafness, and the factors associated with hearing loss, have a slight negative impact on intelligence. Qualitative reports of deaf people's intelligence suggest that deaf people are usually within the low-average range of intelligence. Quantitative results provide a higher estimate of intelligence, suggesting that the distribution of IQ in deaf people is nearly identical to the IQ distribution of normal-hearing people. This is true not only for the center, or mean, IQ, but also for the spread of IQ. Although the cumulative data suggest that deafness has little impact on IQ, there are two important caveats. The first is that the distribution of studies shows a noticeable negative skew, which suggests there are certain features in some studies that lead to lower outcomes. The second caveat is that between-study comparisons inevitably obscure within-study relationships. Consequently, methods of obtaining IQs, and demographic factors associated with subject selection, must be considered when drawing conclusions about the impact of deafness on intelligence.

Methodology plays a substantial role in obtained IQs. IQs of deaf people are substantially lowered by linguistic test content, and oral-language-based test administration procedures. This finding is not remarkable from the perspective of psychologists who work with deaf people, since it has been noted for nearly a century that verbal intelligence tests provide inappropriate estimates of deaf people's intellectual abilities (Pintner & Patterson, 1917). The magnitude of the effect that deafness has on the distribution of verbal IQ (i.e., reducing the mean for hearing-impaired people approximately one standard deviation below normal-hearing peers) is substantial. Other methodological factors affecting IQ include the basis for calculating IQs (e.g., normative, ratio, sample comparison) and the type of nonverbal test (i.e., motor-free nonverbal tests yield somewhat lower IQs than motor-intensive nonverbal tests). It is generally true that, as methods approximate those recommended for research and clinical purposes, IQ differences between deaf and normal-hearing people diminish, although there are two exceptions to this rule. The first is that the use of norms based on deaf samples (i.e., "deaf norms") does not result in meaningful changes in IQ, and second, that motor-free and motor-intensive nonverbal tests do not yield similar results.

Just as the nature of the research affects outcome, so too the nature of the individual being studied affects IQ. Demographic factors known to affect IQ in normal-hearing-populations include age, race, and gender. Gender does not appreciably affect IQ in samples of deaf people, although there are some minor differences that mirror the small differences between genders found in normal hearing populations. Raw score performance on intelligence tests increases with age in deaf children, which is similar to trends found in normal-hearing children. However, as deaf people become older, they fall further behind normal-hearing peers on verbal IQ and academic achievement tests. This "cumulative deficit" is not as pronounced when nonverbal measures of intelligence are used. There is some evidence to suggest that young deaf children organize cognitive operations in a manner that is qualitatively distinct from their normal-hearing age-mates. However, qualitative differences diminish with increasing age, so that the structure of intelligence in deaf teens and adults is quite similar to that of normal-hearing age-mates. Differences in IQ and achievement between normal-hearing racial groups are also found in racial groups of deaf people. Thus, demographic factors appear to exhibit effects in the deaf population similar to those found in the normal-hearing population, with the exception that increasing age is not as strongly associated with increase in verbal IQ and academic achievement in deaf people as it is in normal-hearing people.

Some of the demographic factors unique to deafness affect IQ. The age of onset and degree of hearing loss have a substantial impact on verbal IQ and academic achievement, but have no appreciable impact on nonverbal IQ. To the degree that school placement affects IQ, it appears as though residential programs enhance IQ. However, because residential programs typically select students with low IQs, it is critical to distinguish selection factors from longitudinal changes in IQ when comparing IQ variation between educational programs. The presence of an additional disability (AD) substantially lowers IQ in deaf people. In contrast, children with deaf parents and/or a deaf sibling have higher IQs than other deaf peers. This finding has been widely reported in the literature, but it was not until 1980 that researchers investigated the odd phenomenon that DP have IQs above the normal-hearing average.

The finding that deaf children of deaf parents (DP) have performance IQs *above the mean for normal-hearing peers* is remarkable. Although it might be expected that DP would have higher IQs than HP, in light of their native exposure to sign language, early detection and acceptance of deafness by deaf parents, and reduced prevalence of ADs, it is not at all clear why DP should outperform normal-hearing peers. Normal-hearing children are assumed to have early and consistent exposure to language, their (normal) hearing status is readily accepted by parents, and they are assumed to have few if any undiagnosed disabilities. Therefore, the facts that DP have above average PIQs, and that this finding has been replicated frequently in international samples, raise many intriguing questions regarding the concomitant effects of environment and heredity on the IQs of DP.

The average to above-average PIQs reported for deaf children with hearing parents and a deaf sibling (HP/DS) are also interesting. The similarity of HP/DS and DP IQs allows a refined analysis of the potential causes of above-average IQs in these groups. It is presumed that both groups are genetically deaf, which therefore raises the possibility of a genetic link between hereditary deafness and above-average IQ. Therefore, the HP/DS results are provocative, and will be discussed in greater detail in the following chapters.

The outcomes of deafness as a natural experiment are clearly affected by methodological and demographic factors. However, the most remarkable feature of this meta-analysis is the similarity between deaf and normal-hearing people. Deaf people have similar nonverbal IQs, and their IQs mirror the trends found for demographic groups in the normal-hearing population. However, there are some intriguing differences between deaf and normal-hearing people, such as the differences found on verbal IQ and achievement tests and parental hearing status. These similarities and differences will be exploited in Chapter 4 to determine those scientifically defensible inferences that may be drawn from the natural experiment of deafness, and what implications those inferences may have for the understanding of IQ differences between groups in the normal-hearing population.

4

Evaluating the Outcomes of Deafness as a Natural Experiment

What can the study of deaf people tell us about intelligence and differences in IQ between groups? The data in Chapter 3 are provocative in suggesting ways that environment does, and does not, affect IQ differences between groups. However, there are many factors confounded with deafness, and many alternative explanations of outcomes, that must be considered carefully before drawing conclusions. This chapter is devoted to an examination of three hypotheses that might affect between-group differences in IQ: (1) bias in mental tests, (2) the influence of compensation on IQs, and (3) experimental procedures used to obtain IQs. Each of these rival hypotheses will be considered with respect to their potential to account for the results obtained from deafness as a natural experiment.

Test Bias as an Alternative Explanation of Results

Test bias is frequently cited as a source, if not *the* source, of between-group differences in IQ (e.g., Mercer, 1979; Williams, 1974). Unfortunately, the label of bias invokes strong emotional overtones (connotative meanings) in addition to the technical application of the word in test theory (denotative meaning). Test bias, as presently understood by those people who develop and use psychometric tests, is systematic error in the predictive validity or the construct validity of a test with respect to two groups. In other words, if a test performs differently (with respect to predictive or construct validity) for one group than for another, it may be appropriately labeled "biased." For the purpose of evaluating outcomes of deafness as a natural experiment, it would be possible to conclude that intelligence tests are biased for use with deaf people (1) if the predictive validity of intelligence tests differed for deaf people relative to normal hearing people, or (2) if construct validity indices differed to an appreciable degree between deaf and normal-hearing samples.

Before determining whether test bias if found for deaf people, it is necessary to rule out pseudo-bias, or results given by a test that some may take as evidence of bias even though there may be no systematic error in measurement. There are a number of fallacies regarding the use of intelligence tests with minority groups that are often cited as prima facie evidence of test bias or faulty methodology. These fallacious definitions of test bias appear in the literature on deafness, and must therefore be identified and dismissed as the first step in determining whether test bias affects the differences (or similarities) in IQ between deaf and normal-hearing groups.

Fallacious Assumptions of Test Bias

Three fallacious assumptions commonly drive those interested in discovering test bias. These have been identified by Jensen (1980) as (1) the egalitarian fallacy, (2) the culture-bound fallacy, and (3) the standardization fallacy. Each of these fallacies is explained, and examples showing the presence of these fallacies within the literature on deafness are provided.

The Egalitarian Fallacy

The most common fallacy in test bias research is the egalitarian fallacy (Jensen, 1980). In the egalitarian fallacy, tests are judged to be biased if they produce different mean scores for different groups. In other words, any indication of between-group differences on a trait is taken as evidence that the test is biased. This method of finding "test bias" is fallacious, because it presumes the outcome of the research (i.e., it is presumed that groups have identical distributions of IQ, and therefore any test that does not report such an outcome is necessarily biased). Rigorous application of this method of determining test bias would result in the classification of height as a biased measure (distributions of height differ markedly between genders and some racial groups). Therefore, a test that yields a difference in mean IQ between hearing-impaired and normal hearing groups is not necessarily biased.

The fallacious nature of the reasoning in the egalitarian fallacy occasionally escapes researchers in deafness (e.g., Hirshoren, Hurley, & Hunt, 1977; Vonder-haar, 1977) who have claimed that various subtests of the Wechsler Performance Scale are biased because they yield different means for deaf children than they do for normal-hearing children. Likewise, the fact that deaf people have very low verbal IQs does not necessarily mean that verbal IQ tests are biased. Given good predictive validity and appropriate construct validity, it may be possible to conclude that the between-group differences in verbal IQ, or other intelligence test scores, accurately reflect differences in these traits between deaf and normal-hearing people.

The Culture-Bound Fallacy

A second common fallacy is the culture-bound fallacy. In this fallacy, it is presumed that any test that samples items from a given culture necessarily discriminates against members from another culture. It is certainly possible to create items that do, in fact, favor people from one particular group, and therefore have limited applicability to people from other groups (e.g., the BITCH, developed by Williams [1974], is a highly culture-loaded test that favors urban blacks but that has little predictive or construct validity). The assumption underlying the culture-bound fallacy is that culturally loaded items are relatively easier for members of the culture than for individuals who are not members of the culture. This in turn renders the items more difficult, or biased, for people who are not members of the culture, in turn leading to lower IQs.

The reason that the culture-bound hypothesis is fallacious lies in the assumption that casual, subjective inspection of items can readily identify the item difficulty for members of a given group. For example, in a project to develop Canadian norms for a commonly used test of intelligence, the question "What is the Fourth of July?" was replaced with the question "Why do we celebrate Boxing Day?" because the question about a holiday specific to the United States was judged to be biased against Canadians. However, when the item was changed to "Why do we celebrate Boxing Day?" the item became more difficult than the original item (i.e., fewer Canadian children knew why Boxing Day was celebrated than knew why the Fourth of July was celebrated). This example demonstrates that it is impossible to subjectively and categorically state that a given item or test is biased simply because it samples knowledge from a particular culture.

Evidence of the culture-bound fallacy is found in research regarding deafness. Vonderhaar (1974) assumes that items depicting social interactions necessarily discriminate against hearing-impaired people, because hearing-impaired people have different rules for social interactions. He bolsters his argument by noting that deaf people score slightly lower on the subtest depicting social interaction (i.e., he justifies one fallacy by invoking another). Oddly, Vonderhaar and others do not argue that tests on which deaf people outperform normal-hearing peers are somehow culturally biased in favor of deaf culture. To do so would, of course, reveal the fallacious nature of the culture-bound argument. Comments by researchers that IQ tests unfairly sample knowledge of the normal-hearing world fail to acknowledge that acquisition of such knowledge in deaf people may accurately indicate the intelligence of those people.

The Standardization Fallacy

The third fallacy regarding test bias is the standardization fallacy. This fallacy assumes that any test standardized on one group is necessarily biased when applied to another group. A corollary of this fallacy is that people representing a particular group must be included in the normative sample (e.g., the Kaufman Assessment Battery for Children includes a smattering of disabled children in the normative sample). When viewed from the perspective of time, no test can be appropriately standardized, because it can never sample the population to which it will be applied—individuals in the future. Simply including individuals in the normative sample does not guarantee that the test will be unbiased when used with those individuals; likewise, the exclusion of certain groups does not mean the test will be biased when used with them.

Simply including a handful of deaf children in a normative sample (where they would occupy about 0.03% of a representative North American sample) would not guarantee that the test would be unbiased when used with hearing-impaired people. The characteristics of the test must be evaluated in the particular group (i.e., in groups of deaf people) to determine whether the test systematically produces errors in the measurement of construct or predictive validity. Thus, the call for norms based on deaf people (Anderson & Sisco, 1977; Hiskey, 1966; Sullivan & Vernon, 1979) is premature, because it is not necessarily true that IQs based on deaf norms will produce better indices of construct and predictive validity than IQs derived from normal-hearing norms. In fact, use of norms based on deaf people may obscure important test profile features and skew clinical and educational decisions in unexpected ways (Braden, 1985c, 1990b).

It is unfortunate that most discussions of test bias with respect to deaf people rest on fallacious assumptions about what constitutes bias. When the mean for deaf people on certain subtests falls below the mean for normal-hearing people, many researchers erroneously conclude that the difference constitutes evidence of test bias (i.e., the egalitarian fallacy). Likewise, challenges to test content based on subjective reviews of culture-loading trivialize the search for meaningful indices of test bias. Finally, the call for norms based on deaf people, and the criticism of tests for the inclusion or exclusion of hearing-impaired people in the normative sample, misdirects the search for systematic errors in measurement. The failure to adequately examine test bias still begs the question: Does test bias contribute to, or perhaps even account for, the relative performance of deaf versus normal-hearing people on intelligence tests? The answer to this question requires two steps. The first step is to develop an appropriate definition of test bias, and the second step is to apply this definition to what is known about the characteristics of intelligence tests when used with deaf people.

Appropriate Indices of Test Bias

The fact that there are common misconceptions about test bias does not imply that one cannot find legitimate indices of test bias. Generally, evidence of test bias falls into one or more of three domains: (1) internal, or construct, validity; (2) situational factors, and (3) external validity. Each of these categories, and the index associated with it, is discussed and evaluated to determine whether common tests of intelligence are biased when used with deaf people. The special topic of *compensation*, or the development of special abilities in deaf people that may affect intelligence test results, is also examined as a possible source of error in reported IQs.

Internal Indices of Bias

The definition of internal indices of bias rests primarily with how a given test functions with respect to itself. In contrast, external indices of bias refer to ways in which a test functions with respect to one or more external criteria. Therefore, within-test psychometric characteristics of one group are compared to characteristics in another group. Tests that function differently in a target group than in the standardization group are biased; those tests that have similar characteristics in both groups cannot be classified as biased. It is important to note that it is impossible to prove a test is unbiased. The null hypothesis assumes a test is unbiased until data are presented to refute this hypothesis; therefore, the burden of proof rests on the demonstration that the test is biased. Evidence of internal bias must show that internal test characteristics differ between two groups to a significant, and meaningful, degree.

There are many methods to identify internal bias in tests. These methods range from techniques that examine each test item (e.g., item characteristic curves, group-by-item interactions) to methods that incorporate the test as a whole (e.g., comparison of factor structures, test stability, test consistency). Research describing the internal characteristics of intelligence tests used with deaf people is compared to similar research with normal-hearing groups to determine what, if any, evidence exists for internal bias of intelligence tests when used with deaf people.

Item Bias. Item characteristic curves (ICCs), investigations of item difficulties, group-by-item interactions, and item–total correlations may provide evidence of bias. Each of these methods assumes that the content of an item interacts with group membership to cause the item to act in unexpected, or unusual, ways. For example, an item that is easy for one group may be difficult for another group simply because the former group is exposed to the content in the item more frequently than the latter group.

At the item level, differential exposure to item content may produce an ICC that departs from the normal, or expected, form. ICCs graph the percentage of those passing an item as a function of total test score. Good ICCs resemble the ogive of the normal distribution, whereas poor curves depart from this shape (e.g., a poor ICC might show that very bright and very dull people are equally likely to get the item right, suggesting the item is a poor discriminator of ability).

Difference in familiarity with test content could also cause a juxtaposition in the rank order of difficulty associated with items. Changes in the rank order of items in a test show the test is biased, because the items function differently within the test for one group relative to their rank order in another group. Changes in relative item difficulty can be assessed by correlating rank orders of items between groups, or more precisely, by correlating delta decrements between the two groups (Jensen, 1980, pp. 439–442).

Significant group-by-item interactions also suggest that a given item has a source of variation that is reliable and yet separate from whatever variance in the item may be due to differences in group means. Finally, the correlation between individual items and total test scores may be analyzed to detect evidence of test bias. If the item–total score correlation is significant for one group, but not for another (after consideration of floor and ceiling effects), the discrepancy suggests the item is not as closely associated with intelligence in one group as it is with the other, therefore yielding evidence of bias.

Although a more thorough discussion of each of these methods for detecting bias could be provided, the discussion is rendered moot because there are virtually no reports, with any test, of these indices from samples of deaf people. An exception to this conclusion is a study by Holland (1936), who correlated item difficulties between deaf, blind, and normal-hearing groups. The poor correlation between item difficulties in the deaf group and the normal-hearing group ($r = .20$) is evidence that the test (the Otis Classification Test, which is a verbal test of intelligence) is biased when used with deaf people. The small sample size and the lack of information regarding procedures used to collect and analyze data make this study difficult to interpret, but it at least provides some evidence that verbal tests may in fact be biased when used with hearing-impaired people.

The paucity of test bias evidence is not terribly surprising, given that methods for detecting test bias typically require large numbers of subjects to reliably produce evidence of bias. For example, ICCs (and other methods using latent trait techniques) require hundreds, if not thousands, of subjects for accurate determination of curves. Most of the studies reporting IQs on deaf children use small sample sizes, and therefore could not reasonably apply these methods for detecting bias even if the researchers were so inclined. Large-sample research in the literature is often collected in the form of survey data, in which total scores (not item scores) are provided. Thus, the vast majority of literature simply fails to consider item analyses as a method of establishing test bias.

There are only two studies reported in the literature that could reasonably test for evidence of item bias: (1) Anderson and Sisco's (1977) normative study of the Wechsler Intelligence Scale for Children-Revised (WISC-R) Performance Scale, and (2) Hiskey's (1966) normative study of the Hiskey-Nebraska Test of Learning Aptitude (HNTLA). Both of these studies developed norms for performance tests of intelligence, which are widely used with deaf people in clinical and research settings. However, neither of these studies reports efforts to examine item bias, and the authors have stated that no examinations were conducted (Anderson, personal communication, May 12, 1985; Sisco, personal communication, November 4, 1987; Hiskey, personal communication, October 12, 1984). Therefore, there is simply no evidence that can be brought to bear on the issue of item bias in nonverbal tests of intelligence, and only one study, which used a small sample, poorly described methods, and an obscure test of intelligence, that examined item bias in verbal tests of intelligence. The markedly limited data regarding one verbal test of intelligence is suggestive, but hardly conclusive, evidence for showing that verbal tests of intelligence are biased when applied to deaf people. Although there is no evidence to suggest that nonverbal tests of intelligence contain item bias when used with deaf people, the fact that there have been no investigations of this issue whatsoever provides little comfort in determining the degree to which item bias might affect the IQs of deaf people.

Psychometric Indices of Bias. Other internal methods for detecting test bias include test stability, test consistency, and factor-analytic methods. If a test is found to be less stable in a target group than in the standardization group, it is determined to be biased when used with the target group. Likewise, differences in measures of test consistency between standardization and target groups constitute evidence of test bias. It should be added that the direction of the differences is irrelevant, in that tests that are *more* consistent for a target group than the normative sample are said to be biased, albeit in a positive way. Finally, factor-analytic methods for detecting bias are used to determine whether two groups have similar factor structures. Differences in factor structures imply that the test is assessing different attributes in each group, and is therefore biased, because test scores will not have similar meaning for each group.

Fortunately, there is evidence in the literature regarding the three psychometric methods for detecting bias. Some studies report the stability of IQs (e.g., Birch, Stuckless, & Birch, 1963; DuToit, 1954; Evans, 1966, 1980; Gaskill, 1957; Lavos, 1950; Mira, 1962; Pintner, 1924, 1925; Pintner & Paterson, 1916a) for samples of deaf people. The resulting test–retest correlations are comparable to stability coefficients reported for normal-hearing people (Braden, 1985c). Similarly, the consistency values derived from samples of deaf people are similar to values derived from samples of normal-hearing people (Hirshoren, Kavale, Hurley, & Hunt, 1977; Hirshoren et al., 1979; Reamer, 1921). However, it should be noted that there are no reports of reliability for verbal tests. All of the stability and internal consistency data in the literature are limited to nonverbal tests of intelligence.

Meta-analysis methods may be applied to the stability and consistency coefficients reported across studies. The quantitative summary of reliability data cumulated across studies suggests no evidence of bias when nonverbal tests are used with deaf people. The mean reliability coefficient (for stability and internal consistency coefficients combined) from studies of hearing-impaired people (M = .83, SD = .10, range .64 to .98) is consistent with reliability estimates obtained from normal-hearing populations. In other words, meta-analytic results concur with the results of individual studies in suggesting that nonverbal tests are equally reliable and stable when used with deaf people. However, this conclusion does not exclude the possibility that any given test of intelligence may fail to show adequate reliability when used with deaf people. Likewise, the lack of reliability data for verbal tests does not imply that verbal tests have been found to be unbiased. The gist of the research to date simply fails to show evidence of bias with respect to test reliability, measured either as stability or as internal consistency, for deaf people. The fact that there are few reports of reliability coefficients for nonverbal intelligence tests, and no reports of reliability coefficients for verbal intelligence tests, suggests that the best conclusion to be drawn from reliability and stability research is "no evidence of bias to date."

The examination of factor-analytic studies of hearing-impaired people may also provide some basis for the detection of test bias. Unfortunately, few factor analyses adopt a method that is consistent with theories of intelligence, such as extraction of first principal factors or hierarchical factor analysis. Instead, most studies adopt an orthogonal rotation of factors (e.g., Farrant, 1964; Hine, 1970; Zwiebel, 1988; Zwiebel & Mertens, 1985), although a few studies (e.g., Bolton, 1978) use oblique factor rotations. Differences in factor-analytic methods have a substantial impact on the conclusions drawn from research (e.g., orthogonal rotation of factors is more likely to yield differences between groups than hierarchical extraction of factors). Likewise, factor-analytic investigations adopt widely varying psychometric samples, thus complicating detection of bias for any given test of intelligence.

Fortunately, it is possible to recalculate factors when the original correlation matrices, taken from samples of hearing-impaired subjects, are reported in a study. These factors may then be compared to factors extracted from the matrices taken from the test's normal-hearing normative sample in a consistent, quantitative fashion. Such a reanalysis of four commonly used nonverbal intelligence tests shows that the first principal factors extracted from samples of hearing-impaired people are virtually identical (all coefficients of congruence $r_c > .986$) to the factors extracted from the normative, normal-hearing samples reported in test manuals (Braden, 1985b; Braden & Zwiebel, 1990).

The strong evidence of factorial similarity between deaf and normal-hearing subjects breaks down for younger cohorts. A second principal factor emerges for deaf children aged 3–10 years on the Hiskey-Nebraska Test of Learning Aptitude that is not found for their normal-hearing peers. This leads to quite different factor structures between deaf and normal-hearing groups ($r_c = .487$) for this age range. This anomalous finding could be due to variations in administration, in that the test is given using gestures and pantomime to deaf children, but is given with verbal instructions to normal-hearing children. However, these results have been replicated with confirmatory factor analyses of other tests (Braden & Zwiebel, 1992), which suggests that administration methods per se are not responsible for the factor differences between younger and older deaf children.

These and other data have led Zwiebel (1987; Zwiebel & Mertens, 1985) to stress the role of differential development as a cause of factor differences between normal-hearing and hearing-impaired children. These results have been discussed with respect to understanding the effects of deafness on the development of intelligence, but the question to be addressed in this chapter is whether these findings demonstrate evidence of factor-analytic test bias? On the one hand, the answer is a limited yes, because young deaf children have different factor structures than normal-hearing age peers. On the other hand, large sample studies (which include a wide range of ages), conducted on commonly used performance IQ tests, show little if any evidence of bias. Therefore, the most appropriate conclusion to be drawn is that nonverbal tests appear to measure different constructs in young deaf and normal-hearing children, but there is no evidence of bias when heterogeneous age groups, large samples, or older samples of subjects are used. The issue of developmental changes leading to bias could be investigated using refined techniques for detecting test bias (e.g., pseudo-age groups, as recommended by Jensen, 1980) to rule out interactions between age, group, and ability level, but these analyses have not been conducted to date.

In contrast to equivocal, limited evidence of test bias for nonverbal tests, factor analyses of verbal tests show strong and clear evidence of factor differences between deaf and normal-hearing peers. Verbal tests group together with hearing loss to form a factor that apparently measures degree of language exposure. As such, the loading of verbal tests, and the factor structure underlying verbal tests, differs substantially between normal-hearing and deaf people. There can be no doubt that the factor structures that underlie verbal intelligence tests are quite different from the factor structures of normal-hearing peers (Farrant, 1964).

Summary: Internal Indices of Bias. The search for evidence of internal bias for intelligence tests applied to hearing-impaired children is inconclusive. The available data are fairly consistent in finding no evidence of test bias for nonverbal intelligence tests, although there may be an interaction between hearing status and age (i.e., some evidence of factor-analytic bias is present in studies of young deaf children). The evidence regarding verbal intelligence tests is far more limited, but the available evidence suggests verbal IQ tests are biased when used with deaf people. It is clear that, despite the widespread use of intelligence tests with deaf people, there have been few systematic, sophisticated investigations of test bias. The assumption that nonverbal intelligence tests do not show evidence of internal bias when used with hearing-impaired people rests primarily on the absence of data. The absence of data is hardly an appropriate foundation for empirical research and clinical practice.

Situational Indices of Test Bias

Yet another form of test bias may stem from the situation in which tests are administered. If the directions for administration, or the rapport between the examiner and examinee, interact with the group membership of the examinee, the test setting may introduce bias (i.e., systematic under- or overprediction of performance).

The interaction between examiner and examinee has been a commonly cited source of between-group differences in IQ. For example, it has been hypothesized that black children obtain lower IQs when administered IQ tests by white examiners than when they are administered the same tests by black examiners. Although there is little evidence to support this hypothesis relative to North American whites and blacks (Jensen, 1980), it is possible that the interaction between a deaf examinee and the examiner may affect the deaf examinee's IQ. Therefore, the evidence related to situational bias, and factors involved in test administration and scoring, is reviewed as it pertains to deaf people.

Violation of Standardized Administration Procedures. Nearly every time an intelligence test is administered to a deaf person in a form other than spoken language, the standardized administration procedures are violated. The only exceptions to this statement are tests that were normed with gestural, rather than spoken, directions. These tests include the Hiskey-Nebraska Test of Learning Aptitude (Hiskey, 1966) and the Snijders-Oomen Nonverbal Intelligence Test (Snijders & Snijders-Oomen, 1959). The Leiter International Performance Scale and the Raven's Progressive Matrices test manuals also state that gestural administration of these scales is permissible practice, but the norms obtained for these tests were not based on gestural administration. The most popular tests of intelligence used for assessment of deaf people (e.g., the Wechsler Performance Scale) are typically normed on normal-hearing people using spoken directions for administration.

Despite the fact that the use of signs, gestures, written directions, and other modifications of test administration violate normative administration procedures, the research clearly favors alternative methods of test administration. To examine potential bias in test administration, I will revisit the analysis of test administration procedures presented in Chapter 3. However, slightly different, more refined analyses of the test administration data will be used to determine whether situational bias affects the IQs of deaf people.

The 324 reports of deaf person's intelligence in the literature were assigned to one of the following seven categories of test administration:

1. Combined presentation of signs, gestures, speech, and other visual and/or auditory cues to enhance comprehension ($N = 50$)
2. Simultaneous presentation of speech and signs (no additional cues; $N = 32$)
3. Gestural presentation of directions ($N = 19$)
4. Ray's (1979) method of gestural presentation, which includes additional trial items for the Wechsler Performance Scale ($N = 4$)
5. Oral administration of directions (no additional signs or gestures) ($N = 36$)
6. Written presentation of directions ($N = 5$)
7. Unreported methods used to administer the test ($N = 171$)

Over one-third (36%) of the IQ reports favored use of nonstandardized administration methods, particularly those involving gestural communication. Only 11% of the reports rigidly followed oral administration procedures. Unreported methods (53%) are likely to include a high proportion of signed administration procedures because most of these studies took place in residential schools for the deaf (where signing is usually the primary mode of communication).

Traditional assessment practice mandates strict adherence to standardized administration procedures. Why then would so many studies eschew standardized procedures in favor of nonstandard techniques for administering IQ tests? The answer to this question lies in part in early research and clinical work with deaf people, which strongly discouraged the use of verbal tests, and encouraged the use of signs and gestures, in addition to speech, to insure subjects understood test directions (e.g., Pintner & Paterson, 1917). These practices have since been reiterated by clinicians serving deaf people (e.g., Sullivan & Vernon, 1979; Vernon & Brown, 1964). Therefore, researchers investigating the intelligence of deaf people followed recommended clinical practices, and altered test administration to promote deaf people's understanding of test directions and task demands.

The finding that IQ varies as a function of presentation method ($F_{(6,313)} = 2.20$ $p < .05$) supports the clinical recommendation to alter test directions. Post-hoc analyses show that Ray's method of administration produced the highest IQs ($M = 103.87$), whereas written administration produced the lowest IQs ($M = 88.25$). Mean IQs for other methods, in descending order, are Combined ($M = 99.22$),

Unreported (M = 97.78), Gestural (M = 96.05), Simultaneous (M = 94.41), and Oral (M = 93.60).

The meta-analytic results concur with experimental studies of test administration (e.g., Graham & Shapiro, 1953; Sullivan, 1982) in showing that test administration procedures that adapt the test to the communication modes most often employed by deaf people yield scores quite similar to normal-hearing norms. Much lower scores are found for the same subjects when oral or written administration procedures are used. The findings of experimental procedures concur with meta-analytic findings in suggesting that simultaneous presentation of speech, signs, and gestures is likely to produce IQs that do not differ from those of normal-hearing people.

The one exception to this trend is that Ray's method of administration produced slightly higher than average IQs, even though the method consists of gestures supplemented with additional example items. This exception may be due to the interaction of three factors: (1) Ray's method is only used with the Wechsler Performance Scale, which produces slightly higher IQs than other nonverbal and verbal IQ tests; (2) Ray's sampling methods included relatively large numbers of deaf children of deaf parents, who have higher than average nonverbal IQs; and (3) there are only four reports of IQ in this meta-analysis that used Ray's procedure, thus increasing the likelihood that sampling error may give rise to the slightly higher IQs.

It should be pointed out that none of the administration methods discussed in the preceding paragraphs used techniques such as multiple presentation of test items, coaching, testing the limits, altering basal and ceiling rules, or other administration procedures likely to give an advantage to deaf people. One exception is Miller's (1984) approach to administration of the Verbal Scale of the WISC-R, which was discussed in the previous chapter. Not surprisingly, her method of administration produced the highest mean verbal IQ for deaf people found in the literature. Because the administration procedure confounds translation with multiple presentation of items, it is not possible to determine whether the deaf children in her study fared better because items were appropriately translated, or because they simply had more opportunities to try items. However, the preponderance of evidence suggests that situational bias plays a role in the IQs of deaf people, and that the oral and written presentation of items is more likely to lower IQs than administration using signs.

Examiner Hearing Status and IQ. It is interesting to note that there is no research investigating the effect of examiner hearing status on deaf people's IQs. This is surprising, because the interaction between examiner and examinee race, and its effect on IQs obtained by minority examinees, has been hotly debated in the psychological literature. The lack of investigations regarding the interaction of examiner–examinee hearing status in studies of deaf people may reflect the fact that deaf people have yet to "come of age" as an identified ethnic group. Recent events attesting to a stronger identification with "Deaf Power" and "Deaf Pride" may stimulate research regarding the effects of examiner hearing status on obtained IQs. However, at present there is no evidence to suggest that examiner–examinee hearing status affects examinee IQs, although the lack of any investigation of this issue once again provides a poor foundation from which to draw conclusions.

Summary: Situational Indices of Bias. Perhaps the most important question to be asked of test administration methods is, Do test administration methods result in abnormally low or high IQs? The data show that verbal administration methods (i.e., oral and written item presentation) depress IQs. Although the mean IQ from studies employing gestural methods is not significantly different from other studies, experimental data suggest that gestural administration, without signs or speech, also depresses IQs. Meta-analytic and experimental results concur in pointing toward higher IQs when combined methods are used. Therefore, there is evidence of situational effects on obtained IQs. Rigid adherence to standardized administration procedures depresses IQ, whereas the addition of gestures and signs to oral directions produces nonverbal IQs near average levels for normal-hearing people. This conclusion, which is supported by results from experimental studies, suggests that the outcomes associated with deafness as a natural experiment may be depressed by the use of standardized and less-than-optimal administration methods. There is no evidence to suggest that the hearing status of the examiner affects the IQs achieved by deaf people. Consequently, the research suggests some evidence of bias in the administration of intelligence tests to deaf people, and the direction of the bias is to lower or depress IQs. This bias can be minimized, and perhaps eliminated, when appropriate steps are taken in test administration.

External Indices of Bias

Whereas internal indices of bias are detected primarily by variations within a test, external indices of bias typically investigate how a test relates to external criteria. There are two primary sources of data for detecting external indices of bias: (1) the match between the test and another measure of the same or a related construct (i.e., construct validity) and (2) the ability of the test to predict performance in another domain (i.e., predictive and concurrent validity). If the construct, predictive, or concurrent validity of intelligence tests changes for hearing-impaired people relative to normal-hearing peers, the test is a biased measure of intelligence.

Construct Validity. Fortunately, there are many reports of construct validity for IQ tests used with hearing-impaired people. A popular construct used to validate intelligence tests is the relationship between raw scores on a test and age. It is assumed that, across the childhood to early-adult age range, older people should have higher raw scores (i.e., get more items right) than younger people. The finding that there is a strong relationship between age and raw scores on intelligence tests in deaf people (Anderson & Sisco, 1977; Bond, 1987; Day, Fusfeld, & Pintner, 1928; Drever & Collins, 1928; DuToit, 1954; Goetzinger & Houchins, 1969; Hiskey, 1966; Lavos, 1950; MacKane, 1933; Pintner & Paterson, 1915a; Pintner & Reamer, 1920; Raven, Court, & Raven, 1983; Reamer, 1921; Shirley & Goodenough, 1932; Trybus & Karchmer, 1977; Zeckel & van der Kolk, 1939) provides evidence of acceptable construct validity of intelligence tests for use with deaf populations. It should also be noted that the growth curves for deaf children are not as smooth as those for normal-hearing children, because deaf children appear to lag behind normal-hearing peers at various ages (e.g., between the ages of 10–14 years). However, deaf children show relatively rapid gains at other ages (e.g., increases in the raw scores of deaf people near 16 years of age close the gap between deaf and normal-hearing teens). Despite some interesting deviations in growth of raw scores over age, the data are consistent in showing strong construct validity between age and raw scores on intelligence tests for hearing-impaired people.

Another common determinant of construct validity is the agreement between a test of intelligence and another test of intelligence. There have been frequent reports of correlations among tests of intelligence used with deaf people (e.g., Bonham, 1963; Braden & Paquin, 1985; Brinich, 1981; Brown, 1930; Davis et al., 1986; DuToit, 1954; Evans, 1980; Gaskill, 1957; Gibbins, 1988; Hirshoren, Hurley, & Hunt, 1977; James, 1984; Kearney, 1969; Larr & Cain, 1959; Lavos, 1954; Levine & Roscoe, 1955; MacPherson & Lane, 1948; Meacham, 1984; Myklebust & Burchard, 1945; Phelps & Ensor, 1987; Ross, 1953; Seiler, 1985; Streng & Kirk, 1938; Ulissi & Gibbins, 1984; Wilson et al., 1975). Most studies report favorable comparisons (i.e., substantial correlations between intelligence tests). Preliminary meta-analytic results (based on 50 reports of correlations between tests) show solid evidence of agreement between tests of intelligence when used with deaf people. The mean correlation coefficient (M_r = .68, SD_r = 0.18) is substantial, and compares favorably to correlations between IQs from various tests in normal-hearing populations. The range of values (.16 to .91) suggests significant variation between studies. A perusal of studies suggests that smaller correlations are associated with studies using pantomime administration or restricted variability in sampling (e.g., correlations between tests for mentally retarded deaf people). Studies using more appropriate administration methods and samples yield moderate to high correlations between tests. These meta-analytic results concur with experimental studies, suggesting adequate construct validity for nonverbal intelligence tests used with deaf people.

Convergent and Divergent Validity. The fact that intelligence tests correlate with the constructs of age and other intelligence tests demonstrates an important feature of construct validity. This feature is convergence. In other words, the construct validity of a test is supported if the results of the test and the results of another test converge toward a common finding. Tests that correlate with each other provide evidence of convergence. However, merely knowing that tests correlate with age or other tests only provides half of what a researcher needs to know about tests. The other half is provided by evidence of divergence. Intelligence tests not only must agree with other tests and factors that one can reasonably believe are associated with intelligence (e.g., age); intelligence tests must also be independent of factors that cannot be reasonably associated with intelligence. For example, a test that correlates well with age and tests of intelligence, and also correlates with shoe size, hair length, and arm strength, is probably not a good test of intelligence. In fact, the finding of such a pattern of relationships would raise the question of what the test measures. Therefore, in assessing the construct validity of intelligence tests for hearing-impaired people, the search for factors that do not relate to IQ is as important as the search for factors that do relate to IQ.

The primary nonintellective factor that has been correlated with IQ in samples of hearing-impaired people is degree and onset of hearing loss. Performance and nonverbal tests of intelligence have no consistent association with onset and degree of hearing loss (Bond, 1987; Burchard & Myklebust, 1942; DuToit, 1954; Evans, 1960, 1980; Fuller, 1959; Gaskill, 1957; Habbe, 1936; Madden, 1931; Murphy, 1957; Myklebust, 1964; Pintner, 1928; Pintner & Lev, 1939; Pintner & Paterson, 1915b; Reamer, 1921, Roach & Rosecrans, 1972; Streng & Kirk, 1938; Templin, 1950; Treacy, 1952; Upshall, 1929; Waldman et al., 1930; Watson et al., 1982). An analysis of 12 studies that reported correlations between hearing loss and IQ shows that the average correlation ($M_r = .05$) is not significantly different from chance. These results concur with meta-analytic results reported in Chapter 3, which consistently show no relationship between nonverbal IQ and hearing impairment.

In contrast, verbal IQs are consistently and significantly associated with the degree and onset of hearing loss (Davis et al., 1986; Farrant, 1964; Moores et al., 1987; Roach & Rosecrans, 1971, 1972; Treacy, 1952; cf. Montgomery, 1968; Pintner & Lev, 1939). Four studies reported correlations between degree of hearing loss and verbal IQ. The mean correlation is substantial ($M_r = -.49$), and supports the conclusion that verbal IQ and hearing loss are related.

The association between hearing loss and verbal IQ is accounted for in the following way. Hearing loss is inversely related to oral language exposure and stimulation (i.e., less hearing loss is associated with more language development, and more hearing loss results in less language development). Language development is in turn related to the knowledge of language-based items in verbal intelligence tests, and so verbal IQ and degree of hearing loss are negatively related. In other words, hearing loss restricts the person's access to language, which in turn depresses scores on verbal intelligence tests. Again, these findings are consistent with the meta-analytic results presented in Chapter 3 which show substantial relationships between hearing impairment, verbal IQ, and academic achievement.

These results imply that verbal intelligence tests are biased, because they fail to produce evidence of divergent validity. However, this interpretation presumes that no relationship should exist between degree of hearing loss and intelligence. This leads to a paradox, in that the use of IQ–hearing loss correlations can be interpreted as evidence of differential divergent validity only if one is willing to assume that hearing loss has no effect on verbal reasoning ability.

Most researchers in the field have addressed this paradox by assuming that nonverbal IQ should be unrelated to hearing loss, because there is no *a priori* reason to believe that restricted language exposure necessarily affects performance on nonlanguage tests. Conversely, researchers expect to find a relationship between hearing loss and verbal IQ, because it is presumed that exposure to verbal knowledge bases will affect scores on verbal intelligence tests. If one is willing to accept these assumptions, the lack of relationship between nonverbal IQ and hearing loss provides evidence of divergent validity for nonverbal intelligence tests. The moderate relationship between hearing loss and verbal IQ then provides evidence of *convergent* validity for verbal IQ tests, in that it is assumed that the fund of verbal knowledge should be related to the severity of hearing loss. Unfortunately, the literature does not contain data from other variables that could serve as tests of divergent validity (e.g., correlations between arm strength and IQ) in studies of deaf people. Consequently, the available evidence supports the convergent and divergent validity of nonverbal intelligence tests when used with deaf people, and provides appropriate evidence of convergent (but not divergent) validity for the use of verbal intelligence tests with deaf people.

Predictive Validity. If intelligence tests are unbiased, they should be able to predict a criterion with equal accuracy in hearing-impaired and normal-hearing groups. In this context, prediction refers to the ability of a test to predict some score taken at a later point in time, and the ability of a test to predict a score on another index, whether the prediction is concurrent or prognostic. Therefore, studies reporting how well IQ predicts some future behavior or index, and studies of concurrent validity (i.e., studies assessing the degree of relationship between IQ and other measures), must be reviewed for evidence of test bias.

Predictive bias may be specifically identified in one of three ways: (1) a difference in intercept between two groups; (2) a difference in slope between two groups; or (3) a difference in the standard error of prediction between two groups

(Jensen, 1980; Reynolds, 1982). The technology for determining differences in these indices requires large numbers of subjects, from which regression parameters may be estimated. There are no large-scale studies of predictive or concurrent validity using deaf subjects that would allow for direct, precise comparisons of regression parameters. In fact, none of the studies listed in the bibliography reported regression parameters for any criterion regressed on IQ.

Fortunately, there are other, albeit less precise, means to test for predictive bias. The most common method is to examine the correlations reported between intelligence tests and a criterion, and compare the correlation obtained from one group to the correlation obtained from the other group. If the correlations differ, it can be inferred that there is a difference in slope and/or a difference in the standard error of prediction for the groups. The case in which the correlation between IQ and a criterion in one group is different from the correlation obtained from another group is called "differential validity." Evidence of differential validity leads to the conclusion that the IQ test is biased. Therefore, the search for predictive bias in intelligence tests applied to deaf people is limited to evidence of differential validity, because no direct tests of regression parameters are possible.

The first source of differential validity comparisons is predictive validity studies. True prediction studies, in which scores for a group of individuals are obtained at one point in time and then related to scores taken from the same individuals at another point in time, are rare. Most researchers do not collect longitudinal data because of the inconvenience and problems associated with following a group of individuals over time. The few predictive validity studies conducted with deaf people (e.g., Birch et al., 1963; Braden et al., 1993; Lavos, 1950; Paquin & Braden, 1990; Pintner, 1925; Pintner & Paterson, 1916a) report values equal to or greater than values reported in longitudinal studies of normal-hearing people. Most of the predictive validity studies conducted with deaf participants use an IQ to predict an IQ on the same test at a later point in time. Although this is technically a predictive validity study, the correlations from these studies also reflect the stability of the trait that is measured by the test (i.e., intelligence). Therefore, it is possible to conclude that the trait of intelligence, as measured by performance tests of intelligence, is as stable in hearing-impaired people as it is in normal-hearing people. It also follows that there is no evidence of differential validity provided by longitudinal studies of IQ.

The ability to predict performance in another context, such as using IQ to predict future performance in school, is largely untested. The few studies that use IQ to predict academic achievement (e.g., Birch et al., 1963) and communicative competence (Brinich, 1981) report predictive validity coefficients for nonverbal and performance IQ tests that are well within the range of values expected for normal-hearing people (i.e., $rs > .50$). The evidence regarding predictive validity of IQ tests is limited to nonverbal and performance tests of IQ, and, on the basis of a very limited number of studies, there is no evidence to suggest differential validity (i.e., no evidence of predictive bias). However, it must be noted that none of these studies reported a direct comparison between the predictive validity coefficients from samples of deaf people and the predictive validity coefficients from samples of normal-hearing people. Therefore, the conclusion of "failure to demonstrate bias" is based on indirect tests of differential validity with respect to the use of intelligence tests to predict future IQ, and to predict academic achievement.

Concurrent Validity. There are more reports of concurrent validity than there are reports of predictive validity. A total of 153 reports of concurrent validity were identified, in which IQ was correlated with achievement, teacher ratings, grades, or other indices that could be related to intelligence. The average correlation between IQ and this potpourri of external criteria (M_r = .42) suggests IQ tests perform adequately for concurrent prediction of external criteria. However, the range of correlations (−.06 to .89) attests to substantial variation in the criteria that are concurrently predicted and the methods used to obtain concurrent correlations.

Some criteria have stronger correlations with IQ than other criteria. For example, the average correlation between spelling achievement and a composite achievement index (M_r = .29) is less than the average correlation between IQ and a composite achievement index (M_r = .53). Composite achievement is typically a total score for an achievement battery that is derived from some average including reading, mathematics, and spelling domains. This pattern of correlations (i.e., higher correlations for broader indices, and lower correlations for specific sub-domains such as spelling) is similar to findings in normal-hearing groups. The variation in the criteria predicted, then, are actually congruent with results found in normal-hearing samples. This means that far from offering evidence of differential validity, the variation between IQs and types of achievement scores offers evidence that intelligence tests function similarly for deaf and normal-hearing people.

Correlations between IQ and achievement also vary as a function of the type of intelligence test used in the study. The average correlation between verbal IQ and all concurrent criteria (M_r = .52, N = 26) is higher (Welch-Aspin $t_{(45)}$ = −2.95, p < .01) than the average nonverbal IQ–criteria correlation (M_r = .42, N = 132). The verbal IQ–achievement correlations are higher than nonverbal IQ–achievement correlations in all three academic achievement areas (i.e., reading, mathematics, and language) where verbal IQ and nonverbal IQ data are available. The finding that verbal IQ is a better predictor of concurrent achievement than nonverbal IQ is supported by studies contrasting verbal IQ to nonverbal IQ as a predictor of concurrent achievement within the same sample (e.g., Maller & Braden, 1993). Therefore, it is clear that verbal IQ has a stronger relationship to academic achievement criteria than does nonverbal IQ.

There are at least two viable explanations for the finding of higher verbal IQ–achievement correlations in deaf people. The first is that verbal IQ tests and achievement tests have a greater overlap in content, which would result in a stronger correlation between the two tests. The phenomenon of higher verbal IQ–achievement correlations among samples of normal-hearing children is often attributed to this cause. It is assumed that higher correlations between verbal IQ and achievement are due to the shared effects of verbal reasoning, because verbal reasoning underlies both verbal IQ and achievement scores. The correlation between nonverbal IQ and achievement scores is lower, because nonverbal reasoning is less associated with academic tasks than are verbal reasoning skills.

A second explanation is that verbal IQ, achievement, and degree of hearing loss are correlated in samples of hearing-impaired people (Barron, 1940; Conrad, 1979; Davis, et al., 1986; Evans, 1960; Farrant, 1964; Moores et al., 1987; Pintner, 1928; Reamer, 1921; Seiler, 1985; Trybus & Karchmer, 1977). Therefore, verbal IQ may covary with achievement more than nonverbal IQ simply because both verbal IQ and achievement are related to a third variable (hearing loss). In contrast, nonverbal IQ is not correlated with hearing loss, and therefore may correlate with academic achievement criteria to a lesser degree. These two explanations are not mutually exclusive. It is possible that verbal IQ correlates with achievement better than nonverbal IQ for psychometrically acceptable reasons (i.e., because verbal IQ and academic achievement both require verbal reasoning ability), as well as for psychometrically unacceptable reasons (i.e., inflated correlations due to the association between verbal IQ, academic achievement, and hearing loss). Regardless, the data clearly show that the selection of criteria, and the selection of predictors, affects concurrent validity coefficients.

Other factors also affect concurrent validity coefficients, and in particular, IQ–achievement correlations. One factor affecting IQ–achievement correlations is restriction of range in the criterion variable. Restriction of range in the criterion, or achievement, variable may occur when grade equivalents or other nonstandard scores are used to estimate deaf children's achievement. This is because grade equivalents are not normally distributed in samples of hearing-impaired people. There is a substantial restriction of range in grade equivalents at the lower grade levels (Braden, 1990a; Kelly & Braden, 1990; Trybus & Karchmer, 1977), and a serious attenuation of the IQ–achievement correlation when samples span large age ranges. For example, a bright first grader might earn a grade equivalent of 3.0 on a reading test, whereas a below average teen might earn the same 3.0 grade equivalent. The inclusion of young, talented children with older, less successful children attenuates the IQ-achievement relationship if grade equivalents are used to represent academic achievement.

When grade equivalent scores are replaced with normative-based achievement scores, correlations between IQ and achievement improve to a significant degree (Kelly & Braden, 1990). Also, correlations between IQs and raw scores on achievement tests, with age effects statistically removed, are considerably higher than correlations between IQ and grade equivalents in samples of deaf children (Watson et al., 1986). Therefore, low correlations between IQ and achievement reported in some studies of deaf children may have more to do with the metric used to represent achievement than a lack of close association between intelligence and achievement. Substituting an appropriate, age-based metric for achievement eliminates the measurement problems associated with grade equivalents, and simultaneously increases IQ–achievement correlations.

Conversely, some of the unusually high correlations reported between IQ and achievement are based on samples with excessive variation in IQ and achievement. Such samples are typically composed of children varying widely in age and ability, but for which intelligence is typically represented as a mental age. This approach gives rise to a spuriously high association between IQ and achievement. This is particularly true for studies that select small samples of children ranging from preschool to high school ages (e.g., Birch et al., 1963). There are methods that can be used to statistically correct for excessive range in the predictor variable (e.g., Braden & Paquin, 1985), but these procedures have not been routinely applied to concurrent validity research in deafness.

The issue of differential validity has not been directly tested in the literature. Some researchers have questioned the concurrent validity of nonverbal IQ tests with deaf people (e.g., Hirshoren et al., 1979; Watson et al., 1986) on the basis of low IQ–achievement correlations, whereas others have found substantial correlations between achievement measures and IQ (e.g., Birch & Birch, 1956; DuToit, 1954; Evans, 1980; Lavos, 1962; Maller & Braden, 1993; Porter & Kirby, 1986). Careful inspection of conflicting studies suggests that low correlations are frequently associated with restriction of range due to the choice of achievement metric (grade equivalent), and are therefore poor evidence of differential validity. The moderate to high correlations reported in studies using appropriate metrics, and the absence of direct tests for differential diagnosis, suggests there is inadequate evidence to demonstrate differential validity when IQ tests are used with deaf people. More important, there is fairly consistent evidence showing no differential concurrent validity when intelligence tests are used with deaf people.

Ironically, the failure to show differential validity for intelligence tests, and the simultaneous finding that the distribution of deaf people's verbal IQ is quite different from the distribution of their nonverbal IQ, leads to the unexpected conclusion that nonverbal IQ tests are certainly biased predictors of external criteria. The simultaneous findings of similar IQ–achievement correlations for deaf and hearing samples, and dissimilar nonverbal IQ means, strongly suggest evidence of intercept bias for nonverbal intelligence tests. This conclusion is derived by employing a purely statistical argument.

Because correlations determine the slope of a regression line, but are unrelated to the intercept, similar IQ–criterion correlations for two groups imply similar slopes for their regression lines. When between-group differences are found for both the IQ and criterion measures, and the magnitude and direction of these differences are similar, a common regression line is suggested. This is the case for verbal IQ and achievement, in that deaf people score approximately 1 *SD* lower on both measures relative to normal-hearing peers. Putting this finding together with the observation that they have similar verbal IQ–achievement correlations, it follows that deaf and normal-hearing peers have a similar, or common, regression line for academic achievement regressed on verbal IQ.

However, when group means are different on one measure, but are similar on the other, the two groups must have different intercepts for their IQ–criterion regression lines. In the case of deaf versus normal-hearing groups, the finding that the groups have similar nonverbal IQs, but that deaf children have much lower average academic achievement scores, means that one must systematically predict lower achievement scores for deaf children of a given IQ than for hearing children of a given IQ. This leads to the inescapable conclusion that nonverbal intelligence tests are biased predictors of academic achievement for deaf children.

Perhaps this statistical conclusion can be better illustrated with a clinical example. Suppose two children are given tests of nonverbal IQ, verbal IQ, and achievement. Child A, who is normal-hearing, has a verbal IQ = 100, a nonverbal IQ = 100, and a standard achievement score =100. Child B, who is hearing-impaired, has a verbal IQ = 85, a nonverbal IQ = 100, and a standard achievement score = 85. For Child A, accurate prediction of the criterion (achievement) is achieved regardless of whether verbal IQ or nonverbal IQ is used. For Child B, verbal IQ accurately predicts achievement (both are about 1 *SD* below average), but nonverbal IQ incorrectly overpredicts average achievement. Assuming this pattern would be found in large groups of normal-hearing and hearing-impaired children, nonverbal IQ (not verbal IQ) would be found to be biased as a predictor of achievement. In other words, nonverbal IQ would systematically overpredict deaf persons' achievement, thus demonstrating intercept bias. This example assumes that there are no differences of slope or standard error of prediction, which is a tenable but not directly supported inference from the available research.

It is ironic that the average distribution of nonverbal IQs among deaf people, and their below-average distribution of verbal IQs and achievement scores, makes it likely that nonverbal IQs are biased measures of external criteria, whereas verbal IQs are less likely to be biased predictors. This speculation is based on a rational analysis, and is not yet supported by direct comparison of regression parameters between deaf and normal-hearing samples.

Summary: External Indices of Bias. The pattern of findings associated with external indices suggests no direct evidence of bias when verbal tests are used to predict academic achievement, and other criteria, for deaf people. However, despite the lack of differential validity for either verbal or nonverbal intelligence tests, the available data lead to the conclusion that nonverbal intelligence tests are biased when used with deaf people. The direction of this bias is one favoring deaf people (i.e., the use of nonverbal IQ would lead to overprediction of deaf people's performance on an external criterion relative to normal-hearing people with the same score). However, there are no direct tests of slope, intercept, standard error of prediction, or differential validity in the literature. The literature must therefore be considered to be incomplete in its investigation of test bias with deaf people.

The application of bias methodology to the study of deaf people's intelligence highlights the difference between statistical notions of test bias, and the clinical or casual meaning of the term "bias." Clinicians have long argued that verbal tests are biased measures of intelligence when applied to deaf people. However, clinicians do not mean that intelligence tests systematically under- or over-predict deaf people's performance on some external criterion. Rather, such statements are related to the clinical imperative to differentially diagnose deafness from other causes for delayed language, academic delay, and impaired social interactions (e.g., mental retardation). Thus, clinicians are correct when they encourage the use of nonverbal IQ tests for discriminating deafness from mental retardation, and they are appropriately horrified that exclusive reliance on verbal IQs would lead to misclassification of many deaf people as mentally retarded. These assumptions are quite different, however, from the statistical investigation of test bias. Thus, a test may be valid and useful for differentially diagnosing deafness from mental retardation, but it may be a biased predictor of achievement. Likewise, a test may be an unbiased predictor of achievement for deaf people, yet the same test may be invalid (to the point of being pernicious) for the differential diagnosis of deafness and mental retardation. Thus, clinicians are correct when they discourage the use of verbal IQs for estimating deaf people's intelligence, but they are not statistically correct when they assume nonverbal IQs are unbiased. It is better to say that nonverbal IQs are unattenuated by hearing impairment, which therefore makes them a more reliable and precise estimate of cognitive ability for use with deaf clients. However, it is equally valid to say that because verbal IQs are affected by language exposure, they are actually better predictors of academic achievement (Maller & Braden, 1993) and related domains (e.g., success in college; Falberg, 1983). Thus, nonverbal intelligence tests, although biased predictors of achievement and related criteria, are more accurate indicators of cognitive ability in deaf people than are verbal intelligence tests. Conversely, verbal intelligence tests, although biased in their underestimation of cognitive ability, are more accurate predictors of performance than are nonverbal intelligence tests. Precisely because verbal tests are attenuated by hearing loss, exposure to language, and other nonintellective factors, they provide better empirical prediction of performance than nonverbal intelligence tests. This paradox must be clearly understood in order to distinguish between the clinical and scientific meanings of "bias" applied to intelligence tests used with deaf people.

Summary: Evidence of Test Bias

Is test bias a major influence on the IQs of deaf people? The available literature suggests the answer to this question is "probably not." Although the available evidence largely supports the use of intelligence tests—with some very important exceptions—the literature falls far short in providing direct, compelling investigations of test bias with deaf populations. For example, there is only one antiquated, poorly described empirical study of item bias to be found. The level of evidence provided by the literature falls far short of the level of evidence needed to convincingly answer the bias question.

This is particularly appalling with reference to verbal intelligence tests, which have been uniformly assumed to provide biased (low) estimates of deaf persons' intelligence in clinical practice (Sullivan & Vernon, 1979). There is no question that verbal IQs yield much lower estimates of intelligence than nonverbal IQs for deaf people, and, for this reason, are undoubtedly biased estimates of latent intellectual ability. However, there is also no question that nonverbal tests yield excessively high estimates of academic achievement. The lack of direct examination of test bias in deaf samples is consequently quite appalling, because of the paradox between clinical determinants of bias and statistical indices of bias.

The distinction between clinical and statistical notions of bias should not obscure the major point to be derived from this review: The majority of evidence points toward no evidence of bias. The psychometric indices of bias extracted from studies of deaf people, such as reliability, consistency, and factor structure, are generally similar to values found for normal-hearing peers. Likewise, there is no evidence of differential validity for intelligence tests used to predict IQ over time or external criteria such as academic achievement. Provided one retains the distinctions between clinical versus statistical bias, and nonverbal versus verbal tests, it appears that test bias is not a major influence on the IQs obtained by deaf people.

Compensatory Effects on IQ

It has been proposed at various times that individuals compensate for a disability in ways that change the individual. In the clinical realm, Freud's theories of compensation attributed certain behaviors (e.g., Napoleon's quest for power) to physical deformities (e.g., Napoleon's small stature). Although Freud was careful to note that compensation affected behavior, not necessarily psychological or physical ability, others have generalized theories of compensation to psychological and physical traits. In fact, the representation of disabled people in the popular literature often implies that disabled people develop supernatural physical and psychological features to compensate for their disability (e.g., the blind comic book cartoon character Daredevil reads a newspaper by feeling the impression of the ink on newsprint).

Researchers studying deafness have noted that deaf people adapt and develop many behaviors to compensate for their hearing loss (e.g., sitting in the front of a lecture hall, looking directly at individuals as they speak, obtaining and using sign language interpreters). These changes in behavior as a result of deafness are adaptive and appropriate to the limitations imposed by a hearing loss. However, some psychologists have also proposed that deaf people experience a change in psychological abilities as a result of deafness. For example, it has been proposed that deaf people develop superior eye–hand coordination in order to compensate for their hearing loss (Myklebust, 1964). Compensatory mechanisms developed by deaf people might include adaptations that affect the structure and/or measurement of intelligence. Two types of compensatory mechanisms have been proposed: (1) that the conditions experienced by deaf people lead to qualitatively different forms of intelligence, and (2) deaf people develop superior skills for specific abilities (e.g., superior manual dexterity), which in turn attenuate intelligence test results. Therefore, the possibility of compensatory effects on IQ must be considered as a possible confound in the interpretation of deaf people's IQs.

Changes in Intelligence as a Result of Deafness

A number of theories have been proposed to suggest that deaf people have qualitatively distinct psychological structures relative to normal-hearing people. These theories are generally concerned with ways of processing information rather than intelligence per se, but they nonetheless challenge the notion that the performance of deaf people on intelligence tests can be accepted as an accurate indication of intelligence. Rather, they propose that the intelligence of deaf people differs in kind from the intelligence of normal-hearing cohorts. Examples of the "qualitative difference" perspective include Levine's (1960) experiential deficit hypothesis, Myklebust's (1964) organismic shift hypothesis, and Tomlinson-Keasy and Kelley's (1978) proposal that deaf people organize cognition in ways profoundly different from normal-hearing peers.

Support for the thesis that deaf people develop qualitatively distinct forms of intelligence comes from research using information-processing tasks rather than intelligence tests per se. The results of information-processing tasks are, however, quite heterogeneous. Some researchers (e.g., Belmont, Karchmer, & Bourg, 1983) have found that deaf children use very similar, but immature, memory strategies relative to normal-hearing cohorts. Studies of neurolinguistic functioning have found that deaf adults organize, store, and retrieve language in a manner nearly identical to normal-hearing adults (Poizner et al., 1987). In contrast, Myklebust, Tomlinson-Keasy, Levine, and others cite other experimental data showing deaf people differ from hearing people in their qualitative and quantitative performance on information-processing tasks. Therefore, the evidence regarding a qualitative shift in the intelligence of deaf people is by no means conclusive.

Even if deaf people were known to have distinct methods of information processing, the relevant question is, Would these differences change what is measured by IQ tests? Test bias data offer the empirical grounds to prove whether qualitative differences in intelligence affect IQ. If deaf people develop qualitatively distinct forms of intelligence, it follows that their performance on intelligence tests would be unusual, or show qualitative changes, relative to normal-hearing people. Evidence of abnormality should be especially pronounced in the factor structure underlying intelligence test batteries or subtests (Myklebust, 1964).

As discussed previously, the available evidence regarding internal indices of test bias suggests that nonverbal intelligence tests generally evince similar psychometric characteristics in deaf and normal-hearing populations. This in turn offers little evidence to support the notion that intelligence differs in kind, rather than in degree, in deaf people. It is possible that deaf children have different rates for intellectual development relative to normal-hearing children (e.g., Braden & Zwiebel, 1990; Zwiebel, 1988; Zwiebel & Mertens, 1985), but the preponderance of evidence fails to support the notion that compensation in deaf people leads to qualitatively distinct nonverbal intellectual structures. In fact, the striking similarity of factor structures found between deaf and normal-hearing peers, and the fact that such similarities increase over time, strongly suggests that compensation does not have an appreciable effect on the way deaf people develop and organize nonverbal intellectual skills.

The same conclusion may not be valid with regard to verbal intelligence. The bulk of experimental data suggest that deaf people employ slightly different strategies for encoding, processing, storing, and retrieving verbal information. Although it is questionable whether these differences are of kind, or simply of maturity or degree, there can be no doubt that deaf people process verbal information differently than normal-hearing people. Furthermore, verbally loaded tests correlate substantially with hearing loss, and this phenomenon creates a factor not found in normal-hearing people (e.g., Farrant, 1964). These findings argue against the assumption that deaf people develop and organize verbal reasoning skills in a manner similar to normal-hearing people. Thus, it is at least possible that compensation leads deaf people to develop qualitatively distinct processes for verbal reasoning, and that the effects of compensation create qualitative, rather than quantitative, differences between deaf and normal-hearing people on verbal intelligence tests.

Changes in Specific Skills as a Result of Deafness

On a less sweeping scale, it is also possible that deaf people compensate for hearing loss by developing and refining a particular subset of psychological skills. This argument is a less ambitious version of the qualitative shift in intellect proposed in the preceding section. Instead of large-scale reintegration of cognitive organization, deaf people might compensate for reduced auditory acuity by developing subsets of specific skills. Logical candidates for such compensatory mechanisms include psychomotor skills, such as visual search, eye–hand coordination, or other attributes that are not directly affected by deafness but could serve to offset the effects of hearing loss. If true, intelligence tests that confound the assessment of intelligence with psychomotor skills might provide inaccurate estimates of intelligence.

Despite the hope that deaf people might develop superior vision or coordination to compensate for deafness, there is no evidence to suggest compensation in sensory acuity and physical development among deaf people. In fact, orthopedic, visual, and gross motor disabilities are more prevalent among deaf people than they are among normal-hearing people (Brown, 1986; Schein, 1975). The higher prevalence rate of additional disabilities among deaf people is attributed to the sequelae of the often traumatic etiology of deafness. Therefore, far from compensating for hearing loss by developing superior vision or physical development, deaf people exhibit higher rates of visual and orthopedic disabilities. The greater prevalence of dysfunction in vision and motor skills is attributed to organic, rather than environmental, causes.

However, there is still the possibility that deaf people who do not have organically induced impairments develop superior visual–perceptual or psychomotor skills as a means of compensating for deafness. Some evidence in support of this position has been offered by Bellugi (1989), who has reported that deaf people exhibit superior skills for recognizing and remembering idiographic characters. It is of particular interest to note that Bellugi's work is based on deaf children of deaf parents, who also exhibit above-average nonverbal IQs. Thus, it is possible that superior visual–perceptual skills, which may have been developed via early and consistent exposure to sign language, transfer to nonverbal tests of intelligence, resulting in inflated IQs for this group. Conversely, it is possible that the above-average intelligence of deaf children of deaf parents causes them to do better on visual-perceptual tasks. In the absence of other data, either hypothesis is tenable. However, it is a provocative possibility that the development of superior visual-perceptual skills, perhaps engendered by early and consistent use of sign language, accounts for the above-average nonverbal IQs of deaf children of deaf parents.

A second possibility proposed in the literature is that deaf people with early and consistent exposure to sign language develop superior psychomotor skills.

Specifically, I have proposed (Braden, 1985a, 1987) that exposure to sign language is correlated with speed on psychomotor tasks. Evidence for this hypothesis comes from experimental analyses of movement time. Deaf children of deaf parents are faster than deaf children of hearing parents, who in turn are faster than normal hearing children on experimental tasks. This implies that speeded, psychomotor intelligence tests (i.e., performance tests of intelligence) will produce higher IQs for deaf people than nonspeeded intelligence tests (i.e., motor-free, untimed IQ tests). This hypothesis is partially corroborated by meta-analytic results showing that mean performance IQ is higher than mean nonverbal IQ for samples of deaf people.

However, not all meta-analytic results are compatible with the psychomotor superiority hypothesis. An analysis of Wechsler Performance Scale subtest means shows that deaf people are often below average on the subtest that most directly measures psychomotor speed (i.e., Coding/Digit Symbol) (Anderson & Sisco, 1977; Braden, 1990b). Conversely, they tend to be average or slightly above average on the Picture Completion subtest, which does not reward speeded performance. A similar pattern of subtests performance is found on the Hiskey-Nebraska Test of Learning Aptitude. Deaf children tend to perform below average on speeded subtests (e.g., bead stringing in the Bead Patterns subtest), yet they perform somewhat better on untimed subtests (e.g., Completion of Drawings). Therefore, it is not clear whether deaf people do, in fact, develop superior psychomotor skills. Critical studies using tests of psychomotor skills independent of intelligence (e.g., finger tapping) are needed to identify compensatory psychomotor development, and what influence (if any) such compensation might have on nonverbal IQ.

Summary: Compensatory Effects on IQ

The available data argue strongly against the notion that deaf people develop qualitatively distinct forms of intelligence in compensating for hearing loss. Although it is possible that deaf people may develop information-processing strategies and approaches that are unique, these do not appear to affect deaf people's IQs. More important, if information-processing differences exist, they do not affect the psychometric characteristics of intelligence tests in samples of deaf people. An important caveat to this conclusion is found with verbal intelligence tests, which deaf people may approach quite differently than their normal-hearing peers.

Evidence for specific visual–perceptual and psychomotor compensation is inconclusive. Available data suggest deaf people may develop superior psychomotor skills, which in turn are compatible with the higher IQs obtained on motor-intensive nonverbal intelligence tests. However, even if deaf people developed superior skills in specific areas, the preponderance of evidence suggests the effect on IQ is modest. IQs from nonverbal, motor-free tests are only slightly lower than IQs from tests confounding IQ and psychomotor skills, and the pattern of scores among motor-intensive and motor-reduced subtests within nonverbal batteries does not support the notion of superior psychomotor skills for deaf people. Therefore, the evidence for compensatory effects on IQ is mixed, but there is no reason to believe that compensatory mechanisms have a major effect on the IQs of deaf people.

Experimental Procedures

Although it is unlikely that test bias and compensatory mechanisms seriously attenuate the IQs of deaf people, it is possible that the way in which research is conceived and conducted may affect IQs. If so, it is possible that the outcomes of the natural experiment provided by deafness may be skewed by procedural factors. Therefore, methods employed by researchers must be evaluated to determine what, if any, effect research methods have on obtained IQs.

There are at least four experimental procedures that could affect reported IQs. These procedures are (1) test content, (2) test administration, (3) the scale used to compute IQs, and (4) sampling bias. Because test type (i.e., verbal, nonverbal, or performance IQ tests), test administration (e.g., oral, signed, gestural, combined methods), and IQ scale (e.g., ratio, normative) are discussed in Chapter 3, the only procedure to be examined here is the influence of sampling on reported IQs.

Sampling Methods Affecting IQ

Biases in selecting samples of deaf people may skew the IQs reported in the literature. The degree to which samples select children in a nonrandom fashion increases the probability that IQ results will not represent the population of deaf people. Sampling methods that result in over- or underrepresentation of factors known to relate to IQ, such as socioeconomic or handicapping conditions, will therefore skew the reported results. It is critical to examine what sources of sampling bias may be present in the literature describing the intelligence of deaf people.

Evidence of sampling bias is clearly suggested by the nonrepresentative nature of settings from which samples were obtained. Fully 50% of the studies reporting IQs for deaf people obtained samples from residential schools that serve deaf children, whereas 11% sampled deaf children from public school (commuter) programs. Less than 10% of the studies sampled individuals from noneducational settings. The overrepresentation of residential schools in the literature is distressing, because most deaf children in Western nations attend commuter schools (Conrad, 1979; Schildroth, 1986).

On the one hand, the overrepresentation of deaf people attending residential schools is likely to result in overrepresentation of deaf people with additional disabilities, because residential schools have higher rates of deaf children with additional handicapping conditions (Schildroth, 1986). The overrepresentation of deaf children with additional handicapping conditions should depress the mean IQs reported for residential school samples. On the other hand, residential schools typically enroll more deaf children of deaf parents, and fewer ethnic minorities, than public schools (Schildroth, 1986). These factors should raise IQ estimates, in that they would overrepresent deaf children of deaf parents (who have above-average IQs) and underrepresent ethnic minorities (who typically have below-average IQs).

Meta-analytic comparisons across studies suggest no relationship between the source of samples of deaf children and average IQ ($F_{(6,316)}$ = 1.76, NS). This outcome contradicts studies that directly compare day and residential programs. Direct studies of sampling source consistently report that the IQs of deaf children attending day schools are higher than the IQs of deaf peers attending residential schools (Braden, 1989b; Braden et al., 1993; Conrad, 1979; Day et al., 1928; Madden, 1931; Raviv et al., 1973; Reamer, 1921; Upshall, 1929).

It is impossible to reconcile the conclusions reached in the meta-analytic investigation with those of studies that directly compare deaf children from day and residential schools. Individual studies suggest that the overrepresentation of residential deaf children in the literature is likely to underestimate the intelligence of the deaf population. However, it is impossible to convincingly conclude that there are any sampling effects, and so it is unlikely that reported IQs are substantially affected by sampling methods.

Summary: Experimental Methods

Experimental methods affect the IQs of deaf people. The review in Chapter 3 shows that nonverbal tests yield higher IQs than verbal tests, and that administration of tests using sign language yields higher IQs than oral and/or written administration methods. Use of normative IQ scales yields higher IQs than technically inadequate ratio scales. These factors converge to suggest that IQs in the literature may underestimate the intelligence of deaf people, in that there appear to be no modifications that systematically inflate deaf people's IQs beyond expected levels. A similar pattern is suggested when sampling bias is included as a concern, in that, to the degree it is likely to have any affect on reported IQs, the predominate sampling methods employed in the research are likely to under-estimate the IQ of the deaf population.

There are many reasons independent of the IQs obtained by deaf people for believing that sampling methods, verbal tests, vocal/written test administration, and outmoded methods for calculating IQ would have a deleterious effect on IQ. It is important to acknowledge that the rationale for using one method over another must be independent of the outcomes or IQs obtained. It cannot be assumed that methods that yield higher IQs are necessarily better than those yielding lower IQs. For example, all children will do better on IQ tests in which examiners coach them, provide feedback on answers, or otherwise extend more assistance than is allowed under established administration procedures. This does not mean that established normative procedures "underestimate" the IQs of children! However, independent experimental and clinical research discourages the use of certain procedures independent of their effect on IQ.

Consequently, there is ample reason, independent of the impact such methods have on IQ, to believe that verbal administration, verbally loaded test content, use of ratio or sample-derived IQs, and oversampling from residential schools will negatively skew the IQs reported for deaf people. These factors all point in a direction that strongly suggests that the nonverbal IQs reported in the meta-analysis underestimate the intelligence of the deaf population.

Conclusions: Evaluation of Deafness as a Natural Experiment

The outcomes of the natural experiment of deafness must be considered in light of rival hypotheses. The review of the rival hypotheses of test bias, compensatory effects on IQ, and experimental methods identifies many factors that must be considered in evaluating the IQs reported for deaf people.

To what degree do these rivals confound the impact of deafness on the development of intelligence with other factors? The preponderance of evidence suggests that experimental methods substantially affect deaf people's IQs. Verbal test content, administration procedures that do not use sign language, outmoded methods for calculating IQ, and bias in sample selection depress IQ. The confluence of these factors suggests that the IQs of deaf people reported in the literature are likely to underestimate the intelligence of the deaf population.

There is no compelling evidence to suggest that nonverbal IQ tests are biased estimates of intelligence when used with deaf people, although nonverbal tests may overestimate the performance of deaf people on academic and linguistic criteria. Likewise, there is no consistent evidence regarding the possibility that compensatory effects invalidate or influence nonverbal IQ. More important, the literature regarding the reliability, validity, and predictive power of nonverbal IQ tests lends confidence to the assumption that these tests accurately measure the intelligence of deaf people. Granted, there are many gaps in the literature, but the preponderance of available results suggests tests function quite similarly in deaf and normal-hearing populations. The evidence provides a strong basis for rejecting proposals that intelligence is qualitatively different, or changed, as a result of deafness. Furthermore, the finding that studies using contemporary, clinically recommended methods produce higher IQs than studies using outmoded, clinically questionable assessment methods again lends confidence to the conclusion that deafness has little impact on nonverbal intelligence. Therefore, the minimal impact of deafness on nonverbal IQ is unlikely to be due to test bias, compensatory skills on the part of deaf people, or experimental methods.

It is not yet possible to make such strong conclusions with regard to verbal tests of intelligence. The evidence needed for drawing conclusions is simply unavailable. The limited evidence regarding verbal IQ tests with deaf people yields some indicators of test bias. However, there is a complex, tangled web of factors that surround the use of verbal IQ tests with deaf people. For example, it is known that verbal administration procedures depress nonverbal IQs, and are therefore likely to artificially depress verbal IQs. It is also known that deaf people often fail to acquire native competence in spoken language, which would legitimately lower their verbal reasoning fluency (Conrad, 1979). The limited psychometric data regarding verbal IQ tests with deaf people argue against the psychometric integrity of the tests when used with deaf populations. Experimental comparisons, which match deaf children with normal-hearing children on the basis of verbal measures (e.g., Moores, 1970), suggest that verbal IQ may overestimate deaf children's verbal abilities. If so, test bias and experimental factors may inflate estimates of deaf people's verbal intelligence. Thus, there are many factors that complicate the interpretation of verbal IQs derived from samples of deaf people.

The most conservative conclusion to be drawn from these conflicting data is that it is impossible to determine whether verbal IQ is biased with respect to estimating deaf people's verbal reasoning ability. Further research regarding the use of verbal intelligence tests with deaf people is needed to determine what, if any, conclusions would be defensible. However, there is nothing in the literature to suggest that deaf people have average or above-average verbal reasoning skills, because the bulk of experimental and achievement data consistently shows deaf people performing below normal-hearing peers on measures of verbal information processing and achievement. Ironically, although verbal tests may function as a biased estimate of intelligence for deaf people, verbal tests apparently provide unbiased empirical predictions of criterion performance.

Extraneous factors and rival hypotheses do not appear to exert a substantial impact on the IQs of deaf people. Psychometric findings strongly support the use of nonverbal IQ tests for estimating the intelligence, if not the academic achievement, of deaf people. Situational test factors show that verbally loaded administration procedures, and administration procedures that do not use sign language, are likely to depress IQs. Experimental methods suggest that outmoded and inappropriate procedures for test selection, test administration, IQ calculation, and sample selection depress the IQs of deaf people. Thus, to the degree that extraneous factors or rival hypotheses have an impact on the outcomes of deafness as a natural experiment, the impact is one of underestimating the IQs of deaf people.

5

Implications of Deafness, Deprivation, and IQ for IQ Differences between Groups

The study of deafness helps illuminate the nature and causes of between-group differences in IQ. Deafness offers a powerful paradigm for testing environmental, genetic, and interactionist theories of IQ differences between groups. By examining the IQs of deaf people in the context of IQ differences between groups, theories can be tested, refined, clarified. As such, deafness offers a valuable, and heretofore underutilized, tool for understanding why different groups have different distributions of IQ.

This investigation must note at the outset that the outcomes of deafness (i.e., significant and severe depression of verbal IQ and little if any change in nonverbal IQ) are not readily explained by measurement error, experimental procedures, or test bias. In fact, the evidence reviewed in the previous chapter suggests that, to the extent that experimental factors affect the reported distribution of IQ within the deaf population, these factors are likely to overestimate verbal IQ and underestimate nonverbal IQ. Thus, the impact of deafness on intelligence is to depress verbal IQs, and essentially not affect nonverbal IQs.

Theories accounting for group differences in IQ are analyzed in light of the results of deafness as a natural experiment. These analyses are based on syllogistic reasoning using three premises. First, to the degree a theory specifies a factor or factors as causing a difference in IQ between groups, the factor or factors should affect IQs in other groups. Second, the degree to which deafness as a condition includes the factor(s) specified by the theory should directly impact deaf people's IQs (e.g., if a theory specifies language exposure as a major factor affecting IQ, deaf people's IQs should be affected). Third, the distribution of verbal and non-verbal IQs among deaf people can be used to test the truth of the first premise (i.e., whether the proposed factors do in fact affect IQ).

An application of this syllogism will illustrate my point. First, a theory might propose that auditory stimulation is a key ingredient for the development of verbal intelligence. Without auditory stimulation, areas of the brain related to verbal reasoning will atrophy, thus diminishing verbal reasoning skills. Second, it is hypothesized that deafness as a condition includes auditory deprivation and distortion, and so provides a strong test of the theory. Third, the severely depressed verbal IQs found for deaf people, and the negative correlation between hearing loss and measures of verbal IQ and academic achievement, support the prediction of the original theory. In other words, the outcomes of deafness as a natural experiment would be compatible with the theory. However, the depressed verbal IQs and academic achievement scores of deaf people do not provide a critical test of the hypothesis, because the condition of deafness also includes language deprivation (not just auditory deprivation), as well other factors that might also cause depressed verbal IQ and achievement.

An overview of the types of theories offered to account for IQ differences between groups is provided as a basis for organizing the logical analysis of theories. Specific examples of each type of theory are analyzed to illustrate the potency of deafness as a natural experiment to test accounts of IQ differences between groups.

Overview of Group Difference Theories

There are a multitude of theories attempting to explain why some groups have different distributions of IQ relative to other groups. These theories generally attribute the cause of between-group differences in IQ to one of four causes: (1) experimental or measurement factors, such as tests bias; (2) environmental influences; (3) genetic influences; or (4) gene–environment interaction. Some individuals cite a variety of causes to explain IQ differences between groups, but the theories themselves may generally be separated into the four categories listed above.

Most instances of IQ differences between groups are situations in which a racial or ethnic minority group has a lower distribution of IQ than the dominant racial or ethnic majority group. The instance that has received the greatest attention in the research is the difference in IQ between North American whites and blacks. North American blacks consistently score well below their white counterparts on tests of intelligence. However, not all minority groups score below the majority group. Asians in North America have higher IQs and higher academic achievement scores than the dominant white majority (Jensen, 1980; Vernon,

1982). Therefore, it is not always true that ethnic or racial minorities are at a disadvantage on tests of intelligence and achievement relative to dominant majority peers.

A second caveat is that the magnitude of IQ difference between groups sometimes varies as a function of tests. For example, blacks and whites show smaller differences on certain kinds of intelligence tests than they do on others. One cause of variation in test scores is the metric of the IQ test. If a test is normed so that the standard deviation of the score is small, the difference between any two groups will be smaller than if the standard deviation is large. In order to eliminate IQ scale as a source of variation in between-group differences, IQ differences between groups are typically expressed in standard deviation units. These units are calculated by subtracting the mean for one group from the mean of the other group, and then dividing by the pooled standard deviation (see Jensen & Reynolds, 1982, for a description of this process). Thus, a difference of 3 on a WISC-R subtest between the mean for blacks and the mean for whites is approximately equal to 1 SD unit, which in turn is comparable to a difference of 15 WISC-R PIQ points, which is also approximately equal to 1 SD unit. By converting differences to a common scale, variations in between-group differences due to the metric or scale of the test are eliminated.

When IQ scale is eliminated as a source of variation in the magnitude of IQ differences between whites and blacks, it is consistently reported that blacks score about 0.66 to 1.0 SD units below whites on tests of intelligence (e.g., Jensen, 1980; Loehlin, Lindzey, & Spuhler, 1975). The persistence of this finding, and the magnitude of the IQ difference, has been the subject of intense debate in the psychological literature. Because this phenomenon is so robust, and has been so widely studied, the accounts of IQ differences between blacks and whites are the primary focus of this chapter. In this context, theories attributing the cause of black–white IQ differences to experimental procedures, environmental influences, genetic influences, and interactionist theories are examined with respect to how well they account for IQ differences between normal-hearing and deaf people.

Experimental Sources of between-Group Differences

The methods, procedures, and tools used to collect data regarding black–white differences in IQ have come under scrutiny as possible causes of group differences. If the methods used to obtain information in some way systematically skew the results, it is possible that the resulting differences in IQ reported for blacks and whites are falsely exaggerated or diminished. In other words, if the magnitude of black–white differences in IQ is due to experimental factors, it is unreasonable (and unethical) to interpret the differences as indicating different distributions of intelligence.

Two experimental procedures have been offered to account for variations in the magnitude of black–white differences in IQ. The first is test bias. Systematic error in the measurement of IQ, particularly when the error is more prevalent among one group than among the other, could skew estimates of IQ for one or both groups. The second experimental factor that might lead to erroneous estimation of IQs is sampling bias. Systematic error in the selection of samples for study could skew the estimates of IQ for blacks or whites, and thus affect the magnitude of IQ difference. Each of these conditions has been proposed to account for variations in the magnitude of black–white differences, and so each will be considered in light of the outcomes of deafness as a natural experiment condition.

Test Bias

Test bias is one of the most commonly cited causes of between-group differences in IQ. In fact, the sheer volume of literature on this topic is overwhelming, and a thorough review of test bias literature is well beyond the scope of this book. Curious readers who wish to understand test bias will find that Jensen's (1980) book and a companion volume of edited works by Reynolds and Brown (1984), provide lucid and exhaustive treatment of the topic.

These works define two basic definitions of test bias. The first definition is statistical, and the second is polemic. Each of these approaches to test bias has been cited as a cause of between-group differences in IQ. Fortunately, the study of deaf people has a great deal to offer in examining polemic theories of test bias, and their ability to account for black–white differences in IQ.

Statistical Theories of Test Bias

Before discussing polemic theories of test bias, it is important to understand why the presence of test bias with deaf people has no bearing on whether a test is biased for or against other groups. The statistical definition of test bias (e.g., Berk, 1982; Jensen, 1980, Chapter 9) specifies the internal and external psychometric conditions that constitute bias. Test bias is defined as the presence of the conditions indicating bias. Because one can only affirm or demonstrate the presence of test bias, the "no-bias" hypothesis can never be proved. In other words, one can only show there is evidence of bias; the absence of such evidence means that it is impossible to reject the null hypothesis of "no bias."

Furthermore, statistical definitions of bias can only be applied to a particular test used with a particular group. Should a given test systematically err in estimation of a trait within a given group, there is reason to believe that test is biased for that group. However, demonstration of test bias does not generalize to other tests, or to other groups. Therefore, the finding that intelligence tests are biased, or unbiased, for groups of deaf children does not affirm or deny the proposition that the tests may be biased measures of intelligence in racial or ethnic minority groups. Therefore, there is little that the study of deaf people's intelligence can offer to statistical studies of test bias as a source of between-group differences in IQ.

Polemic Theories of Test Bias

The performance of deaf people on IQ tests has significant import for polemic theories of test bias. Polemic theories of test bias attack the failure to find statistical bias by arguing that statistical tests of bias, which are based largely on the psychometric congruence of IQ tests (predictors) with tests of achievement (criteria), find no evidence of bias because IQ and achievement tests are indistinguishable. Polemic theorists argue that intelligence tests are unbiased predictors of academic achievement because intelligence and achievement tests measure the same construct, which is usually posited to be culturally specific competence and knowledge common to dominant majority groups. Therefore, there are no differences between groups in terms of slope, intercept, or standard error of prediction when IQs are used to predict achievement. Likewise, the finding that blacks score well below whites on both intelligence and achievement tests is cited as proof that achievement and intelligence cannot be reasonably considered two separate constructs. Instead, polemic theorists (e.g., Mercer, 1979; Williams, 1974) suggest that the lack of test bias is simply due to the fact that IQ and achievement tests measure knowledge of the dominant culture to the same degree, and are therefore: (1) biased against nondominant cultural groups and (2) show no evidence of statistical bias, since they measure cultural knowledge to approximately the same degree. Even those who propose blacks and whites differ for reasons in addition to test content (e.g., Ogbu, 1988) often argue that intelligence tests are largely tests of cultural achievement. The argument proposes that intelligence tests fail to separate culturally specific outcomes from psychobiological outcomes (i.e., intelligence). Thus, black–white differences in IQ are due to differential knowledge of the dominant culture, and are not due to differential distributions of intelligence.

Deafness certainly restricts knowledge of the dominant culture. North American deaf people are cut off not only from all social customs involving Standard American Speech, but from all secondary sources of the dominant version of spoken English (e.g., television, radio). Speech-reading is nonstandard because it severely restricts the amount of information flowing across the communication channel, and because speakers often simplify, edit, and otherwise alter their communication behavior when speaking to hearing-impaired people. Sign systems either represent an altogether different language than the dominant language (i.e., American Sign Language), or a nonstandard dialectical variant of standard speech (i.e., pidgin sign English). Signs and speech are also presented to deaf children in nonstandard media (i.e., visual or gestural/visual rather than oral/auditory).

Consequently, it is logical to assume that all deaf people, even those deaf people who are members of the dominant ethnic group, are likely to be deprived of knowledge of the dominant culture. Although they could be assumed to observe nonverbal aspects of the dominant culture (e.g., modes of dress), the primary modes of cultural transmission (e.g., language, parental interaction) are severely restricted for deaf people. If the polemic arguments of test bias are correct, deaf people should score far below average on tests of intelligence and achievement. A corollary of this proposition is that deaf people's performance on tests of achievement and intelligence should be consistent (i.e., because tests of achievement and intelligence measure the same things, they should yield similar scores).

The performance of deaf people on tests of academic achievement, and on verbal tests of intelligence, is congruent with polemic arguments that deprivation from the mainstream of the dominant culture severely depresses knowledge of that culture. In other words, the markedly low verbal IQs and achievement scores of deaf people is consistent with the polemic arguments of test bias, because deaf people typically receive limited, nonstandard language input, and are generally isolated from the mainstream of the dominant culture by virtue of their hearing loss. Likewise, there is no difference in performance between achievement and verbal intelligence tests, further supporting arguments that these tests do not distinguish between verbal reasoning ability (presumably a psychobiological trait) and culturally specific knowledge.

However, the findings that deaf people have average nonverbal IQs, and that deaf children of deaf parents (i.e., children of a nondominant minority who are economically and socially isolated from the dominant majority culture) have above-average IQs, are incompatible with polemic arguments of test bias. In fact, the average performance of deaf people on nonverbal tests of intelligence, coupled with their below-average performance on verbal tests of intelligence, offers strong evidence of construct validity for tests of intelligence and achievement. Tests that measure knowledge to determine success on a criterion (i.e., achievement tests) and tests that measure acquisition of knowledge to infer underlying abilities (i.e., verbal intelligence tests) both yield scores well below average when used with deaf people. In contrast, tests intended to be culture-reduced estimates of psychobiological functioning (i.e., nonverbal or performance IQ tests) yield average IQs when used with deaf people. Thus, polemic propositions of test bias are valid insofar as tests measure culturally specific knowledge to estimate intelligence (i.e., achievement scores and verbal IQs are depressed by the lack of exposure to the dominant culture). However, polemic arguments that attempt to lump nonverbal intelligence tests with verbal intelligence tests are misleading, for it is clear from the nonverbal IQs of deaf people that reliable and meaningful distinctions must be made between nonverbal and verbal tests of intelligence.

The performance of deaf people on nonverbal intelligence tests offers a critical test of the polemic account of black–white differences in IQ. Blacks score about 1 *SD* unit below whites on verbal intelligence tests, on tests of achievement, *and on nonverbal intelligence tests.* The magnitude of black–white difference is often larger on nonverbal intelligence tests than on verbally loaded tests of intelligence (Jensen, 1980, 1985; Jensen & Reynolds, 1982). Polemic theories of test bias propose that nonverbal tests somehow measure knowledge of the dominant culture, which is possible even if the test content does not appear to sample cultural knowledge. The finding that deaf people have average nonverbal IQs, and below-average verbal IQs and depressed academic achievement, strongly implicates the polemic theory of test bias as the cause of black–white differences in IQ. If knowledge of the dominant culture is measured on nonverbal intelligence tests, then deaf people should score below average on these tests, because they certainly lack that knowledge of the dominant culture. The fact that they have average nonverbal IQs suggests that knowledge of dominant culture has little if any impact on nonverbal IQ, and thus cannot account for black–white differences in nonverbal IQ.

Polemic theories could be salvaged by evidence demonstrating how deaf children from dominant majority homes would somehow have greater access to the type of knowledge measured on nonverbal tests than normal-hearing minority children. It is possible that deaf children might play more than black children with puzzles, blocks, geometric designs, and other stimuli used to measure nonverbal intelligence. However, this scenario is unlikely for two reasons. First, the presence of such objects has not been linked to nonverbal IQ, and thus it is questionable whether play with such objects substantially improves performance on nonverbal intelligence tests. Second, experimental observations and biographical accounts of deaf children suggest their parents actually restrict deaf children's play time in order to saturate them with language (via signs, speech, written labels, or other means) and otherwise control their children's interactions with the environment.

Thus, polemic theories of IQ differences between groups anticipate the poor performance of deaf children on verbally loaded tests of achievement and intelligence, but fail miserably when applied to deaf children's performance on nonverbal intelligence tests. This application of deafness as a natural experiment condition highlights the psychological value of the distinction between verbal and nonverbal intelligence tests, and in so doing refutes critics who attempt to argue that all black–white differences in IQ are due to the cultural content of intelligence tests.

Sampling Bias

The magnitude of the black–white difference is affected by sampling methods. Bracken (1985) proposes that the relatively small difference in IQ between whites and blacks on the Kaufman Assessment Battery for Children (K-ABC)

(Kaufman & Kaufman, 1983) is due in part to sampling methods. The black–white difference on the K-ABC Mental Processing Composite (a term synonymous with IQ) is about 0.5 *SD* units, which is smaller than the 0.66–1.0 *SD*-unit difference reported for most popular tests of intelligence. Bracken notes that the inordinately high number of mid- to high-SES blacks in the K-ABC normative sample positively skews the estimated IQ for blacks, which overestimates black children's IQs.

A second source of sampling bias resulting in a diminished black–white difference is the inclusion of large numbers of young children (2–5 years of age) in the normative sample. Because the IQs of blacks and whites are more similar at early ages than at later ages, large numbers of young children in the normative sample minimize the black–white differences in IQ. Although Bracken cites other factors in addition to sampling methods as causes of diminished black–white differences, the demonstration of sampling bias as a source of variation in IQ differences between blacks and whites is likely to be affected by inappropriate sampling.

It is important to note that Bracken shows how sampling bias diminishes the magnitude of IQ difference between blacks and whites. Sampling bias is not likely to exaggerate differences between blacks and whites, because stratified random sampling techniques are unlikely to overrepresent low-SES blacks and high SES whites. Although normative samples based on census figures are, in fact, likely to underrepresent low-SES minorities (e.g., low-SES people of minority status are more likely than high-SES people of majority status to be excluded from household-based census procedures), such underrepresentation would diminish black–white IQ differences. The use of public schools as the primary source of children in normative samples is also likely to reduce black–white differences in IQ, because low-SES black children are less likely to regularly attend school, and thus be included in normative samples, than higher SES whites. Likewise, high-SES white children are likely to attend private boarding schools, and therefore are excluded from normative samples. Thus, sampling characteristics are likely to minimize, rather than exaggerate, black–white differences in IQ.

The ability of deafness as a natural experiment to test the impact of experimental sampling procedures on IQ differences between groups is essentially nil. The fact that excessive sampling of residential school populations probably lowers the mean nonverbal IQ for deaf people does not imply that sampling procedures used with blacks and whites are similar to, or better or worse than, those used to select samples of deaf people. Therefore, although sampling procedures may diminish the magnitude of black–white differences in IQ, and may exaggerate deaf–hearing differences in IQ, there is no logical connection between methods used to sample deaf children and methods used to sample majority and minority children. Also, most major tests of intelligence exclude residential populations from their normative samples, which also diminishes the value of deafness as a natural experiment for understanding sampling effects on black–white differences. Therefore, the application of deafness as a natural experiment to accounts of black–white IQ differences due to differential sampling is a barren exercise.

In summary, the findings from the study of deafness are relevant for evaluating the polemic version of test bias as an account of between-group differences in IQ, and are irrelevant for evaluating the viability of statistical bias and sampling accounts of between-group differences in IQ. The fact that deaf people score well below average on verbal intelligence and academic achievement tests is consistent with polemic theories of test bias. Such a pattern shows that knowledge of dominant culture is sampled by verbal IQ and achievement tests. However, the average nonverbal IQs of deaf people refute the notion that all tests of intelligence are inherently tests of culturally specific knowledge, and therefore validate the importance of distinguishing between verbal and nonverbal intelligence tests. These conclusions offer some insight into the value of deafness as a natural experiment for methodological theories of between-group differences in IQ.

Environmental Accounts of between-Group Differences

Environmental explanations of black–white differences in IQ abound in the professional and lay literature. Indeed, the North American psyche is so profoundly influenced by philosophies stressing environmental causes of individual differences that those who have proposed genetic causes for black–white differences in IQ have been attacked and ridiculed in the lay and professional press (Herrnstein, 1982; Snyderman & Rothman, 1986). Consequently, there are many popular environmental explanations of IQ differences between whites and blacks. The degree to which these explanations overlap with deafness (a form of environmental deprivation) is explored in this section.

Before beginning this review, it is worthwhile to recall some of the environmental characteristics that differ between groups representing the normal-hearing majority, the normal-hearing disadvantaged minority, deaf children of hearing parents, deaf children of hearing parents with a deaf sibling, and deaf children of deaf parents. The relative advantages and disadvantages experienced by each of these groups on the seven factors associated with deafness is presented in Table 5.1. These qualitative rankings provide an admittedly limited summary of environmental differences and similarities between groups, which will be helpful for evaluating the degree to which environmental theories of group differences make consistent predictions across majority, disadvantaged minority, and deaf groups.

Two types of environmental theories have been proposed to account for black–white differences in IQ. The first type is the single-factor theory. These

TABLE 5.1. Deafness as a Natural Experiment in Differences between Groups

	Group				
Condition	Norm	Minority	HP	HP/DS	DP
Auditory deprivation	+	+	−	−	− −
Language exposure	+++	++	− − −	− − −	+
Medical trauma	+	−	− −	− −	− −
Genetic endowment	+	?	−/+	−/+	−/+
Family dynamics	+	+	− −	−	+
Social interactions					
Majority/proximal	+	−	−	−	−
Majority/distal	+	−	+	+	+
Family ethnicity	+	+	−	−	+
SES	+	−	+	+	−

Note: + = relative advantage; − = relative disadvantage; −/+= advantage or disadvantage, depending on circumstances; ? = unknown or insufficient data.

theories posit the primary cause of black–white (or minority–majority) IQ differences to be a single factor, that varies as a function of ethnic or racial group membership. The second type of theory is the multiple-factor theory. These theories attribute the primary cause of between-group differences in IQ to multiple causes that vary as a function of racial or ethnic group membership. Because group membership embodies many interrelated environmental variables, theories stressing the effects of culture, and those proposing a constellation of single-factor theories as the cause of between-group differences in IQ, are considered multiple-factor theories. Single-factor and multiple-factor theories are considered and examined with respect to deafness as a natural experiment in environmental conditions.

Single-Factor Environmental Theories

Single-factor theories of intelligence typically draw from one of four environmental domains. The first environmental domain could be considered organic, in that these theories propose that environmental differences between groups lead to different rates of organic difficulties between groups that are later expressed as differences in IQ. The second domain of environmental theories is linguistic, in which linguistic differences between groups are believed to affect performance on tests of intelligence. The third environmental theory domain comes from social interactions, or the way in which minority groups are treated by the dominant or majority culture. Finally, the fourth domain of environmental theories comprise essentially descriptive approaches, which attempt to infer environmental causes by examining the nature of between-group differences in IQ. Each of these domains will be considered with reference to the distribution of IQs in deaf and normal-hearing people.

Organic-Environmental Accounts of IQ

Organic accounts of between-group differences in IQ stress prenatal, peri-natal, and postnatal trauma as factors affecting distributions of IQ. Because ethnic and racial minorities are often born into low-SES environments, they are more likely to experience malnutrition and other forms of trauma before, during, and after the birth of children. These traumata may affect their offspring in small, sometimes hidden ways. However, organic theories stress that although there may be no readily observable clinical indices of organic impairment as a result of poor diet, substandard medical care, or other forms of environmental deprivation, the organic damage is nonetheless present. The consequences of these sub-rosa trau-mata may be expressed in difficulties with learning tasks, particularly the abstract and artificial types of learning required for success on tests of achievement and intelligence. Therefore, between-group differences in IQ could be due to the prevalence of sub-rosa traumata in minority group people. In contrast, members of the majority group have lower rates of organic traumata, due to the better health care and nutrition at all ages and stages of life afforded by their privileged socioeconomic status.

Deaf people offer a potentially valuable test of the effects of certain organic traumata on IQ. Nearly half of the deaf people in North America have hearing losses due to organic trauma so severe that it caused a permanent auditory impair-ment. It is likely that there would be sequelae associated with the trauma of deafness. The most common forms of traumata leading to deafness are maternal illness during pregnancy, (e.g., rubella), low birth weight, and postnatal disease (e.g., spinal meningitis). Therefore, the rates of organic traumata among deaf people should exceed, or at the very least be equal to, rates of sub-rosa traumata among ethnic minorities. However, the exact rates of traumata among deaf people, as well as those among minority groups, are a matter more of speculation than of fact. Surveys of deaf people report organic traumata as the cause of deafness in 49% of all cases (Brown, 1986), clearly documenting trauma in half of the deaf population. Furthermore, over 30% of the deaf population exhibits at least one disability in addition to deafness. Therefore, the prevalence of organic trauma is certainly high within the deaf population, but exact rates are unknown.

By definition, it is not possibly to directly assess and compare rates of sub-rosa organic traumata. However, epidemiological studies of minority groups also show higher than average rates of disabilities among ethnic minorities. North American blacks are no exception. However, because most studies of between-group differences in IQ exclude disabled subjects, clinically diagnosable disabilities are unlikely to seriously influence the IQs reported for blacks and whites. The rate of subclinical, or sub-rosa, trauma is therefore the primary culprit in organic accounts of between-group differences. Because these traumata are, by definition, not diagnosable, it is impossible to estimate their prevalence in minority groups. However, there is no reason to believe that the prevalence of subclinical traumata due to disease would be higher among blacks than it is among deaf people, given that at least half of all deaf people are known to have experienced severe medical trauma. This does not mean other environmental hazards, such as lead poisoning (e.g., lead-based paints, high levels of lead in the air), do not vary between deaf people and people raised in low-SES areas (e.g., inner-city settings).

The IQs of deaf people therefore allow a partial test of the organic accounts of IQ differences. Organic accounts of between-group differences in IQ predict that any group that experiences a higher than average prevalence of medical trauma should have below-average intelligence. The pattern of deaf persons' IQs is inconsistent with the organic or trauma-based theory. Although deaf people certainly have below-average achievement and verbal IQs, their average non-verbal IQs argue against the effects of organic trauma as the cause of between-group differences in IQ. Furthermore, experimental and clinical studies of in-dividuals with diagnosed traumata show that nonverbal tests are usually more sensitive to organic trauma than are verbal tests. The probability that organic trauma therefore affects only verbal measures of intelligence is small, and even if it does, it would still fail to account for the below-average distribution of non-verbal IQs found for North American blacks.

The application of deafness as a natural experiment to test organic trauma accounts of between-group differences in IQ suggests such accounts have difficulty accurately accounting for the data. However, operationally defining the prevalence of subclinical trauma and comparing the means of traumatized and nontraumatized people within and across minority groups would provide a better test of the theory. As such, the outcomes of deafness as a natural experiment question the adequacy of organic trauma to account for between-group differences in IQ. This should not be construed to mean that the sequelae of sub-rosa organic traumata have no important effects. Rather, it means that the group means derived from intelligence tests, particularly nonverbal intelligence tests, do not appear to be particularly sensitive to sub-rosa organic impairments. Nonverbal intelligence tests are, however, sensitive to diagnosable, additional disabling conditions. It is unlikely that differential rates of organic traumata account for black–white dif-ferences in IQ, because deaf people should be affected as much as minority groups with respect to organic traumata.

Language-Based Environmental Theories

Some accounts of the cause of IQ differences between groups attribute the root of the cause to language. At least two types of linguistic theories have been proposed in this context: (1) Bernstein's theory of restricted and elaborated codes and (2) theories attributing differences to dialectical variations in the speech used by the dominant group. The critical distinction between these two types of linguistic theories lies in the syntactic elements of language models versus the dialectical, phonetic differences of language models. Each of these features of language exposure has been proposed to account for group differences in IQ.

Bernstein (1961) proposed that children of low SES are exposed to less elaborate syntactical language models than their middle- to high-SES peers. Consequently, it was proposed that black parents use directive, concrete interrogative, and overtly descriptive statements (i.e., restricted codes) more often than white parents when talking to their children. In contrast, white parents use abstract interrogative questions, self-directive statements, and explanations (i.e., elaborated codes) with their children more often than black parents. Bernstein classified the language used primarily for concrete, directive functions as exemplars of a "restricted code," in that the primary language use is immediate and tends to be expressed in short, grammatically simple statements. The language used for abstract functions, such as self-direction, questions, and explanations, relates to subjective or abstract states, and is classified as "elaborated code," because language use is abstract and tends to include extended discourse and grammatically sophisticated statements, and because the parent tended to expand on the utterances provided by the child.

Because whites and blacks differ with regard to their experience with elaborated codes, whites were hypothesized to have an advantage on tests of intelligence, which typically ask abstract questions or require explanations for a response. Furthermore, differences in achievement between blacks and whites could also be due to early exposure to elaborated and restricted codes. Schools often use elaborated codes in the classroom and reward students who demonstrate facility with elaborated responses. Therefore, linguistic differences could account for black–white differences in IQ and achievement.

The study of deaf children appears to offer an excellent test of the elaborated–restricted code hypothesis. Observational studies of teachers and parents communicating with deaf children show that language models are markedly restricted. The content of linguistic interchange (e.g., a strong emphasis on compliance and commands), as well as the fluency of the language model (most parents fail to acquire substantial sign vocabularies, much less fluid expression), suggests that deaf children are exposed to severely restricted linguistic codes as they grow up.

This is not, however, true of all deaf children. Deaf children of deaf parents (DP) are assumed to experience adequate language models, albeit in American Sign Language. Observational studies of deaf parents suggest they may, in fact, provide somewhat restricted models relative to normal-hearing parents (Galenson et al., 1979), but there are insufficient data to assume that the language models provided by deaf parents are more or less restricted than the models provided by normal-hearing parents.

The outcomes of deafness as a test of the restricted–elaborated code hypothesis is congruent with the speculation that exposure to restricted codes inhibits the development of verbal IQ and academic achievement. Deaf children perform at or below levels comparable to North American blacks on measures of verbal achievement and verbal reasoning.

However, the average performance of deaf children on nonverbal tests is inconsistent with the restricted–elaborated code hypothesis. If it were true that limited exposure to elaborated codes, or excessive exposure to restricted codes, resulted in depressed nonverbal intelligence, deaf people should have nonverbal IQs far below normal-hearing norms. The fact that the distribution of nonverbal IQs in deaf people is quite comparable to the distribution of nonverbal IQs in normal-hearing people suggests that exposure to restricted or elaborated codes plays little part in the development of nonverbal intelligence. The fact that DP perform better than deaf children of hearing parents (HP) also suggests that exposure to elaborated codes may facilitate development of nonverbal intelligence. This hypothesis has been echoed by educators in deafness, who have pointed to the above-average IQs of DP as evidence that early exposure to signs and speech fosters cognitive development to a greater extent than speech alone (e.g., Brill, 1969; Vernon & Koh, 1970). This is quite unlikely, however, because the difference between deaf and normal-hearing minority children to exposure to elaborated codes is unrelated to differences on nonverbal intelligence tests. Therefore, it is illogical to invoke the hypothesis to account for DP–HP differences, when the hypothesis cannot account for the differences between deaf people and normal-hearing minority group members.

The power of deafness as a test of the restricted–elaborated code hypothesis is limited by the fact that there are no direct comparisons of language models between the normal-hearing parents of deaf children, the deaf parents of deaf children, and the parents of normal-hearing majority and minority groups. A study that used consistent methodology across these groups would lend far more power to the viability of restricted–elaborated codes as an account of IQ differences between groups. At present, it is only possible to note that the outcomes of deafness as a natural experiment challenge the elaborated–restricted code theory, as they appear to be incompatible with the outcomes predicted by such a hypothesis. It should also be noted that Bernstein (1970) later changed his views on the impact of restricted and elaborated codes, further suggesting the theory cannot adequately account for between-group differences in intelligence and achievement.

The restricted–elaborated code hypothesis has been attacked on other grounds, not least of which is that of cultural stereotyping. It has been argued that Bernstein's characterization of the language used by North American black parents is inappropriate because it fails to consider the richness of expression in alternative dialects. Critics citing cultural stereotyping point to the consistent and systematic ways in which blacks alter the dominant form of spoken language as evidence of a dialectical, not superior–inferior, difference in language expression. For example, North American blacks frequently use "be" for all forms of the verb "to be," so that "he is walking" is appropriately expressed in the Standard Black Dialect as "he be walking."

Following this line of reasoning, nonstandard language theories have been proposed to account for black–white differences in IQ. It is argued that groups who are raised in a nonstandard language environment (e.g., blacks) are at a disadvantage when tested on instruments that are administered, scored, and normed using the standard language dialect (e.g., the dialect used by North American whites). To attempt to prove this point, Williams (1974) developed a test (the Black Intelligence Test for Children in Harlem, or BITCH) that used dialectical patterns used by North American blacks, and that sampled content associated with the cultural experience of blacks. The fact that he reported that blacks did much better on his test than on tests of intelligence administered, scored, and normed using the dialect of North American whites has been cited as evidence that dialectical differences in language lead to black–white differences on tests of IQ (which are uniformly administered, scored, and normed using the dialect of the dominant white majority). The viability of this proof is questionable on logical and empirical grounds (e.g., Jensen, 1980), but the hypothesis is nonetheless one alternative that may account for between-group differences on tests of intelligence and achievement.

Once again, the linguistic experiences of deaf people argue in favor of considering them as a test of this hypothesis. Deaf children are exposed to nonstandard linguistic dialects in nonstandard language modalities. Studies of teachers and others working with deaf children show that adult language models systematically delete English markers and simultaneously incorporate characteristics of ASL, resulting in a linguistic pidgin. Because pidgins are a blend of two or more languages, they typically differ from the dominant language more than do regional or ethnic dialects. Therefore, North American deaf children experience language models that differ substantially from the dialect used by North American white children.

However, unlike ethnic minorities, deaf children also experience another major departure from standard language models. This departure is one of medium. Whereas ethnic minority children typically experience a nonstandard dialect in the same medium as their ethnic majority counterparts (i.e., oral/auditory speech), deaf children are exposed to language primarily via gestural/visual channels. A deaf person may receive some auditory input, and develop some vocal expression, but the input and output via oral/auditory modes are typically distorted due to the deaf person's hearing loss. Therefore, deaf children confound a test of nonstandard dialectical exposure with nonstandard language modality. Furthermore, many of the adults modeling language for deaf children are not even fluent in the nonstandard sign pidgin, unlike native speakers of ethnic dialects. Therefore, the test provided by deaf children confounds nonstandard dialectical exposure and usage, nonstandard linguistic media, and unskilled language models. Given that none of these has been proposed as an advantageous situation, these conditions should combine to lower deaf children's IQs, according to the nonstandard dialect hypothesis.

There are two ways in which users of a nonstandard dialect will be at a disadvantage on an intelligence test. The first is understanding and following directions, which are usually given in the dominant (not dialectical) form of the language. The second is the content of items in the test, which would draw on standard (rather than nonstandard) dialect. Both of these have been proposed as factors lowering the IQs of speakers of a nonstandard dialect.

The impact of test administration in standard language on nonstandard language users is clearly demonstrated by the strong relationship between administration procedures and IQs obtained by deaf people. As has been shown in the previous chapter, rigid adherence to standard language directions (in oral or written form) substantially depresses IQ. In contrast, test administration using the nonstandard pidgin and media used by deaf people (i.e., administration combining signs and speech) results in higher IQs. Experimental evidence, meta-analytic findings, and clinical recommendations all concur that administration in standard modalities severely depresses the IQs obtained by deaf people.

However, it is not clear whether it is the nonstandard dialect, or the nonstandard medium, that affects deaf people's IQs. When people sign, they commonly engage in systematic deletions and distortions of the message, which mirrors nonstandard pidgins. Consequently, the shift in medium is often confounded with nonstandard pidgin usage, and thus the effects of the medium cannot be isolated from the effects of nonstandard dialect. It is clear that combining nonstandard media with pidgin usage enhances deaf people's ability to understand the test, and thus improves performance on IQ tests.

Although the IQs of deaf children suggest that nonstandard dialect and media can play a substantial role in test administration, the average nonverbal IQs of deaf children (and the above-average nonverbal IQs of DP) suggest the content of nonverbal intelligence tests does not penalize nonstandard language users. Thus, assuming that individuals understand task demands, nonverbal IQs appear to be unrelated to nonstandard language background. This is not true for verbal IQ and achievement scores. Even when task demands are clearly understood, nonstandard language users perform poorly on test content that draws heavily on standard language use. The fact that a nonverbal IQ test does not penalize nonstandard language users once again affirms the important distinction that must be made between verbal and nonverbal intelligence tests.

The concomitant failure to demonstrate that black children achieve higher IQs when tests are administered in nonstandard dialects familiar to black children (e.g., Crown, 1970; Quay, 1971, 1972, 1974) challenges dialectical, nonstandard language accounts of black–white IQ differences. Thus, the strong effects that administration procedures have on deaf children's IQs suggest that nonstandard language use may significantly impair test performance within a group, but it does not automatically impair performance within all nonstandard language or non-standard dialect users. Consequently, the nonstandard dialect or language theory cannot adequately explain the below-average nonverbal IQs of North American blacks and simultaneously account for average nonverbal IQs among North American deaf children. The study of deaf people as a test of the nonstandard language or dialect account of IQ differences between groups provides three conclusions. First, administration using standard language ordialects may substantially impair the performance of nonstandard language or dialect users due to problems understanding test directions. However, not all groups who use nonstandard languages or dialects (in particular, North American blacks) are necessarily penalized by test administration procedures using standard language or dialects. Second, test content based on standard language models may skew scores of nonstandard language users. It is unclear that results are always depressed, however, as it has been found that academic achievement scores tend to overestimate deaf children's actual achievement and verbal reasoning skills. Third, there is no evidence to show that nonstandard language exposure interacts with the content of nonverbal intelligence tests. These findings partially support, and partially refute, linguistic accounts of between-group differences in IQ.

Sociological Environmental Theories

Some theories have proposed that black–white differences on tests of intelligence are brought about by the different social status experienced by blacks and whites in North America. Specifically, Katz and his colleagues (Katz, Epps, & Axelson, 1964; Katz & Greenbaum, 1963) have proposed that blacks experience greater anxiety than whites on tests of intelligence due to the fact that being black is held in less esteem that being white. The difference in esteem brings about anxiety, which in turn depresses performance on intelligence tests. Thus, blacks score lower on IQ tests because they internalize the disadvantaged status of their minority status, which then inhibits successful completion of IQ tests.

To the degree that deaf people internalize their membership in a lower-status ethnic minority, deaf people's IQs could be used to test Katz's social status theory of between-group differences in IQ. The issue of whether deaf people identify to the same degree, and in the same way, with their physical status as do racial minorities with their racial status, is unknown. Certainly, there are ample references in the literature to deaf people as a disadvantaged subculture (e.g., Humphries & Padden, 1988). Likewise, it is clear that deaf people have been badly treated by normal-hearing society (witness labels still in use, such as "deaf and dumb" or "dummy," for deaf people). Deaf people internalize some aspects of their status. For example, deaf people exhibit a high degree of learned helplessness, which in turn is related to depressed performance on tests of academic achievement (McCrone, 1979).

It is unknown whether deaf people identify more with their deafness or with their racial group membership, or how identification with disability and ethnicity might interact. Qualitative accounts suggest that both disability and ethnicity are important to deaf people's self-identity. Jacobs (1974) and other spokespeople for the deaf community have argued eloquently and passionately for the need to embrace hearing status as a part of the deaf person's persona. Bowe (1971) has noted that racial prejudice remains active in the deaf subculture, suggesting that, despite the common disability of deafness, race is still a salient variable to deaf people. The outcomes of deafness as a natural experiment therefore have some vitality with which to test Katz's theory of IQ differences between groups, in that deaf people apparently internalize some negative aspects of their social status, and these internalized traits are related to performance on tests of academic achievement.

The pattern of scores across verbal IQ, achievement, and nonverbal IQ measures is inconsistent with the notion that minority status per se interacts with testing to yield low scores on all intelligence tests. Internalized perspectives on social status do not depress nonverbal IQs. However, the lack of data examining test anxiety as a function of normative group, experimenter hearing status, or other procedural manipulations associated with sociological research renders deafness a limited test of Katz's theory. Because Katz has also questioned internalization of minority status as an exclusive account for differences in IQ (Katz, 1969), the relative lack of power for testing the internalization of minority status renders outcomes associated with deaf children an ambiguous test of Katz's theory. To the degree deafness, internalized low social status, and nonverbal IQ test performance overlap, the study of intelligence in deaf people suggests that social status per se has little impact on nonverbal IQ.

Another sociological theory offered to account for between-group differences in intelligence is Thoday's (1973) "Factor X." The Factor X theory essentially proposes a construct, "X," to represent the factor(s) associated with lower social status due to race and ethnicity. This construct could then be used to account for the disparity in IQs between social groups. Factor X would typically have a negative weight for disadvantaged minorities, and a positive weight for advantaged minorities. Unlike many other social–environmental theories, this theory also accounts for the fact that some minorities score higher than the dominant majority on tests of intelligence and achievement (e.g., North American Asians and Jews score higher than whites on tests of intelligence and achievement). Although Factor X could encompass many attributes of the environment, it is essentially a single-factor theory, and is therefore considered in this section.

There are serious problems with Thoday's proposal, not least of which is the difficulty in devising appropriate tests of the theory (Urbach, 1974). Essentially, Factor X could be invoked post hoc to explain any difference noted between groups. However, the refinement of factors associated with Factor X could assist in the delimitation of Factor X from an ill-defined, hypothetical construct to an operationally defined set of variables.

There is no reason to suspect that deafness would not contain some (if not all) of the relevant variables composing Thoday's Factor X. Deaf people are certainly a disadvantaged minority group in terms of SES, employment, opportunity for advancement, and isolation from the dominant group. Added to this constellation of negative factors is deaf people's delayed, inconsistent, nonstandard language exposure, auditory deprivation, prevalence of organic trauma, family dynamics, and negative proximal social interactions. Taken together, these variables ought to yield a negative valence for Thoday's Factor X.

The results of the deafness as a natural experiment are incongruent with a Factor X account of between-group differences in IQ, once again because of the average nonverbal IQs found for deaf people. These results challenge Thoday to describe the factors, and their interactions, that could account for between-group differences in IQs for deaf and normal-hearing groups, and at the same time account for black–white differences in IQ. Although it may well be possible to assign values to various factors to yield a neutral or even positive value for deafness, such an exercise begs the central question: What are the factors, and what are the effects (positive or negative) of the factors? The outcomes of deafness as a natural experiment demand that the constellation of such factors be specified so that the theory can be tested. Until such time as that occurs, it appears that a Factor X model is no better than other models reviewed to date in accounting for black–white and deaf–hearing differences in mean IQ.

Descriptive Environmental Theories

Descriptive environmental theories are essentially empirical theories, in that they match between-group differences in IQ to a host of observable factors. However, descriptive theories explain environmental effects as though environment, which could be composed of one or many factors, exerted a single effect. There are two descriptive theories that will be considered. The first is the cumulative deficit theory, and the second is the threshold theory. Each is described and then evaluated using deafness as a test of the theory.

Cumulative Deficit Theory. The cumulative deficit theory (Jensen, 1977) proposes that generalized environmental deprivation (or enrichment) exerts a cumulative effect on IQ. Early in life, individuals in enriched and deprived conditions have similar IQs, but over the course of time, the cumulative effects of the environmental conditions experienced by enriched and deprived groups gradually separate the distributions of IQ. In other words, those in an intellectually impoverished environment have a slower, flatter growth curve of cognitive development relative to those in stimulating environments, which in turn leads to wider separation between groups as age increases. The IQs of North American blacks in deprived conditions exhibit a cumulative deficit, relative to the IQs of North American blacks and whites in enriched environments, across the developmental age span (Jensen, 1977). It is impossible in this model to isolate a factor or factors that account for this phenomenon; rather, the theory essentially posits that active environmental factors exert a cumulative effect over time. This means the IQs of people in dissimilar environments will gradually diverge over time.

Cross-sectional and longitudinal studies of deaf people should offer a strong test of the cumulative deficit theory. It could certainly be argued that deaf children experience unstimulating or understimulating environments relative to normal-hearing peers, in terms of auditory input, language exposure, and opportunities for incidental learning. Consequently, it should follow that the cumulative effects of the environmental deprivation experienced by deaf children should magnify differences as age increases (i.e., deaf children should fall further behind normal-hearing peers as a function of age due to the cumulative effects of deprivation).

Cross-sectional comparisons of deaf children's academic achievement clearly show that deaf children fall further behind normal-hearing peers as a function of age. Comparisons between young deaf children and their normal-hearing peers show that deaf children are behind and that they fall further behind at each advance in chronological age (Allen, 1986; Reamer, 1921; Vernon & Koh, 1970). Trybus and Karchmer (1977) describe the difference between deaf children and normal-hearing children in academic grade level in this way: "the difference . . . increases from about a grade and a half at age 9 to more than 5 grades by age 14" (p. 64). The slope of growth in deaf children's academic achievement relative to norms for normal-hearing children is clearly a negatively decelerating function, meaning the growth mirrors the shape of the curve hypothesized to occur when environment exerts a cumulative effect on development. In absolute terms, the cumulative effect on deaf children's academic achievement is substantially larger than the cumulative environmental effect noted for black children's IQs (Braden, 1989c).

However, there are problems associated with cross-sectional research in establishing cumulative deficit. Older subjects may be influenced by historical effects (e.g., substandard schools in earlier years), whereas younger cohorts are raised in more stimulating environments and thus will eventually show growth curves more consistent with stimulating environments. Unfortunately, there are few longitudinal studies of deaf children's academic achievement that can overcome these methodological limitations. However, those few studies that do report longitudinal research on deaf subjects typically show growth trends similar to those found in cross-sectional comparisons. For example, a 3-year follow-up study showed that deaf children gained less than 0.3 grade levels per year relative to the 1.0 annual grade-level gain experienced by normal-hearing peers (Trybus & Karchmer, 1977). Furthermore, this rate of gain was constant over the age span studied (9–17 years), suggesting a consistent cumulative deficit phenomenon. However, smaller, local studies do not necessarily mirror the national survey data of Trybus and Karchmer. In some schools, longitudinal gains in achievement are substantially larger than gains expected from cross-sectional comparisons (Bone & Delk, 1988), suggesting that environmental effects may be mitigated by some educational programs. Likewise, some small-scale longitudinal studies show small gains for deaf children over time (e.g., Pintner, 1925), whereas others show gains comparable to normal-hearing children (e.g., Pintner & Patterson, 1916a). Longitudinal studies are mixed in their support of the cumulative effects of environment on achievement, although the larger the sample size, the more likely it is that the results mirror a cumulative deficit phenomenon.

It is interesting to note that more recent studies show smaller deaf–hearing achievement differences than older studies. The relative gain over the past eight decades may be due to improvements in the education of deaf children, the decline of achievement skills in normal-hearing children, or a combination of both factors. However, most deaf children are still functionally illiterate, even though most deaf adolescents complete 12 or more years of schooling (Commission on Education of the Deaf, 1988).

How do academic achievement results compare to longitudinal studies of verbal and nonverbal IQ? This question cannot be answered, because I could find no longitudinal or cross-sectional studies of deaf children's verbal IQs. Although it might be expected that changes in verbal IQ with age would mirror the patterns noted for academic achievement across ages, there are no data to test this assumption.

The issue of cumulative deficit in nonverbal IQ can be answered. The growth of nonverbal IQ in deaf children is quite different from growth of academic achievement. Cross-sectional comparisons of deaf children's nonverbal IQs (Anderson & Sisco, 1977; Davis et al., 1986; MacKane, 1933; Myklebust, 1964; Pintner & Paterson, 1916b; Raven et al., 1983; Reamer, 1921; Ries & Voneiff, 1974; Springer, 1938; Watson et al., 1982; Zwiebel, 1988) are far less consistent than the cross-sectional comparison of deaf children's academic achievement. In part, the variation in outcomes can be explained by the type of test used to assess nonverbal IQ. Performance tests of intelligence generally produce no evidence of cumulative deficit (Anderson & Sisco, 1977; Davis et al., 1986; MacKane, 1936; Ries & Voneiff, 1974; cf. Myklebust, 1964; Watson et al., 1982). In contrast, motor-free tests of nonverbal intelligence show that deaf children tend to fall further behind normal-hearing children as age increases (Pintner & Paterson, 1916b; Raven et al., 1983; Reamer, 1921; Springer, 1938; Zwiebel, 1988). However, the cumulative deficit phenomenon is not consistent for deaf children's motor-free nonverbal IQs; deaf teens from 17 to 20 years of age are closer to normal-hearing peers than are deaf children from 9 to 16 years of age. This "catching up" has been attributed to consolidation and application of verbal mediation strategies in late adolescence and early adulthood among deaf teens (Reamer, 1921; Zwiebel, 1988). However, it could also be due to differential attrition rates for bright and dull students (e.g., dull deaf students may be more likely to leave school than bright students, thus raising the mean nonverbal IQ for older deaf students). Because studies uniformly examine deaf people in school settings, the data are confounded with the differential drop-out rates known to exist for bright and dull students (Ries & Voneiff, 1974).

Taken as a composite, longitudinal studies of nonverbal intelligence do not follow a cumulative deficit hypothesis. Unfortunately, there are only five longitudinal studies of deaf children's nonverbal intelligence (Braden et al., 1993; Lavos, 1950; Paquin & Braden, 1990; Pintner, 1925; Pintner & Paterson, 1916a). Four of the five studies show that deaf children show *gains* in nonverbal IQ over time relative to norms based on normal-hearing age peers. Only the study by Pintner (1925) reports a slower than expected gain in IQ for deaf people over time. Therefore, longitudinal studies of nonverbal IQ do not show a cumulative deficit in nonverbal IQ as a result of the environmental deprivation experienced by deaf children. In fact, deaf children placed in residential schools experience a cumulative benefit, in that IQ gains continue with increased length of placement (Braden et al., 1993; Paquin & Braden, 1990).

In summary, cross-sectional and longitudinal studies of deaf children's academic achievement clearly support the notion that environmental deprivation acts in a cumulative fashion with regard to the acquisition of culturally specific knowledge and skills. No data are available to show whether environmental deprivation also acts in a cumulative fashion on verbal IQ. However, deaf children's nonverbal IQs provide inconsistent evidence of a cumulative deficit. Deaf children of different ages have different motor-free nonverbal IQs, but the pattern of change across ages is inconsistent with a cumulative deficit hypothesis (i.e., the significant gains noted for 17- to 20-year-old adolescents contradict the cumulative deficit phenomenon). Longitudinal research suggests that the gains noted for deaf people in their late teens might well represent improvement in motor-free nonverbal IQ, rather than the higher drop-out rate for below-average deaf students. Thus, the study of intelligence in deaf people suggests that environmental deprivation acts in a cumulative fashion on learned information and skills, but has relatively little effect on the development of nonverbal intelligence. The data regarding a cumulative environmental effect on motor-free nonverbal intelligence are inconclusive.

Threshold Theory. The second descriptive theory of environmental effects on IQ is threshold theory. Simply put, threshold theory proposes that the effects of environmental stimulation are essentially dichotomous. Either a sufficient amount of environmental stimulation is provided for the development of intelligence, or it is not, in which case intelligence is not expressed. An example of threshold theory is found in the study of eye color. Either there is sufficient food for the organism to survive, in which case eye color develops, or there is not, in which case eye color does not develop. Increases in environmental stimulation (e.g., diet, oxygen) over the threshold have no effect on eye color. Likewise, it has been proposed by those who believe that intelligence is largely genetically determined that the environment acts in a threshold fashion with regard to intelligence. Either there is sufficient stimulation for cognitive development, or there is not; variations in environment beyond a threshold are believed to have little impact on the development and expression of intelligence.

Threshold theory functions as a complement to genetic accounts of IQ differences between groups. As such, it is not used to explain IQ differences between groups, as it is assumed that any child raised in any known society or culture would be provided the minimum threshold of environmental stimulation. Threshold theory is invoked to account for the intellectual development of feral or "closet" children. Although rare, there are instances in which children have been raised with little or no contact with other people. Although these studies run the risk of confounding organic defects with environmental deprivation (i.e., the children may have been abandoned or isolated because they were organically deformed), studies often show remarkable gains in IQ following the children's inculcation into society. However, these gains quickly level off as the children's mental age nears their chronological age, at which time they then proceed at a rate representative of most children (e.g., Fromkin et al., 1974). This pattern of growth is accounted for by threshold theory, because it is proposed that the minimum amount of environmental stimulation had been missing from the child's environment. Once provided, intellectual development occurs at a rapid rate because the biological development of the organism essentially provides the basis for intellectual growth.

In contrast, cumulative theories of environmental effects cannot account for the rapid growth of intelligence following the return of the child to society, because the rate of growth is not a cumulative or incremental function. The fact that mental age levels off as it approaches chronological age suggests a largely biological basis for the development of intelligence, for which there must be a minimum amount (i.e., threshold) of environmental stimulation in order for the intelligence to be expressed by the organism.

Because of the severe environmental deprivation experienced by deaf people, the study of intelligence in deaf people may be used to evaluate threshold theory and its ability to account for variations in IQ as a function of environment. Ideally, threshold theory would specify what factors would need to be present, and their intensity, frequency, and duration to provide the minimum environmental threshold for the expression of intelligence. Following such specification, one could then determine whether deafness as a condition would be likely to include the minimum threshold, or whether deafness would prevent the environmental threshold from being achieved.

In the absence of a specific definition of environmental threshold, the application of deafness as a test of threshold theory tests only whether deaf people receive enough environmental stimulation to develop intelligence. If the IQs of deaf people are similar to the IQs of people who have greater environmental stimulation, the threshold theory would be supported. In other words, there would be no evidence that the difference in stimulation between deaf and normal-hearing people has a meaningful effect on IQ. In contrast, if deaf people were below their normal-hearing counterparts, the threshold theory would be implicated because it would imply that simply meeting the threshold (i.e., being a member of a known society or culture) is insufficient environmental stimulation for the complete expression of intelligence.

Given this standard, the study of intelligence in deaf people argues for and against the threshold hypothesis. The fact that the distribution of nonverbal IQs in deaf people is little different from the distribution in normal-hearing people supports the notion that the development and expression of nonverbal intelligence is little affected by environmental stimulation over and above the threshold. Or, to state the case more precisely, the difference in stimulation between the deprived conditions imposed by deafness and the enriched conditions experienced by normal-hearing people has little or no effect on nonverbal intelligence, which implies environmental effects may well function in an all-or-none threshold fashion with respect to the development of nonverbal reasoning abilities.

In contrast, the fact that deaf people have below-average verbal IQs suggests that environmental factors beyond a minimum threshold play an important role in the development and expression of verbal intelligence. The fact that deaf people's verbal IQs are below average, but not so far below average to be considered nonexistent, further implicates threshold theory as an explanation of environmental effects on verbal intelligence. The fact that deaf people are below average, but not totally outside the range found for individuals who can be assumed to have met the threshold for environmental stimulation, implies that deaf people have also surpassed the minimum environmental threshold.

Therefore, the study of intelligence in deaf people is a valuable test of threshold effects. Results support threshold theory as an account of environmental effects on *nonverbal* intelligence. However, threshold theory cannot account for environmental effects on *verbal* intelligence.

Multiple-Factor Environmental Theories

Multiple-factor theories of between-group differences in intelligence differ from single-factor theories primarily in their orientation to the study of environmental effects. Few, if any, single-factor theories propose that between-group differences are accounted for solely by differences in a single factor (i.e., the theories do not deny the existence of other factors). The critical distinction between single-factor theories and multiple-factor theories is that multiple-factor theories assume that environmental variables interact with each other in nonadditive ways. In other words, environmental factors do not act in a cumulative fashion such that the total effect is merely the sum of the individual environmental factors. The whole is not equal to the sum of its parts, proponents argue, and so environmental effects must be studied from a multiple-factor framework.

There are essentially two types of multiple-factor accounts of between-group differences in IQ. The first is the cultural-difference approach (e.g., Ogbu, 1988), and the second is the eclectic synthesis of environmental factors to account for between-group differences. Each of these is considered in the following sections.

Cultural Difference Theory

The finding that ethnic minority groups score lower on tests of intelligence than the ethnic majority has been explained in terms of cultural factors. Ogbu (1982, 1988) has proposed that when ethnic groups constitute a majority, they create a social climate that supports their culture and its competencies. In turn, other, potentially competitive, cultures and their competencies are diminished. Thus, human competence is defined in ways that confer advantage to members of the majority group, which in turn leads to depressed performance of minority groups on a wide variety of measures, including intelligence tests.

The issue of cultural loading of intelligence tests is synonymous with polemic theories of test bias. As such, it has already been demonstrated that tests of verbal intelligence and academic achievement do, indeed, confound psychobiological and maturational outcomes with culturally specific competencies. In contrast, nonverbal intelligence tests do not appear to measure culturally specific competencies (i.e., nonverbal tests apparently discriminate psychobiological and maturational outcomes from learned outcomes). Therefore, the study of deafness refutes one component of Ogbu's position (i.e., that nonverbal intelligence tests fail to discriminate psychobiological and maturational outcomes from culturally specific outcomes), while supporting his position with respect to verbal intelligence and academic achievement tests. In fairness to Professor Ogbu, it should be noted that most of his work relates to academic achievement in school settings and does not specifically address nonverbal intelligence. However, his work as been cited as an explanation of IQ differences between North American blacks and whites, and therefore can be legitimately applied to all types of intelligence tests.

Deaf people constitute a sociocultural, ethnic group (Heider & Heider, 1941; Humphries & Padden, 1988). They share common folklore, customs, and a language. Because the culture of deaf people is distinct from that of normal-hearing people, and because deaf people do not constitute a majority in any region of the world, they are a minority group. However, the means of entry and socialization into this minority group is profoundly different for deaf children of hearing parents (HP) and deaf children of deaf parents (DP).

The socialization process of DP is presumed to be similar to the socialization process for most minority groups. Children are raised by parents who are members of the minority group, the children are members of the minority group, and it is presumed that most of their social contacts are with other members of the minority group. It is usually assumed that deaf parents are members of the deaf community, are knowledgeable in the folklore and customs of deaf people, and are fluent ASL models. That these assumptions have not been empirically investigated is regrettable. However, it is known that DP do acquire a non-standard language, are raised in a family where deafness is the norm, and are placed in a larger societal context where deaf people are a disadvantaged, disenfranchised minority group. As such, DP embody many of the characteristics associated with minority group status, and should therefore reflect the effects of being raised in a minority culture.

The socialization process of HP is quite different. HP are born into a family where no members of the family use ASL, and where the parents are (by definition) not a member of the child's minority group. The sociological effects of this situation are unknown. The closest parallel to the sociological situation of HP is transracial adoptees who are adopted into a family at an early age. Transracial adoptions have been criticized in recent years for failing to provide adopted children with a congruent childhood experience (i.e., children are raised in a family with cultural expectations that conflict with the expectations of their biological group membership). Although transracial adoption studies have shown that rearing in a majority household raises IQ on tests of intelligence (Scarr & Weinberg, 1983), the improvement in IQ diminishes over time so that children tend to resemble their biological parents more than their adoptive parents as they approach maturity.

The unique situation of HP complicates the analogy to transracial adoptions. HP have extreme difficulty acquiring the language used in the home, and thus require that the parents learn a different language system. Also, HP are of the same race as the parents. HP therefore present a complex cultural situation, in that they are members of their parent's racial group, but due to the language barriers imposed by deafness, they cannot become full members of the racial or ethnic group into which they are born. Consequently, many HP opt to become members of the deaf community, and are socialized into that community via educational and social institutions serving deaf people (rather than being socialized into the culture by the family unit).

The power of deafness as a test of cultural-difference theory rests on the logic that deaf people are a powerless minority group. HP are probably at a greater disadvantage than DP simply because it is assumed they would have the most difficult time identifying strongly with any culture (i.e., they are a disadvantaged minority within their own families). In contrast, DP should reflect the effects of membership in a disadvantaged minority culture.

Examination of the IQs of deaf children are inconclusive with regard to the cultural-difference theory. On the one hand, verbal IQs and academic achievement scores are depressed for all deaf children, which would be compatible with the theory because deaf children are unlikely to acquire culturally specific competencies. In addition, DP do better on measures of achievement, verbal IQ, and nonverbal IQ than HP, suggesting that DP are more likely than HP to be taught and to acquire culturally relevant competencies in the home. On the other hand, the fact that deaf children of normal-hearing parents have IQs similar to the dominant majority is not predicted by the cultural-difference theory. The finding of above-average nonverbal IQs among DP and deaf children of hearing parents with a deaf sibling (HP/DS), is also unexpected because DP and HP/DS are not members of a dominant majority, and should therefore achieve lower nonverbal IQs than the members of the dominant majority (for whom the tests were developed). It is difficult to imagine how families could support the conflicting competencies needed to bring about the profile of differences noted for groups of blacks, whites, normal-hearing people, and deaf people across tests of verbal intelligence, academic achievement, and nonverbal intelligence.

Eclectic Syntheses of Environmental Factors

Eclectic syntheses of environmental theories are, by definition, unsystematic in scope and function. Proponents of environmental theories often cite single theoretical accounts of between-group differences in IQ (such as those discussed in the preceding sections), and then add that many specific circumstances act together to yield between-group differences. Although the citation of many individual theories creates an impressive rhetorical argument, the scientific arena demands that relationships among variables be specified, and their effects measured, in order to test accounts of between-group differences in IQ.

Eclectic syntheses of environmental factors (e.g., Thoday, 1973; Williams, 1974) imply that many environmental factors interact to cause IQ differences between racial or ethnic groups, yet they often do so without saying exactly how these factors interact. It is important to note that genetic and environmental factors are often correlated. For example, SES is correlated with IQ. Proponents of genetic models argue that genotypes underlie adult SES, adult IQ, and offspring IQs. Environmentalists argue that a common environment, that is, SES, underlies adult and offspring IQs. Eclectic syntheses of environmental factors are therefore difficult to test, because (1) many variables are cited as causal, (2) the effects among variables are not specified, and (3) the potential relationship between environment and genotype is usually ignored. However, eclectic theories are popular, and realistically acknowledge the complex web of factors that affect intelligence.

The common feature of eclectic syntheses of environmental factors is the proposition that environmental conditions are correlated (e.g., low SES, poor prenatal and postnatal health care, substandard education, and social discrimination often co-occur). Although isolated inspection of any one of these factors may suggest a small impact on IQ, the combined effect of all of the correlated environmental factors is believed to be at least as large as the sum of the individual effects. It therefore follows that members of ethnic or racial minorities may experience a multitude of correlated environmental factors, and that these factors interact to lower the distribution of IQ relative to the IQs of dominant racial or ethnic groups. To the extent that deaf people represent individuals who experience a host of correlated environmental effects, the study of IQ among deaf people could be considered as a potential test of eclectic syntheses of environmental theories.

Deaf people do, indeed, experience a host of environmental circumstances that are correlated, or co-occur. In a sense, the very confounds that make deafness a poor test of any single factor (e.g., auditory deprivation on IQ) make it an attractive test of correlated, multiple environmental effects on IQ. The many environmental disadvantages known to co-occur with deafness have been reiterated many times in this book. In fact, on nearly all standard indices of environmental factors, deaf people are disadvantaged relative to the majority of unimpaired peers (whether majority or minority group members). However, on two variables (i.e., SES and distal social interactions), deaf people are believed to experience the same conditions as normal-hearing peers of the same racial or ethnic group. In this sense, deaf children make up a strong test case for one constellation of multiple, correlated environmental effects on IQ.

Results of IQ research show the impact of environmental factors on the development of verbal intelligence and academic achievement. At least one interaction is also supported by the data: the combined effects of deafness and an additional disability lower verbal IQ and academic achievement scores beyond the effect of either of these variables in isolation. In other words, deaf people with additional disabilities have lower verbal IQs than deaf people without additional disabilities and normal-hearing people with only one disability, even when neurological disabilities (e.g., cerebral palsy) are excluded from consideration. The combined effects of deafness and behavior disorders, deafness and blindness, or deafness and other disabling conditions not specifically associated with neurological lacunae lower verbal IQ and academic achievement more than either condition in isolation.

The coincidence that verbal IQs for deaf people are near the mean noted for some minority groups (e.g., North American blacks) could be construed as evidence that the environmental factors associated with deafness interact to produce effects similar to those induced by environmental factors associated with minority group status. However, this interpretation ignores the likelihood that verbal IQs and achievement scores overestimate deaf children's abilities. A better inference would be that deafness may well depress verbal IQ and academic achievement more than minority group status.

Deaf people perform far less well than black people and most other minority groups on standardized tests of academic achievement. This finding is all the more surprising when one considers that standardized tests appear to overpredict deaf children's achievement skills (Moores, 1970). Furthermore, deaf people exhibit substantial deficits in pragmatic skills or adaptive behaviors, in contrast to the adaptive behavior skills of minority groups (Mercer, 1979). Thus, deaf people are not merely low scorers; they are genuinely poor performers, and apparently suffer substantial academic, verbal, and adaptive behavior deficits as a result of their hearing impairment. In contrast, minority groups have low average scores on verbal intelligence tests and achievement, and typically exhibit adaptive behavior within the average range.

The average distribution of nonverbal IQs found for deaf people is inconsistent with eclectic syntheses of environmental factors. Environmental factors believed to act on verbal IQ and academic achievement have little effect on nonverbal IQ in deaf people. Eclectic syntheses of environmental factors are an insufficient account of between-group differences in IQ, because they cannot explain the finding of average nonverbal IQs in a group known to experience a host of correlated environmental disadvantages.

Eclectic synthesis accounts of between-group differences in IQ could be viable if one of three conditions existed. First, they could emphasize differences between deaf and normal-hearing minorities, such as SES or distal social interactions. Second, eclectic syntheses could specify how factors unique to deafness might interact to mitigate correlated environmental effects (e.g., proposing that auditory deprivation somehow promotes compensatory development of nonverbal intelligence). Third, environmental factors common to minorities, but not to deaf people, could be identified to account for between-group differences in IQ. None of these avenues is particularly promising at present, but all offer potential avenues of investigation to clarify the relationship between environment and intelligence. The value of deafness as a natural experiment lies in its apparent ability to show that many factors believed to lower IQ have a major impact on verbal IQ and academic achievement, but simply do not have an appreciable impact on nonverbal IQ.

Genetic Theories

Despite the negative connotations associated with genetic accounts of IQ differences between groups (as noted by Herrnstein, 1982), a majority of scientists consider genetic accounts acceptable and worthy avenues of inquiry (Snyderman & Rothman, 1986). However, genetic theories have been invoked to justify discriminatory social practices and suppression of minorities (Gould, 1981). Therefore, genetic accounts of IQ differences between groups must be carefully examined to insure they are not used simply to promote the hegemony of the dominant majority over racial and ethnic minorities.

Two areas of inquiry are associated with genetic accounts of IQ differences between groups. The first is the additive effects model, which proposes that IQ differences between and within groups can be explained using principles common to the field of genetics (e.g., the effects of alleles at specific genetic loci). Additive effects are cited by proponents of genetic factors as the major factor leading to between-group differences. Additive effects specify the biological foundation for genotypes, which in turn are believed to strongly affect IQ.

The second area of inquiry associated with genetic theories is the search for correlates of genetic activity, such as nonadditive effects, mating patterns, or evidence of association between intelligence and traits known to be genetic in origin. The presence of genetic correlates can enhance or undermine the credibility of genetic proposals. The additive effects and correlates of genetic activity models are discussed with reference to deafness as a test of genetic accounts of IQ differences between groups.

Additive Effects Model

The logic of environmental models is familiar to students of psychology. Experimental designs, treatments, reinforcement schedules, interventions, and other aspects of research and practice in psychology specify environmental effects and measure their impact on behavior. However, behavioral genetics is less commonly taught in psychology, and certainly does not receive the attention that environmental variables are given. Therefore, a brief overview of additive genetic models is provided as a basis for genetic accounts of IQ differences between groups.

Genetic Effects

The additive effects model proposes that genes at certain loci work together to produce the variability within and between groups. Two genes are present at each locus. Each gene may assume a value, called an allele, which is typically coded as a positive or a negative effect on the trait. The joint effect of the two genes may be thought of as the sum of the alleles at each locus. Therefore, each gene locus has a value of a negative effect (two negative alleles), zero effect (a positive plus a negative), or a positive effect (two positives). With more than one locus involved in the genotype for intelligence (current estimates propose about 7 loci), the distribution of genotypes quickly approximates a normal curve, with a mean of zero (i.e., the population mean). There are very few highly positive or highly negative genotypes. Nonadditive effects (e.g., dominance, partial dominance) are also possible in this model, but may be unnecessary to explain the normal distribution of IQ.

IQ differences between groups are consequently determined by the prevalence of positive or negative alleles in a group's gene pool. Mating patterns over time (e.g., isolation of the group from others, customs regarding mating and families) increase, decrease, or stabilize the prevalence of alleles within a group. For example, cultures that actively encourage mating on the basis of educational or intellectual achievement encourage individuals who have genotypes with positive allele values to have offspring. Such a pattern would be likely to increase the prevalence of positive allele states in the gene pool, and consequently raise the mean for the group. In contrast, customs could encourage mating on traits unrelated or negatively related to intelligence, which would stabilize or reduce the prevalence of positive alleles. Such patterns would, in turn, lower the mean for the group. Continental Europe during the Dark Ages has been cited as an example of a pattern that encouraged poorly educated people to have large families (because large families were economically advantageous for agriculture), while at the same time demanding celibacy from its most learned members (because the Catholic Church controlled higher education, and demanded celibacy from its priests and nuns). This pattern of mating would eventually lower the prevalence of positive alleles, in turn lowering intelligence.

In contrast, European Jews isolated in ghettos during the same time period adopted different mating patterns. Jews encouraged scholars to have large families, and discouraged poor and uneducated people from having families. Over successive generations, the mean of the two groups drifted apart, resulting in between-group differences in IQ.

It is often overlooked that the additive genetic effects model is ultimately an *environmental* account of between-group differences in IQ. The environmental factor accounting for group differences is mating patterns. In other words, geneticists believe that the cumulative effects of mating patterns over time determine the distribution of genotypes within a group, whereas environmentalists believe that the experiences people have during their lives (i.e., following conception) cause between-group differences in IQ. Thus, it should be noted that the additive effects model need not postulate any innate superiority nor genetic defect for between-group differences in IQ; rather, it proposes that the differences are due to the prevalence of positive and negative allele states, which may in turn be caused by the mating patterns operating in a group over successive generations.

It is important to dispute some popular misconceptions about genetic effects. First, no scholarly sources propose that one racial group is inherently inferior to another. Racial groups are created by specific adaptations to environmental conditions within a gene pool, not by some preordained hierarchy. A corollary of this observation is that whatever relationship might exist between race and IQ would most likely be due to the prevalence of alleles within the racial gene pool, rather than a specific phenotypic expression of race per se. Therefore, IQ differences between racial groups could be due to the prevalence of allele states in the racial gene pool, and need not assume IQ difference as an inherent or immutable condition of race.

Second, nobody proposes that traits with substantial genetic components are unaffected by environment. Obesity has been found to have a substantial genetic basis (Strunkard et al., 1986), yet body fat is certainly affected by environmental factors such as diet and exercise. To state that a trait is substantially influenced by genetic factors is not equivalent to saying that it cannot be changed by environmental factors. Rather, a substantial genetic basis for a trait means that the environment, as it is currently distributed among members of the population, has relatively less effect on the phenotypic expression of the trait than the distribution of genotypes. The irony of this truism is that, to the degree that social programs insure similar environmental conditions for all people in society, the degree to which a trait is influenced by genotype increases (i.e., variation in environment is decreased, which decreases the impact of environmental variation on the trait).

The biggest problem with genetic accounts of between-group differences in IQ is that genetic conditions are often confounded with environmental conditions. This is particularly true for race. For example, blacks in North America are a racial group, and are subjected to virulent social and economic discrimination because of their race. Thus, the finding that blacks have lower IQs than whites cannot be easily interpreted as evidence for either genetic or environmental accounts of IQ differences between groups, because race (and the likelihood that the person has genes drawn from a specific gene pool) is confounded with environment (i.e., the likelihood that the person will experience environmental hardships and disadvantages). Genetic models acknowledge this confound (as do some environmental models), and attempt to discover ways to isolate genetic and environmental effects (e.g., adoption studies, twin studies).

Finally, it is not true that genetic accounts "justify" racial discrimination. Geneticists note that variation within groups far exceeds the differences among groups, and therefore any discrimination on the basis of racial or ethnic group membership is scientifically unwarranted, as well as morally abhorrent.

A consequence of the genetic model is that genotype is primarily responsible for determining phenotype, or measured IQ. Therefore, the genetic model predicts that intelligence should be relatively unaffected by variations in environment. Of course, even staunch geneticists acknowledge that environmental conditions are necessary for any organism to grow and develop, and that variations in the environment will affect variations in the expression of a trait. Therefore, the most radical genetic account proposes that a minimal threshold of environmental stimulation is present in all normal environments, keeping intelligence unaffected by variations in the environment such as those associated with minority group membership. Threshold theory has been discussed earlier in this chapter, but it is introduced again as a complement to genetic accounts of IQ differences between groups.

Deafness as a Test of Additive Genetic Effects

Deafness offers an exciting opportunity to test genetic accounts of IQ differences between groups. Deafness is, in essence, the quasi-experimental complement to adoption studies. Adoption studies are a valuable test of genetic models, because the IQ of the adopted child is a function of genotype (which is presumably little correlated with the adoptive family) and environment (which is presumably shared by the adoptive family). Thus, similarities between adoptive children and adoptive family members reflect environmental effects, whereas differences between adopted children and adoptive family members reflect genetic effects.

In contrast, deafness provides a condition in which the genotype is presumably correlated with the family, but the environment experienced by the deaf child is quite different from that of other family members. Thus, similarities between deaf children and family members argue in favor of genetic effects, whereas differences between deaf children and family members argue in favor of environmental effects. It should be noted that within-family environments differ primarily for deaf children of hearing parents without deaf siblings; deaf children with deaf parents and/or a deaf sibling will probably share environmental conditions with family members to a higher degree, because family members will be more likely to use sign language, accept deafness as a normal part of the family, and the like. What makes deafness unique as a quasi-experiment is that it accomplishes the similar genotype–different environment condition without removing the child from the family. Remaining within the family overcomes some common threats to the validity of adoption studies (e.g., placement of children with relatives), and also mitigates some problems associated with the study of feral children or severe childhood deprivation (e.g., abandonment of the child due to mental dysfunction of the parent).

As promising as deafness might be as a complement to adoptive studies, there is one potential problem with characterizing deaf children as sharing genetic similarity with their parents. One cannot rule out the possibility that the genotype for deafness, and the genotype for intelligence, are correlated. Such a confound would render deaf children of hearing parents not only different in terms of their shared environment, but also different in terms of their genotype.

This confound may be overcome by disaggregating nongenetically deaf people from genetically deaf people. About half of all deaf people are estimated to be deaf due to factors not associated with genetics (e.g., illness, maternal trauma). Deaf people whose deafness was induced by nongenetic causes would presumably represent a random genetic sample of the gene pool from which they are drawn. Nongenetically deaf people therefore provide a powerful test of additive genetic effects if two more assumptions are made: (1) that genotype for intelligence is not correlated with a predisposition for insult or injuries resulting in deafness and (2) that the trauma leading to deafness does not include neurological sequelae that affect intelligence. The former assumption is untested; in the absence of data showing a link between susceptibility to illness or trauma and intelligence, the safest assumption is that no relationship exists. The second assumption, which proposes that organic trauma is limited only to deafness, is questionable. Certain traumata leading to deafness, such as maternal rubella or Rh incompatibility, are known to negatively affect nonverbal intelligence (Chess & Fernandez, 1980; Vernon, 1967a). Therefore, nongenetically deaf people represent a complement to adoption studies (i.e., a change in within-family environment without a change in genotype), but the study of nongenetically deaf people confounds deafness with a greater prevalence of neurological sequelae. Other problems associated with nongenetic deafness include accuracy of diagnosis of nongenetic deafness (i.e., some genetic deafness mimics or may be misdiagnosed as nongenetic in etiology) and sampling error (e.g., frequent use of samples from residential programs may yield lower mean IQs). Although the examination of IQs for nongenetically deaf people with no additional disabilities embodies a less than perfect complement to adoption studies, it nonetheless approaches adoption as a quasi-experimental condition from which to explore genetic and environmental effects on intelligence.

The Evidence for or against the Model

The below-average verbal IQs and academic achievement of HP fail to support the radical version of the additive genetic effects model. The difference between HP and normal-hearing peers suggests that environment plays a strong role in the development of verbal intelligence and achievement. The fact that verbal IQ and achievement is strongly correlated with degree of hearing impairment also implicates the threshold model of environmental action by implying that environmental exposure to language functions as a continuous, not discrete, variable. Additive genetic effects are also implicated by the fact that deaf people are below average, but not severely retarded, on measures of verbal IQ and achievement. There is no *a priori* reason to believe that deaf people should inherit a predisposition toward below-average verbal intelligence along with their deafness, and so the below-average performance on verbal IQ and achievement measures cannot be readily explained by an additive effects model.

In contrast, the nonverbal IQs of HP lend strong support to the threshold effects model and, by implication, the additive genetic effects model. The fact that the distribution of IQ among HP appears to be little affected by environmental variables strongly supports the notion that additive genetic effects are primarily responsible for variation in nonverbal intelligence. The genetic model is further supported by the finding that physiological factors, in the form of additional disabilities, substantially affect IQs within the deaf population. The similarity of nonverbal IQ distributions between normal-hearing and deaf populations and the lower nonverbal IQs of deaf people with additional disabilities are congruent with theories proposing that intelligence has a substantial biogenetic basis.

The finding that DP have above-average nonverbal IQs relative to normal-hearing peers is most interesting from a genetic perspective. At least two genetic accounts are possible. The first could propose that deaf parents meet and mate in a fashion that encourages more intelligent deaf people to have children and/or discourages less intelligent deaf people from mating with other deaf people. This genetic function, called assortative mating, would produce higher nonverbal IQs among offspring as a consequence of the higher IQs of the parents. Partial support for this theory is offered by Paquin (1992), who found that deaf parents of deaf children indeed have above-average nonverbal IQs. Consequently, the higher IQs for DP could simply be a function of their parents, who are brighter than average and therefore have brighter than average offspring. However, assortative mating is an unlikely explanation for the above-average IQs of deaf children of hearing parents with a deaf sibling (HP/DS), because their parents would be unlikely to select each other on the basis of recessive genes for deafness. Mating patterns in the deaf community might account for above-average IQs among DP, but it is not at all clear how such patterns could account for high performance IQs among HP/DS.

The second possibility is that alleles for genetic deafness are physically linked or related to alleles for above-average intelligence, so that children who receive an allele for deafness are also likely to receive an allele(s) for high intelligence (called a pleiotropism). Pleiotropic effects have been found to link myopia and IQ, and could function within populations of deaf people. Such a linkage would confer genetic deafness, along with higher intelligence, to children of deaf parents.

The issue is even more intriguing when the IQs of HP/DS are considered. HP/DS also have above-average IQs on motor-intensive nonverbal intelligence tests. Although DP and HP/DS are both believed to be deaf due to genetic causes, they have quite different alleles causing their genetic deafness. DP are assumed to inherit at least one allele for dominant genetic deafness, whereas by definition, HP/DS must inherit two recessive alleles to cause their deafness. Thus, a single pleiotropic model is unlikely to explain the above-average IQs of both groups, because different alleles are involved in the inheritance of deafness for the groups.

The outcomes of deafness as a natural experiment yield three conclusions pertinent to additive genetic effects models. First, additive genetic effects do not provide a complete account for between-group differences in IQ. Environmental factors are clearly responsible for differences between HP and normal-hearing groups on measures of verbal intelligence and academic achievement. Second, additive genetic effects are supported by the similarity between HP and normal-hearing groups on nonverbal intelligence measures. Third, the nonverbal IQs of genetically deaf children differ from nongenetically deaf and normal-hearing children. Assortative mating and pleiotropy are both viable accounts for this phenomenon, yet the distinction between the types of genetic deafness experienced by DP and HP/DS suggests that separate accounts of above average IQs will be needed to explain the above-average IQs of genetically deaf children.

None of the outcomes is a direct test of black–white differences in IQ. Support for genetic effects found in the study of deaf people's nonverbal IQs does not necessarily generalize to blacks or other ethnic minorities. For example, the failure of genetic models to account for the verbal IQs of deaf people does not mean that genetics has no role in black–white differences. The failure of the additive genetic effects model applied to verbal intelligence and achievement in deaf people merely means that environment can, and in at least one case does, act in a continuous fashion to depress IQs. It should be acknowledged that the radical version of additive genetic effects posed in this inquiry has not been promoted by any serious scholar of intelligence. Even strong proponents of genetic accounts of between-group differences in IQ recognize that exposure to language is related to scores obtained on verbal intelligence tests, or tests of academic achievement.

Rather, the results of deafness as a natural experiment condition confirms the important distinction between measures of crystallized ability (i.e., intelligence as reflected on culturally specific cognitive tasks) and measures of fluid ability (i.e., intelligence as reflected on novel problem-solving tasks). Crystallized ability is expected to reflect opportunities to learn, and the depressed verbal IQs and academic achievement scores for deaf people validates this assumption. The best test of the genetic hypothesis is found on tests of fluid abilities, which are purportedly measures of intelligence that do not tap prior learning.

In this regard, the outcomes of deafness research support an additive genetic effects model. It cannot be concluded that because additive genetic effects are supported for this group, they therefore account for black–white differences in IQ on fluid ability measures. Environmental factors not associated with deafness, but found in minority groups such as North American blacks, could lead to black–white differences on fluid ability measures where no differences are noted between deaf and normal-hearing groups. However, the viability of the genetic hypothesis is bolstered by the finding that not all groups with different environments, and in the case of deafness, substantially deprived environments, suffer ill effects on measures of crystallized ability.

Correlates of Genetic Effects

The investigation of deafness as a direct test of environment and heredity is elegant, yet simplistic. The characterization of deafness as a test of severe environmental deprivation on consequent IQ overlooks some important additional tests of the genetic model. These tests include the use of kinship correlations, prediction of the direction and magnitude of differences in IQ between parent–child pairs (i.e., regression to the mean), similarity of IQ across the developmental age span, nonadditive genetic effects, and the search for genetic traits that could serve as markers for the transmission of genotypes associated with intelligence. The comparison of IQ distributions between deaf and normal-hearing people offers only part of the evidence needed to test genetic models.

Kinship Correlations

Additive genetic effects specify a number of conditions in addition to the proposal that environmental differences have little impact on IQ. These conditions include the prediction that the degree of genetic kinship among individuals essentially determines the degree to which IQs are correlated within these groups. For example, IQs should be more strongly correlated within pairs of identical twins than within pairs of dizygotic twins. A hierarchy of values can be clearly determined and tested for a wide variety of kinship values, ranging from unity (monozygotic, or identical, twins have identical genotypes) to near zero (unrelated individuals). If true, a similar rank order of correlation values should be found for nonverbal IQ irrespective of hearing loss. For example, the IQ correlation between normal-hearing parents and children should be the same for normal-hearing parents and deaf children, particularly when nonverbal intelligence tests are employed.

Paquin (1992) tested this theory using DP and found that, indeed, the observed correlation between parent and child nonverbal IQs was quite similar to the genetically anticipated correlation of $r = .50$. Likewise, sibling correlations were not statistically different from (and were actually quite close to) genetically anticipated values. This suggests that, within DP, additive genetic models of intelligence accurately anticipate kinship correlations using nonverbal intelligence tests. It is simply not known whether similar results would be achieved with HP, but the additive genetic model would predict such an outcome. As yet, there are no data to test kinship correlations among HP, but thus far preliminary research supports additive genetic effects as an account for kinship correlations among DP.

Regression to the Mean

Another test of the genetic model is the presence of regression to the mean on the part of deaf children. In families of normal-hearing people, the child's IQ is expected to be closer to the population mean than the parents' IQ (usually calculated as the average, or midpoint, of the parental IQs). The degree and direction of difference is based on the construct of regression to the mean. Children whose parents have above-average IQs are expected to have lower IQs (approximately one-half the distance between the parental IQ midpoint and the mean), whereas children whose parents have below-average IQs are expected to have higher IQs. This phenomenon is called regression to the mean, and it is based on the assumption that additive genetic effects follow a binomial probability model that is congruent with the biology of genetic transmission. Deaf children are expected to regress toward the mean to the same degree as their normal-hearing siblings in a genetic model. Therefore, the direction and magnitude of IQ difference between parents and their deaf children could also be used to test an additive genetic model.

Paquin (1992) also tested children's regression toward the mean using DP and their parents. His results were inconclusive, in that (1) he found slightly lower IQs among the DP relative to their parents, but (2) there was insufficient statistical power to determine whether this difference was significantly different from the genetically anticipated value (i.e., half the distance from the midparent IQ to the mean). The magnitude of difference between deaf children and their deaf parents was smaller than anticipated, but the lack of statistical power in the study precludes drawing any firm conclusions. Thus, the jury is still out on regression to the mean among DP, and there are simply no data to investigate the possibility of regression to the mean among HP or HP/DS.

Similarity of IQs across Development

A genetic model of intelligence anticipates that environmental factors play a role in the development of intelligence, but these environmental factors essentially "wash out" over time. The consequence of this model is that children in different environments will probably exhibit different IQs early in life, but the differences will diminish over time so that the children become more similar, rather than more different, with age. In contrast, environmental accounts predict that continued exposure to different environments should maximize differences between groups, so that groups will grow more dissimilar with age. The finding that the IQs of adoptive children regress toward their biological parents' IQs over time, or the finding that adults adopted as children have body fat indices quite similar to their biological parents (and totally unrelated to the body fat indices of adoptive parents), is anticipated by genetic accounts of intelligence and obesity.

Fortunately, there are data to evaluate the convergence or divergence of intelligence over the developmental age span. The cumulative deficit noted for scores on verbal intelligence and academic achievement tests argues against a genetic account of the poor performance of deaf people on these tests. However, the lack of cumulative deficit on nonverbal tests argues in favor of a genetic account. Furthermore, the finding that deaf and normal-hearing children become more similar in the structure of nonverbal intelligence across the developmental age span offers support for the genetic basis of nonverbal intelligence. Findings related to nonverbal intelligence tests support biological or genetic accounts of intelligence, because differences in environment between deaf and normal-hearing children are diminished, rather than exacerbated, over the course of time.

Nonadditive Genetic Effects

Nonadditive effects may also be used to test whether a trait is inherited, and if so, to what degree dominant genetic transmission plays a role. For example, if consanguineous matings between related pairs (inbreeding) results in lower IQs among offspring, it is evidence that IQ is at least partly determined by dominant genetic effects. Therefore, consanguineous matings within the deaf community, and deaf offspring produced by inbreeding, should show inbreeding depression if intelligence is at least partly determined by dominant genetic factors. There are simply no data investigating consanguinity and its effects on IQ among deaf people.

Marker Traits

Finally, inherited physical traits have been used as markers to determine whether inheritance of a trait is also associated with inheritance of intelligence. The correspondence of marker traits lends further support to the notion that genotypes are the primary determinants of variation in IQ. One example of this application is the finding of a pleiotropic relationship between myopia and above-average intelligence. This relationship suggests that the locus of the trait for myopia, which is known to be a recessive genetic trait, is adjacent to the locus for the trait of intelligence. Furthermore, the allele for myopia is therefore likely to be accompanied by an allele for above-average intelligence, resulting in a pleiotropic connection between myopia and high IQ.

Pleiotropic transmission could explain why HP/DS tend to have above-average IQs. In a pleiotropism, the allele for above-average intelligence would be adjacent to the allele for recessive deafness, thus resulting in a connection between recessive genetic deafness and high IQ. This implies that HP/DS would have IQs higher than their normal-hearing siblings. Pleiotropic effects could also account for higher IQs in DP. In this scenario, deaf offspring of deaf and of normal-hearing parents would have higher IQs than their normal-hearing siblings.

These predictions could be tested if the data were available. However, there are no studies of within-family variability contrasting normal-hearing and deaf siblings. Without these data, it is impossible to investigate nonadditive, or pleio-tropic, genetic effects on intelligence.

It is unfortunate that kinship studies using deaf subjects are lacking in the literature. The genetic hypothesis makes a number of specific, testable predictions with respect to kinship relationships in IQ. The presence of supportive data would obviously strengthen the genetic argument, whereas findings that conflicted with correlates of the genetic model would challenge the ability of the model to account for IQ differences within and between groups.

Summary of Additive Genetic Predictions

The limited data regarding the correlates of the genetic model are similar to the conclusions reached for the "direct" test of the genetic model. First, correlates of the model fail to support its viability as an account of verbal IQ and academic achievement scores. Second, the available evidence strongly supports a biogenetic model for nonverbal intelligence. However, the evidence regarding genetic cor-relates is limited, and is therefore not a conclusive "tour de force" in support of additive genetic accounts.

Interaction Theories

There is no serious student of intelligence that proposes that intelligence is either entirely a function of environment or entirely a function of genetics. Serious scholars on both sides of the issue acknowledge that environment and genetic factors work together to produce intelligence. The most extreme position advo-cated from an environmental perspective is that genetics plays a role only insofar as genotypes determine species, but that within-species differences are determined by environmental circumstances. Chromosomal anomalies (e.g., Down's syn-drome) and rare recessive genetic syndromes are also acknowledged as the pri-mary causes of individual differences in intelligence within people who inherit these unusual genotypes. An extreme environmental perspective presumes that, aside from a genotype for species and chromosomal anomalies, genotype does not account for variation in intelligence. This position is often associated with a Marxist political perspective, because it implies that any inequities between groups have a foundation in the sociopolitical order.

Conversely, the most extreme genetic position proposes that individual dif-ferences are due primarily to genotypic variation, not to variations in environment. "Radical" geneticists presume that a minimum threshold of environmental succor must be provided for the organism to thrive and develop (e.g., food, water, sensory stimulation). Although environmental factors are seen as a necessary condition for intelligence to develop, their effect on individual differences in intelligence is small because all people (except for feral children) receive this minimal threshold of stimulation. Therefore, an extreme genetic position recognizes that some environmental conditions must be present for intelligence to develop, but given these threshold conditions, environmental factors do not account for variation in intelligence. This view has been associated with a capitalist or social Darwinist political perspective, because it implies that inequities between groups are due to preexisting biological factors (i.e., they are part of the "natural order").

Extreme positions on both sides of the nature–nurture debate presume that factors on the opposing side influence intelligence solely as a threshold effect. Strong environmental perspectives propose that genotypes create thresholds, such as differences between species or unusual genetic anomalies associated with mental retardation. Likewise, strong genetic perspectives propose that environmental conditions form a threshold, beyond which additional nurturing or variation in environment has little if any effect on intelligence. These extreme positions, however popular they may be with certain political constituencies, are unpopular with scientists who struggle to understand the complex phenomenon of intelligence. Instead, scientists accept that environmental and genetic factors interact to affect intellectual development, and seek to identify and test models of interactive effects.

There are at least two theories that attempt to define how environmental and genetic factors interact in a continuous, rather than discrete, fashion. One theory, which has been called mediated learning experience, attempts to identify how individual differences in genotype interact with particular environmental variations to affect intellectual performance. The second theory, called the heritability model, is based on statistical estimates of heritability within a population. Each of these theories is described in the following sections.

Mediated Learning Experience

Feuerstein and his colleagues in Israel (e.g., Feuerstein, Rand, & Hoffman, 1979), as well as Haywood and his colleagues in the United States (e.g., Haywood & Switsky, 1986), have proposed a model that accepts the interaction between environmental and genetic factors in the development of intelligence. The theory posits that intelligence is malleable, and since one cannot modify genotypes, the phenotypic expression of intelligence (which may be affected by an underlying genotype) is modifiable through environmental intervention. The key ingredient in the environment that modifies intelligence has been called mediated learning experience (MLE). Intellectual abilities may be improved by increasing the amount of MLE in a person's environment. Experiments with individuals whose low intelligence is clearly due to genetic causes (e.g., adolescents with Down's syndrome) have claimed remarkable gains in IQ as a result of intensive exposure to MLE. The fact that these gains have yet to be systematically replicated in a setting other than Feuerstein's laboratory raises questions regarding the generalization of results (Frisby & Braden, 1992). However, there is at least preliminary evidence that MLE can interact with genetic influences to change intelligence.

Based on laboratory interventions showing powerful effects for MLE, Feuerstein and others have reasoned that between-group differences in intelligence may well be due to differences in exposure to MLE. In Feuerstein's model, MLE is the proximal cause of intelligence; genotype and environmental factors such as SES exert distal effects on intelligence (i.e., they are associated with the frequency, intensity, and duration of MLE). Therefore, between-group differences in IQ are attributed to between-group differences in exposure to MLE, although it is acknowledged that genetic differences between groups may affect the degree to which MLE is offered and received in the environment.

MLE has been defined as the act of cultural transmission. It has five characteristics, which are (1) intentionality, (2) transcendence (i.e., generalization to other settings and tasks), (3) meaningfulness, (4) competence and (5) regulation of the child's behavior. Thus, parents or other caretakers of children provide MLE by selectively filtering and amplifying certain characteristics of the environment for the child. In this selective buffering, caretakers assign meaning, intention, and so on to the myriad of environmental experiences encountered by children. The content of the interaction (e.g., the meanings assigned to experiences, the choice of behaviors to regulate) is determined by sociocultural values. From the perspective of intellectual development, the content is irrelevant to the development of intelligence. The child's participation in MLE develops the cognitive abilities that make up intelligence.

Using this model, it has been proposed that members of nondominant cultures may provide less MLE to their children than members of the dominant culture. This is because minority cultures are devalued by the dominant culture, whereas the dominant culture is valued as "the" model to transmit to children. Members of minority cultures consequently refrain from passing along the culture of their ancestors to their children, because the minority culture is inadequate or inferior in the context of the dominant culture. This in turn creates a situation in which children in minority cultures experience less frequent and less intense MLE than dominant majority peers.

MLE theory does not assume that dominant and nondominant cultural groups have similar genetic constitutions with regard to intelligence (as assumed by environmental theories), but MLE proponents have not suggested that there are genetic differences between cultural groups. Therefore, although the theory proposes that IQ differences between groups are the consequence of environmental factors (specifically, exposure to MLE), it is an interactionist theory because it allows for the possibility that genetics exerts a distal effect on between-group differences in IQ.

The study of deaf people provides a strong test of the proposal that exposure to MLE is the proximal cause of between-group differences in IQ. The characteristics of MLE stress cooperative interactions between care givers and children that convey understanding of the world to the child. Thus, although language exposure per se is not part of MLE, the communication of MLE characteristics (i.e., intention, transcendence, meaningfulness, competence, and the regulation of the child's behavior) requires some medium for exchange. This medium is typically language. Because deaf children of normal-hearing parents (HP) cannot readily understand their parents or caretakers, and because their caretakers must learn a method of communication in which they are typically not proficient, it is quite likely that HP would receive much less exposure to MLE than their normal-hearing peers. In fact, observational studies of mother–child interactions, and qualitative descriptions of HP family life, suggest that most interactions between normal-hearing parents and their deaf children are punitive, nonsupportive, and oriented toward compliance rather than understanding.

Deaf children of deaf parents would be likely to receive exposure to MLE because their parents can communicate to them with relative ease. However, because deaf adults are members of a cultural minority, it is possible that they are less likely than normal-hearing parents to provide MLE to their children. Consequently, it is expected that HP would be far below average on tests of intelligence, because they receive little MLE from parents or care givers due to communicative difficulties. DP would be expected to outperform HP on tests of intelligence, because deaf parents do not have the communication barriers to providing MLE. However, DP would still be likely to be at or below average, because their parents (who are members of a devalued minority) are less likely to pass along their culture to their children.

Deaf people's performance on tests of verbal IQ and academic achievement are compatible with MLE predictions. The mean for HP is well below average, and the mean for DP is somewhat better than HP, but still well below the average for normal-hearing people. However, deaf people's nonverbal IQs are incompatible with MLE predictions. Not only do HP have average nonverbal IQs, but the mean nonverbal IQ for DP is above the average for normal-hearing children. It is interesting that, in the research on MLE, nonverbal tests (particularly Raven's Progressive Matrices) are commonly used to measure intelligence. Gains in IQ resulting from MLE are typically gains as measured by the Raven's. Therefore, nonverbal tests are of greater value to the MLE model for measuring intelligence, yet the results of research using these nonverbal intelligence tests with deaf people are clearly incompatible with MLE predictions.

The study of intelligence within deaf people consequently implicates MLE as an explanation of differences in IQ between groups. Although the research on deafness clearly leads to the conclusion that MLE cannot account for between-group differences in IQ, these results do not implicate the potential benefit that exposure to MLE might have for changing IQs in individuals. Response to treatment does not imply causality (e.g., aspirin is an effective treatment for a headache, but aspirin deprivation is not the cause of the headache). Likewise, stating that MLE cannot explain why groups have different distributions of IQs does not mean MLE could not be an effective means to ameliorate or reduce between-group differences in IQ. However, it is clear that MLE theories cannot account for the outcomes of deafness as a natural experiment, and is therefore suspect as an account of between-group differences in IQ.

Heritability Approach

The heritability approach does not explicitly identify which environmental or genetic factors interact to produce differences in IQ within and between groups. However, it is assumed that, even after threshold effects are taken into consideration, variation in environment and genetics contributes to variations in intelligence. The model is derived primarily from the hereditarian position, which proposes that IQ is largely, but not entirely, heritable. Many estimates of heritability of intelligence have been offered in the literature. They range from 1 to 0, with most estimates hovering between .50 and .80. A heritability index of .60 means that approximately 60% of the variation in IQ is accounted for by hereditary factors. It must be emphasized that heritability estimates are a group statistic (i.e., it is impossible to conclude that 60% of an individual's IQ is due to genetic effects), and most heritability estimates have been derived from white populations in North America and Western Europe. Heritability studies of North American blacks are rare, but provide similar estimates (e.g., Osborne, 1980).

Unfortunately, there is inadequate information to estimate the heritability of intelligence in deaf populations. The only study to date investigating kinship relations (Paquin, 1992) provides results that are compatible with current heritability estimates for the general population, but there are insufficient analyses of the kind needed to develop a heritability estimate for DP and HP groups (e.g., kinship correlations, adoption, twin studies).

There is one way the heritability model may be explored using data from deaf people. The exploration uses model-building by positing established and estimated values, and then estimating the impact of a factor on the outcome. For example, one can estimate the impact of the environment on between-group differences in IQ by (1) stating the magnitude of the between group difference in standard deviation units, (2) assuming that the genetic difference between the population is zero, (3) proposing that the trait has a heritability index of .60, and then (4) working backwards to estimate the impact of environmental conditions needed to cause the between-group difference in IQ when two groups have the same genetic distribution.

An example may illustrate this point. First, assume that the difference between deaf and normal-hearing people on verbal intelligence tests is 0.96 *SD* units (the value obtained from the meta-analysis). Second, assume that the genetic endowment of deaf and normal-hearing groups is similar with respect to verbal ability (i.e., deaf people are a representative random sample of the normal-hearing gene pool with respect to the genotypes for verbal reasoning). Third, assume that the heritability of verbal intelligence is .60 (i.e., 60% of the variation in verbal IQ is produced by variation in environment). Fourth, work back to estimate the impact of the environment needed to yield the between-group difference on verbal IQ. Because 60% of the variation in a trait is due to hereditary factors, 40% must be due to environmental factors. Therefore, the net impact of the environment on the development of verbal intelligence in deaf people would be 2.4 *SD* units (i.e., .96/.40 = 2.4 *SD* units).

The estimate of environmental impact provided by these assumptions is incredibly large in comparison to effects achieved by deliberate experimentation (Wolf, 1986). Consequently, it suggests that the heritabity model is an unreasonable one. Either (1) deaf and normal-hearing people have different genotypes with regard to verbal intelligence or (2) the estimate of heritability is too high. Given that there is no *a priori* reason to suspect genetic difference in verbal ability between deaf and normal-hearing groups, and given the substantial correlation between verbal IQ and degree of hearing impairment, it is likely that the estimate of heritability in the model is too high (i.e., the substantial relationship between hearing impairment and verbal IQ attenuates the correlation between genotype and verbal IQ, thus lowering the heritability of verbal IQ in hearing-impaired populations).

The same model may be applied to estimate environmental impact on nonverbal intelligence. Using the same process, the nonverbal IQ difference between deaf and normal-hearing people of 0.19 *SD* units implies that the net impact of the environment would shift nonverbal IQ 0.475 *SD* units. The estimate of environmental impact is well within the range expected for experimental effects on a trait, and thus is more likely to be a viable account of between-group differences in nonverbal IQ.

The data from this hypothetical model could be compared to data from a similar model of black–white differences in IQ. First, the difference between blacks and whites on verbal and nonverbal tests of intelligence is typically 1.0 *SD* units. Second, assume that there are no genetic differences between the two groups. Third, assume that heritability within groups accounts for 60% of the variation in intelligence. Fourth, work backwards to estimate the approximate effect of environment on intelligence (i.e., $1.0/.40 = 2.5$ SD units).

Once again, the magnitude of the environmental impact value suggests that the model is flawed in one or more of its assumptions. Given that there are independent data supporting a heritability estimate of .60 in black and white populations, proponents of genetic models would doubt the assumption that the two groups have similar genotype distributions. This finding relative to nonverbal IQ is also surprising, in that it predicts that environmental differences between normal-hearing groups of blacks and whites have 5 times the impact that environmental differences between groups of normal-hearing and deaf groups have on nonverbal IQ. To retain the hypothesis that between-group differences in nonverbal IQ are brought about by environmental differences (assuming a heritability estimate of .60), one would have to conclude that black people are subjected to environmental variables with 5 times the impact of those experienced by deaf people.

The consequence of the model-building and estimation of parameters provides three conclusions regarding the heritability model of gene–environment interactions. First, the assumption that verbal intelligence is equally heritable in deaf and normal-hearing populations is very unlikely. Environmental variation in the deaf population is likely to attenuate, or lower, the heritability of verbal intelligence. Second, it is possible that environmental differences among deaf people, and between deaf and normal-hearing people, have a small to modest impact on nonverbal IQ. It is reasonable, but as yet insufficiently supported by research, to assume that nonverbal IQ is moderately heritable within deaf populations. Third, it is unlikely that environmental factors solely account for black–white differences in IQ. To retain an environmental account of black–white nonverbal IQ differences, one would need to argue (1) that the heritability of nonverbal IQ was much lower for blacks than for other groups and/or (2) that the environment experienced by blacks is 5 times more detrimental than the environment experienced by deaf people with respect to the development and expression of nonverbal intelligence.

Racial Differences among Deaf People

Thus far in the chapter, the only between-group differences in IQ that have been discussed are those of deaf versus normal-hearing and black versus white groups. There are, however, some data regarding the differences between deaf blacks and deaf whites. The data are limited, but they are nonetheless valuable for determining the stability of between-group differences across radical changes in environmental conditions. The reasons why these data are of value will be discussed before the data are presented, in order to frame the nature and logic of investigations of racial group differences in IQ within the deaf population.

Theoretical Implications of Racial Differences among Deaf People

Why should the mean IQs of racial groups within the deaf population be examined? The logic of the answer is straightforward: Whatever causes differences between racial groups in normal-hearing populations ought to cause differences in deaf populations *to the degree those causes are shared by both deaf and normal-hearing populations.* For example, it has been proposed that due to unequal health conditions blacks and whites have different proportions of organic trauma. Presumably, deaf blacks and whites would also mirror this pattern. Consequently, the finding of between-group differences in IQ within the deaf population would be congruent with differential rates of organic trauma, whereas a finding of no racial difference would not be congruent with the theory. Investigation of between-group differences in IQ within deaf populations should help focus the search for environmental variables affecting IQ. Conversely, changes in the magnitude or direction of black–white differences among deaf people would suggest the environmental factors active in normal-hearing populations are changed by, or interact with, deafness.

Although unexpected outcomes may challenge theories, it cannot be inferred that expected outcomes imply similar causes. Black–white differences in IQ may be similar across normal-hearing and deaf populations, but for different reasons. The point is that the investigation of racial group differences in IQ within deaf populations could shed light on how environmental characteristics, race, and deafness interact to yield between-group differences (or similarities!) in IQ. The study of such factors might well suggest novel, as yet untested, environmental factors leading to between-group differences in IQ.

Variability of black–white differences in IQ within the deaf population also offers an exciting test of genetic models. Assuming additive effects without interactions among genetic conditions associated with deafness, the genetic model predicts that black–white differences in IQ should be stable across changes in environment. This would be particularly true when IQs are obtained from deaf people known to be deaf for nongenetic causes. Alternatively, changes in the magnitude or direction of between-group IQ differences among deaf people would challenge genetic researchers to specify interaction effects which covary race, hearing impairment, and intelligence. Likewise, interactionist accounts of black–white differences in IQ could be tested by analyzing black–white differences in IQ among deaf populations. Once again, the potential outcomes of such a search could offer exciting new ideas for developing and testing genetic accounts of black–white group differences in IQ.

The study of racial group IQ differences among deaf people offers an exciting proving ground for theories of black–white differences in IQ. Although black–white differences within the deaf population are not a critical test for any theory (i.e., all theories could accommodate either stable or changed black–white differences in IQ), there are radically different ramifications for the viability of various theories implied by stable or distinct outcomes.

Black–White Differences among Deaf People

Only 11 of the 193 studies in the meta-analysis separately investigated or reported the performance of black and white deaf people. None of the studies reported intelligence test data for any other nonwhite racial groups. Of the 11 studies, 7 reported nonverbal IQs, and 4 reported other descriptions of cognitive performance. The mean nonverbal IQs for black deaf people in these 7 studies ranged from 60 to 90, with a mean of 75.98. There was no relationship between IQs and study characteristics, such as the site where subjects were selected or degree of hearing loss. The small number of studies reporting data makes it unlikely that relationships between study characteristics and outcomes could be readily identified. Nearly all of the studies reporting nonverbal IQs for black deaf children were conducted in the southern part of the United States, and those few studies reporting data for white deaf children from the same geographic region suggested that black–white differences in IQ among deaf people were similar to values found in the normal-hearing population (i.e., about −1.0 SD units).

The 4 studies not reporting IQs also noted that black deaf people were below average, and were lower than white deaf people, on cognitive measures other than intelligence tests. Specifically, Adler (1985) reported black–white differences on the WISC-R Performance Scale subtests and PIQ, but did not report the magnitude of the differences. Allen (1986) noted substantial (−0.60 to −0.88 SD units) differences between white and black deaf children on tests of reading and mathematics achievement. Kaltsounis (1971) found smaller but substantial black–white differences (average difference = −0.44 SD units) on tests of creative thinking, and Wolff and Harkins (1986) reported a substantially higher proportion of black deaf students in classes for mentally retarded children relative to their enrollment in programs serving deaf children. Wolff and Harkins noted that the proportion of black deaf children in classes for the mentally retarded was similar to proportions noted for black normal-hearing children found in national annual surveys.

Given these admittedly limited findings, the data suggest that the direction and magnitude of black–white differences on intellective tests are stable across variation in hearing loss. There are no data to suggest that the magnitude of racial group differences among deaf people is substantially different from the magnitude of racial group differences among normal-hearing people. However, the limited number of direct comparisons between white deaf children and black deaf children on tests of intelligence argues in favor of caution.

The implications of these findings challenge environmental theories of black–white differences in IQ. By suggesting that the direction and magnitude of racial group IQ differences are unchanged by deafness, it is implied that environmental factors other than those associated with deafness bring about between-group differences in IQ. Environmental differences between whites and blacks that cause different distributions of IQ must therefore cross the hearing barrier relatively unchanged, or interact in unexpected ways to produce the same net effect. The invariant nature of black–white IQ differences should help environmentalists locate and test environment factors that affect distributions of IQ within and between racial groups.

The apparent stability of racial group differences in IQ supports main-effects or additive genetic accounts of black–white differences in IQ. By finding apparently similar results, despite the substantial differences in the environments experienced by deaf and normal-hearing people, it is implied that the factors causing black–white IQ differences are not substantially affected by changes in environment. Because there is no reason to assume a three-way interaction between the genotypes for race, hearing loss, and genetics, the consistency of black–white differences in IQ is anticipated by additive genetic models.

On closer inspection, however, there are some anomalies in the data that warrant further attention from a genetic perspective. Surveys of deaf children in North America consistently show that the prevalence of black DP is substantially lower than the corresponding prevalence of white DP. In fact, about 96% of DP are white and only 4% are black (Karchmer et al., 1977). This is quite different from the proportions of 67% whites and 18% blacks found in the general deaf population (Wolff & Harkins, 1986). It is unknown whether reporting methods, sampling methods, or actual prevalence rates cause the discrepancy in racial proportion with DP. Therefore, it is possible (but by no means proven) that hereditary deafness may be more rare among North American blacks than whites, and this fact may be related to the below-average distribution of IQs found among black deaf children. If so, this would raise intriguing possibilities for genetic accounts of black–white differences in IQ.

Finally, interactionist accounts of between-group differences in IQ are challenged by findings of stable racial group differences in IQ. Essentially, the stability of IQ differences between blacks and whites suggests that none of the genetic or environmental factors that interact to produce IQ differences act differently when major changes in language exposure, auditory stimulation, prevalence of medical/organic traumata, and other factors are changed. For example, the proposition that mediated learning experience (MLE) transfers unchanged across the deafness barrier to cause between-group differences in IQ seems highly unlikely, because the characteristics of MLE are so closely bound to language and communication between parent and child. Interactionist theories, like environmental theories, are challenged to explain how black–white differences in IQ remain unchanged despite the substantial changes in environmental and organic factors brought about by deafness.

Conclusions

How well do theories purporting to account for between-group differences in IQ actually account for the pattern of differences found between deaf and normal-hearing groups? In general, not well. I have undoubtedly oversimplified many of the theories in my desire to show how deafness could be used to corroborate or reject hypotheses. My intent is merely to illustrate how deafness could be used as a foil against which to test various hypotheses of between-group differences in IQ. The explicit testing and careful research needed to definitively test these theories must be conducted by researchers who are steeped in the theories, and therefore would have a better basis on which to make and test inferences regarding deaf people. My hope is that the preceding discussion will act as a catalyst to spur additional research aimed at refined and responsible tests of these and other theories. In order to encourage future research, I will draw some conclusions regarding the models considered in this chapter (and perhaps spur other researchers to show me the error of my ways!).

None of the theories reviewed in this chapter are sufficient explanations of between-group differences in IQ, when the groups subsumed by the theories are broadened to include groups defined by race, hearing, and racial–hearing status. However, some theories more readily account for the data than others. To facilitate an evaluation of the theories here considered, I am proposing a "score card" that ranks the ability of the theories to account for outcomes of deafness as a natural experiment, in addition to accounting for racial or ethnic group differences in IQ.

The study of intelligence among deaf people yields six findings that are of value in assessing theories of between-group differences in IQ. These findings are the following:

1. Below-average verbal IQ for deaf people (Low VIQ).
2. Below-average academic achievement for deaf people (Low Ach.).
3. Average nonverbal IQ for deaf people (Avg. PIQ).
4. Black–white differences within deaf people (B–W diff.).
5. Above-average nonverbal IQs for deaf children of deaf parents (High DP).
6. Above-average nonverbal IQs for deaf children of normal-hearing parents with a deaf sibling (High HP/DS).

The first three findings are those relating to the performance of deaf people relative to normal-hearing peers, and the next three findings relate to the performance of distinctive subgroups within the deaf population.

Table 5.2 summarizes the ability of various theories to account for the six findings offered by research on deafness. If the theory cannot reasonably account for between-group differences in IQ, and simultaneously account for findings derived from studies of deaf people's intelligence, the theory was rated as unable to account for the finding (i.e., "No" was entered in the table). If the theory predicts the finding, or is neutral with regard to the finding, the theory was judged to account for the finding (i.e., "Yes" was entered in the table). This rating system is sensitive to anomalies, but it is insensitive to the distinction between theoretical predictions (e.g., additive genetic effects theory predicts a black–white difference in IQ within deaf people) and theoretical possibilities that have yet to be established (e.g., the language exposure theory was rated "No," although future research could account for black–white differences in IQ within deaf people if it was found that black parents signed differently to their black children).

Essentially, the outcomes of deafness as a natural experiment offer two important and concentric tests for theoretical accounts of between-group differences in IQ. The first test is the ability to account for the radically different scores that deaf people achieve across measures of verbal intelligence, academic achievement, and nonverbal intelligence. As has been shown, this test finds most theories wanting. The robust nature of deaf people's psychometric profile on these tests does not allow the finding to be dismissed, and forces theorists to acknowledge and

TABLE 5.2. The Ability of Theories to Account for Deaf Persons' IQs

Theory	Differences between deaf and hearing			Differences within the deaf population		
	Low VIQ	Low Ach.	Avg. PIQ	B-W diff.	High DP	High HP/DS
Polemic test bias	Yes	Yes	No	No	No	No
Organic/environmental	Yes	Yes	No	Yes	No	No
Language exposure	Yes	Yes	No	No	No	No
Socio-environmental	Yes	Yes	No	No	No	No
Cumulative deficit	Yes	Yes	No	No	No	No
Threshold factors	No	No	Yes	Yes	Yes	Yes
Cultural difference	Yes	Yes	No	No	No	No
Eclectic syntheses	Yes	Yes	No	No	No	No
Additive genetic effects	No	No	Yes	Yes	Yes[a]	Yes[a]
Mediated learning experience	Yes	Yes	No	No	No	No
Heritability approach	Yes[b]	Yes[b]	Yes	Yes	Yes[a]	Yes[a]

[a]Pending evidence supporting a genetic link between intelligence and some form(s) of hereditary deafness.
[b]Pending evidence of lower heritability of verbal intelligence and achievement in deaf populations.

accommodate the distinction between measures of crystallized ability (i.e., intelligence reflected in skills that are acquired through acculturation and learning) and measures of fluid ability (i.e., intelligence reflected in novel problem-solving situations).

The second concentric test of theoretical accounts of between-group differences in IQ is the ability to account for black–white differences within the deaf population. Essentially, the second test requires specification of factors that maximize differences between normal-hearing blacks and whites, minimize differences between deaf and normal-hearing people with respect to nonverbal intelligence, and simultaneously maximizes differences between normal-hearing and deaf groups with respect to measures of verbal intelligence and academic achievement. The reason that most theories reviewed in Table 5.2 are rated as failing to accommodate black–white differences within the deaf population is because, at present, they have not specified the factors that would lead to black–white differences on nonverbal intelligence tests and still account for differences in verbal intelligence and achievement in normal-hearing and deaf groups.

This does not mean that factors meeting these concentric tests cannot be specified. In fact, the primary goal of this book is to prompt consideration of what those factors might be, so that scientists can refine the search for environmental and/or genetic factors that account for between-group differences in IQ. However, there are few theories at present that can be reasonably construed to account for the outcomes of deafness as a natural experiment in environment and intelligence.

The review in Table 5.2 shows that none of the single-factor theories adequately accounts for all of the relevant outcomes of deafness research. In particular, none of the single-factor theories accounts for the first three findings (low verbal IQ, low achievement, and average nonverbal IQ). The single-factor theories therefore appear to be unlikely contenders as consistent accounts of between-group differences in IQ, as they apparently cannot account for deaf people's performance on measures of intelligence and achievement.

Multiple-factor environmental theories also fail to predict the outcomes of the natural experiment of deafness on intelligence, and for much the same reasons. The concentric tests of between-group profiles on measures of verbal intelligence, academic achievement, and nonverbal intelligence, along with black–white differences on nonverbal intelligence measures, pose a difficult set of criteria for theories to meet.

Genetic theories are more likely to meet criteria that environmental theories find difficult, and vice versa. The likelihood that genetic theories can account for differences in IQ among groups of deaf people may be excessively generous. In the absence of data corroborating a genetic link between deafness and intelligence, genetic theories are no better than environmental theories in accounting for differences between groups. One might argue that environmental theories could also account for differences between groups of deaf people, if those theories were allowed to leave open the possibility that environmental conditions could be discovered that correlated with subgroup status. The reason that genetic accounts are judged as "Yes," and environmental theories are judged as "No," is that there are results in the literature that (1) propose genetic hypotheses and (2) argue against environmental accounts of subgroup differences in IQ. There are no corresponding data or arguments regarding environmental theories, and so they were judged not to account for subgroup differences in IQ within the deaf population.

Finally, it appears that the interactionist theories yield quite different accounts of between-group differences in IQ. Mediated learning experience accounts of between-group differences appear to function much the same as single-factor environmental theories. This is true primarily because the proximal factor believed to account for between-group differences (MLE) is essentially a single environmental factor. MLE holds open the possibility of positing between-group differences in genotype, which could then be used to account for a host of related factors. MLE theorists have not, however, proposed genetic differences between groups, and have instead emphasized the primary impact of MLE on intellectual development.

In contrast, heritability approaches could account for all of the major findings if minor allowances were tolerated. The allowances with regard to heritability estimates are congruent with the available data. The allowances with regard to a link between genetic deafness and intelligence are less tenable, but have been proposed and, to a small degree, empirically supported in the literature. Therefore, the heritability approach offers a likely but incomplete account for the available data.

This analysis should not imply that theories failing to account for all of the outcomes are bankrupt. For example, it is quite plausible to propose that cultural difference theory should only apply to linguistic or learned material, in which case it could be compatible with the pattern of deaf people's achievement, verbal IQ, and nonverbal IQs. However, without such an exclusion, it cannot simultaneously account for the low (and successively slow growth in) verbal IQ and achievement, and the relatively normal development of nonverbal IQ, in deaf people. Cumulative deficit theory could likewise be delimited to learned material, and thus retain its value as an account of a smaller subset of psychological phenomena. The delimitation of theories, however, inhibits their viability as accounts of between-group differences in intelligence, and so begs the question of why groups differ (or are similar) on other measures.

The goal of this theoretical review is to support the value of deafness as a test of theories, and to test the value of theories as accounts of between-group differences in IQ. I have argued that deafness is an important proving ground for accounts of group differences in IQ. The issues raised by this proposal, and their broader context, will be explored in the next chapter.

6

Conclusions: The Value of Deaf Children as a Natural Experiment for Understanding IQ Differences between Groups

Deafness is a natural experiment condition that can offer much to the study of IQ differences between groups. Research regarding the causes of IQ differences between groups has been plagued by confounds of environment and genotype since its inception. As I have argued in this book and elsewhere (Braden, 1988), the study of intelligence in deaf people offers a fresh perspective to address the question of why groups have different distributions of IQ. However, the research regarding deaf people is by no means free from problems and controversies associated with studies of between-group differences in IQ, and so it is worthwhile to review the strengths and limitations of this line of inquiry.

Deafness as a Natural Experiment

The characterization of deafness as a condition in which the primary independent variable is language deprivation is an oversimplification of reality. Many factors are confounded with deafness, and many of them (e.g., prevalence of organic dysfunction, abnormal family dynamics) are factors that are likely to have some impact on intellectual development. Therefore, the first conclusion to be drawn regarding deafness as a natural experiment is that previous characterizations of deafness are too simple, and the factors associated with deafness form a tangled and intricate web.

On the one hand, the fact that deafness is not a neatly characterized, isolated set of conditions complicates its value as an unintentional psychological experiment. On the other hand, the complexity and interdependence of factors associated with deafness are similar to the complex myriad of factors associated with ethnic and racial minority groups. I have argued that the confounds and intricacy of conditions associated with deafness make the study of deafness even more appealing to those who are concerned with the scope and causes of IQ differences between groups. Although correlated and confounded factors make it difficult to isolate specific cause-and-effect relationships, the many factors associated with deafness replicate many of the conditions associated with minority group status, and thus make deafness a valuable adjunct to adoption studies and other natural experiments.

However, deafness has some environmental and genetic characteristics not shared by racial or ethnic groups. Although deaf people use a common language and frequently choose to join the subculture formed by deaf adults, most deaf children are raised in families that are members of another culture. The study of deafness is analogous to adoption studies, except that the within-family environment, rather than within-family genetics, is the primary characteristic that is manipulated. However, even this analogy breaks down when it is noted that a significant proportion of deaf children are deaf due to genetic causes, and there may be a genetic connection between inherited deafness and intelligence. Although complicated and complex, the fact that deafness occurs across traditionally recognized ethnic and racial boundaries provides a unique and powerful perspective with which to test accounts of between-group differences in racial and ethnic groups.

The fact that deafness occurs within racial and ethnic groups allows the study of environmental factors associated with deafness to be combined with the study of ethnic and racial conditions. Thus, the study of deaf people from traditionally advantaged groups (e.g., white, middle-class North Americans) should provide insight into the effects of environmental deprivation and abnormal genetic factors on intelligence, without the confounding effects of low SES, minority status, and other confounding factors. Likewise, comparison of racial or ethnic groups within the deaf population should shed light on the effects of group membership that are unaffected by the factors associated with deafness. The gist of this book, then, is the proposition that much can be learned regarding environmental and genetic influences on intelligence through the study of deaf people that cannot be achieved by investigating existing racial and ethnic groups. The fact that this unique perspective is not absolute, and that there are factors confounded within this search, should not obscure the potential value and promise offered by deafness as a natural experiment.

Outcomes of Deafness as a Natural Experiment

The outcomes of deafness as a natural experiment are surprisingly robust across time and cultures, and are consistent within general categories of tests. However, there are some important variables associated with outcomes, and these factors can be grouped into bibliometric factors, experimental factors, and demographic factors.

Bibliometric Factors

There are factors associated with the dissemination of studies regarding deafness that are related to results. Although there is no evidence of publication bias, there is a slight relationship between the year the study was published or presented and the reported IQ. This means that more recent studies tend to report higher IQs, whereas older studies tend to report lower IQs.

This finding could be interpreted as evidence that deaf persons are "catching up" to normal-hearing peers on tests of intelligence. This possibility is congruent with studies of academic achievement that show deaf children making some progress toward closing the "achievement gap" between themselves and normal-hearing children. However, the relationship between year of study and experimental factors known to influence IQ argues in favor of ascribing the "catching up" to better, more sophisticated experimental methods in more recent studies.

I explored the possibility that year of publication and quality of experimental methods used in the study led to the correlation between reported IQ and year of publication (Braden, 1992). By assigning "quality ratings" to studies, I was able to show a strong correlation between study quality and outcome (i.e., studies rated high for using appropriate tests and administration methods yielded higher IQs than studies with poor methods). Furthermore, study quality showed a substantial relationship to year of publication, supporting the notion that more recent studies used better methods. When the effect of study quality was statistically removed from the correlation between year of dissemination and IQ, there was no relationship between year and IQ. This analysis suggests that it is changes in study quality, and not changes in the actual status of deaf people relative to normal-hearing peers, that led to the relative gains of deaf people over time. However, studies using similar tests over a longer period of time (i.e., studies with behavioral "anchors") are needed to confirm this account of the literature.

Another finding of bibliometric analyses is that the vast majority of studies appear in deafness-related publications and other media unlikely to come to the attention of psychological researchers. This is a truly unfortunate state of affairs. The isolation of research on deafness from the mainstream of psychological science has undoubtedly hurt both fields. Much of the research in deafness is atheoretical, in that correlations between measures and other results are simply reported without regard to their theoretical meaning. There are some notable exceptions to this conclusion (e.g., Furth, 1966; Vernon, 1967c), but the exceptions prove the rule.

The inaccessibility of deafness data to mainstream psychologists has also damaged the vitality of psychological research, particularly in the area of between-group differences on psychological tests. The substantial and meaningful differences in IQs achieved by deaf people on verbal and nonverbal tests of intelligence have apparently escaped those who argue that the distinction between verbal and nonverbal intelligence tests is trivial. In fact, the major premise of this book is that by bringing knowledge of deafness as a natural experiment to such scholars, the research regarding between-group differences in intelligence, and other fields of psychological research, will be improved.

Experimental Methods Affecting Results

There are a number of experimental factors associated with reported IQs. These factors include the content or type of test used, the way in which tests are administered, the method used to derive IQ, and the setting from which subjects are sampled.

The distinction between tests of verbal intelligence, academic achievement, and nonverbal intelligence tests has been made repeatedly, and need not be reiterated. However, the fact that deaf people score higher on performance tests of intelligence than they do on motor-free nonverbal intelligence tests is often overlooked in the literature. The finding that deaf people achieve higher IQs when tests are administered using sound clinical practices is reassuring, and testifies to the importance of appropriate administration procedures to groups using nonstandard language. The importance of IQ scale is also shown by experimental methods, which suggests that deaf people achieve higher IQs when more sophisticated scales (e.g., normative deviation) are used to calculate IQs. Essentially, both sound clinical administration practices and appropriate IQ scale calculation yield higher IQs among deaf people. This in turn suggests that the better the methodology, the less likely one is to find IQ differences between deaf and normal-hearing people.

Demographic Factors

The study of differences between demographic groups of deaf people can be divided into two categories of demographic factors. The first category contains factors that occur in normal-hearing and deaf populations, such as those defined by gender, race, and age. The second subset of factors are demographic variables unique to deafness, such as degree and onset of hearing loss, type of school attended, additional disability, and the hearing status of family members.

Demographic factors shared by deaf and normal-hearing populations yield similar effects in the two populations. There are few stable differences between genders with regard to intelligence, and the difference in performance between young and old deaf people validates the belief that intelligence increases with age across the developmental span. Racial group (i.e., black–white) differences in IQ are also found in the deaf population.

Demographic factors associated with deafness yield some provocative findings. The fact that hearing loss onset prior to 5 years of age has a substantial impact on verbal intelligence and achievement, but has little effect on nonverbal intelligence, suggests that early learning experiences have a profound influence on the acquisition of verbal reasoning and academic success. The relationship between degree of hearing loss and measures of verbal intelligence and achievement further suggests that the degree of exposure to language has a continuous effect on acquisition of verbal knowledge and academic skills. Conversely, the finding of no relationship between degree of hearing loss and nonverbal achievement suggests hearing loss has little effect on the development of nonverbal intelligence.

The contrast in mean IQs between residential and day schools yields inconsistent results. Although meta-analytic findings suggest that studies in residential and day programs do not differ in average reported IQ, direct studies consistently show residential deaf students to have IQs lower than deaf peers attending day schools. Direct studies attribute this finding to selection factors, noting that deaf children attending residential schools have a higher prevalence of additional disabilities. Thus, sampling factors are a possible source of differences in IQ between deaf and normal-hearing groups, in that the majority of studies reporting sampling methods recruited participants from residential schools for deaf children.

Finally, the relationship between the hearing status of family members (i.e., parents and siblings) and IQ are most provocative. They raise important questions regarding potential genetic and environmental effects on IQ. The consistency of above-average IQ for DP and HP/DS argues that these phenomena raise important questions regarding group differences in IQ.

Evaluation of Deafness Outcomes

The evaluation of the outcomes associated with deafness must consider whether the outcomes do, in fact, reflect conditions associated with deafness, or whether outcomes reflect factors not necessarily associated with deafness. Thus, rival hypotheses must be considered before the results of deafness as a natural experiment may be applied to theories of between-group differences in IQ.

Rival hypotheses include test bias, compensatory effects on IQ, and experimental factors affecting IQs. Despite its popularity as an account of IQ differences between groups defined by race, ethnicity, and even hearing impairment, there is no evidence that test bias significantly influences outcomes of deafness as a natural experiment condition. There is little evidence to show that test bias affects measures of academic achievement and nonverbal intelligence, although the evidence regarding the lack of bias for verbal intelligence tests is less persuasive. Some have argued that verbal IQ tests overestimate the verbal intelligence in deaf populations. However, experimental evidence and studies of academic achievement suggest that, to the degree verbal intelligence tests are biased for deaf people, the bias is probably in the direction of overpredicting verbal reasoning abilities.

A critical distinction must be drawn between scientific and clinical definitions of bias. The scientific approach to bias investigates groups to establish whether the statistical behavior of the test in one group is comparable to the statistical behavior of the test in another group. The clinical approach to test bias stresses the validity of clinical decisions drawn from test results. Thus, it is possible to argue that verbal intelligence tests may not be statistically biased, because verbal IQs have similar meaning when predicting deaf and normal-hearing people's achievement. At the same time, it is clear that verbal intelligence tests are clinically biased, because they might often suggest mental retardation or diminished intelligence when, in fact, the deaf person may have average or above-average nonverbal intellectual abilities. Ironically, nonverbal tests appear to be statistically biased (i.e., nonverbal IQs do not yield similar achievement predictions for deaf and normal-hearing people), but these same nonverbal tests do not appear to be clinically biased (i.e., nonverbal IQs have similar meaning for inferring the intellectual ability of deaf and normal-hearing people). This paradox must be kept in mind when issues of test bias are discussed with respect to the use of tests with deaf people.

Compensation does not seriously affect IQ results in deaf people. Compensatory effects may yield slightly higher IQs on performance tests of nonverbal intelligence, but the impact is slight. Other experimental factors, such as methods of data collection and sampling procedures, do impact IQs and therefore offer potential rival hypotheses.

To the extent that experimental procedures skew outcomes of deafness as a natural experiment, the effect is apparently one of underestimating nonverbal IQ, and overestimating verbal IQ and academic achievement. Joint consideration of all rival hypotheses suggests there are factors that attenuate IQs found in deaf people, but these factors do not substantially affect the pattern of performance found for deaf people on measures of verbal intelligence, academic achievement, and nonverbal intelligence.

Implications of Deafness for IQ Differences between Groups

There are many interesting implications of these results for the study of IQ differences between groups. The fact that some groups have below-average distributions of nonverbal IQ, in contrast to the average distributions noted for deaf people, suggests that many of the commonly cited environmental "causes" of between-group differences in IQ cannot explain why deaf people have average nonverbal IQs, and normal-hearing ethnic or racial groups do not. Another interesting implication is that differences between North American blacks and whites appear to cross the hearing barrier (i.e., white deaf children perform better on nonverbal IQ tests than black deaf children). Still another implication is that arguments equating verbal and nonverbal IQ tests (because the IQs are highly correlated and similar) are invalidated by the substantial differences between verbal and nonverbal IQs found among deaf people. These and other implications associated with the outcomes of deafness as a natural experiment shed light on controversies associated with IQ differences between groups, and help to evaluate competing claims in an open, empirical fashion.

The best conclusion to be drawn from the study of intelligence in deaf people is that it raises many intriguing questions for future research. Although some results conflict with popular accounts of between-group differences in IQ, it may be that such accounts could explain the performance of deaf people on tests of intelligence if environmental factors were specified in a more precise fashion, and the environments of deaf people were observed to evaluate the presence and valence of these factors. I have argued that many accounts of between-group differences in IQ are inconsistent for explaining results associated with deaf people. However, these conclusions are limited by the fact that most current versions of theories have little awareness of research with deaf people. Perhaps increased awareness of outcomes associated with deaf people will assist proponents of theories in specifying to what degree theories ought to apply to deaf people, and what outcomes would subsequently be predicted from theoretical models. I may have erred in the ways in which I anticipated that theories could be applied to deaf people, and I may have erred in the types of predictions that the various theories would make. However, I still believe there is value for using deaf people as a group to form and test theories of between-group differences. The study of deafness can help theoreticians and researchers to develop theories that generalize to all groups sharing specified conditions, rather than limiting the scope of generalization to a smaller spectrum.

Conversely, I may be accurate in my assumptions and predictions, in which case, deaf people offer anomalous data with respect to many theoretical predictions. Such anomalies are the beginning of discovery. By presenting a group that experiences unique environmental settings, and whose environmental and genetic characteristics cut across traditional racial and ethnic boundaries, the study of deaf people provides a proving ground for theories of between-group differences in IQ. The proving ground would require more precise measurement of environmental conditions. For example, "minority status" is a factor that appears in many theories of between-group differences in IQ. Specification of what that factor might be, and how it could be measured, would help determine whether deaf people could, in fact, be considered an ethnic minority group, or whether they are treated as a minority by the general population. The specification and accurate measurement of important, but currently ill-defined environmental constructs is an important challenge in the search for causes of between-group differences in IQ. Because deafness cuts across socially determined minority group status, it is an excellent foil against which to specify and test social factors and their effects on intelligence.

Another implication provided by the study of intelligence in deaf people is the likelihood that biologically related environmental factors are needed to account for between-group differences in nonverbal IQ. The fact that deaf people exhibit similar nonverbal IQs, and that the development of nonverbal intelligence across the developmental age span results in increasing similarity between deaf and normal-hearing peers, suggests a strong biological basis for nonverbal intelligence. Therefore, if environmental factors do in fact account for between-group differences in nonverbal IQ, then the search for factors is probably best directed toward environmental conditions known to affect biological maturation (e.g., ingestion or inhalation of toxins, nutrition).

Another implication that many individuals may find uncomfortable is that environmental factors not directly related to biological maturation (e.g., societal customs, language, patterns of social interaction) are unlikely to account for between-group differences in nonverbal IQ. Such theories may need to be set aside, or reexamined, to determine whether cultural factors might facilitate or inhibit biological maturation. Given the findings associated with deaf people's intelligence, sociocultural factors do not appear to be a very promising avenue to account for between-group differences in nonverbal IQ.

The study of deafness also offers opportunities to study genetic accounts of intelligence. Results describing different distributions of IQ within genetic and nongenetic deaf children and their family members could be used to isolate genetic conditions (e.g., pleiotropy). Also, traditional studies of within-family genetic correlations would be enhanced with the addition of deaf people, because they represent a within-family cohort with a radically different environmental history. Thus, environmental and genetic accounts of IQ differences between groups could benefit by expanding their range of inquiry to include the study of intelligence among deaf people.

Therefore, the real value of deafness as a natural experiment lies in its ability to provide a fresh perspective and unique vantage point for the study of IQ differences between groups. The real problem of deafness as a natural experiment lies in determining the veracity of assumptions needed to apply deafness to a given theory. Given that a theory can reasonably be construed to make predictions regarding deaf people, theoretical predictions may be compared to outcomes obtained by deaf people. Findings that are anomalous for environmental and genetic theories should challenge researchers to refine the theory, in terms of specification of factors, measurement of relevant environmental attributes, or in structural shifts regarding the impact of factors. I believe the research on deafness to date challenges many of the commonly held assumptions regarding the causes of between-group differences in IQ. Deaf people provide a proving ground to sharpen and refine environmental and genetic accounts of between-group differences in IQ. This proving ground has the added advantage of testing transfer across boundaries defined by race, ethnicity, and hearing status. Difficult though it may be to tease apart factors in the complex web called "deafness," the search is likely to shed light on an issue that is important to psychology and society: the nature and cause of IQ differences between groups.

Afterword: Deafness and
the Nature of Mental Abilities

Understanding the nature of cognition and the developmental role of environmental factors in those who are born deaf is an important subject for research. Professor Braden, however, also suggests that a wider range of implications for psychology, particularly differential psychology, is to be found in this specialized field of research. Besides providing a comprehensive review of what is known about the characteristics and development of cognitive abilities in persons who are born deaf, Professor Braden has brought this knowledge to bear uniquely on hypotheses concerning the causal factors in individual differences and racial group differences in mental abilities. His main findings about the pattern of abilities in the deaf generally fit quite neatly into the predominant view of the nature of abilities that has come clearly into focus over the past two or three decades of research on this subject.

The most widely accepted theory of what is technically referred to as the *structure* of mental abilities is based on the combination of two fields of empirical study: psychometrics and neurophysiology. By means of factor analysis, psychometricians analyze the pattern of correlations between an extremely wide variety of mental tests on which scores have been obtained from a large sample of some population. Factor analysis reveals the main independent dimensions (or *factors*) of individual differences (technically called *variance*) found in the tests. Neurophysiologists attempt to discover, among other things, the localization in the brain of the processes associated with the various factors, or types of ability. Damage in different parts of the brain, for example, may adversely affect particular abilities. Some of the affected abilities are associated with certain broad factors, or constellations of abilities, such as verbal ability and visual-spatial ability. Abilities that are found to be closely related to localized regions of the brain are known as *modules*. Some of these modules roughly correspond to the ability factors revealed by the factor analysis of psychometric tests. Some modules, such as immediate face recognition and the perception of three-dimensional space, are so universal and "hard-wired" as to show almost no individual differences except in rare pathological conditions, and thus have too little variance in the population to be able to show up in a factor analysis. Also, not all of the factors discovered by the factor analysis of psychometric tests have corresponding modules in the strict neurological sense of this term. Modules are uniquely characterized by the various ways that information or knowledge is represented by the neural activity of the brain, and they are localized in different regions of the brain. The main modules that have been identified in neurophysiological studies are *linguistic* (i.e., verbal/auditory/lexical/semantic), *visual-spatial, object recognition, numerical-mathematical, musical,* and *kinaesthetic.*

A hierarchical structure results from the factor analysis of virtually all known and measurable abilities (provided there are individual differences in these abilities). The hierarchy can be pictured as a wide-based isosceles triangle comprising four tiers, each tier representing a greater range of generality. Along the base of the triangle are an indefinitely large number of tests of highly specific mental abilities. These abilities are all positively intercorrelated to varying degrees. Tests with the higher correlations cluster together; these clusters of the most highly intercorrelated correlated tests, then, are called *first-order factors* (also called primary factors or group factors). There will of course be far fewer first-order factors than tests. (About 30 such first-order factors have been reliabily identified.) The first-order factors constitute the next higher level of the triangle-shaped hierarchy. Each of the primary factors, then, represents a broader or more general ability than any one of the specific tests.

But these first-order factors are also intercorrelated to varying degrees. So the first-order factors form several clusters based on their degree of intercorrelation. These, then, are the *second-order factors*. They are the next higher level of the hierarchy. They are of course far fewer than the number of first-order factors, and each of the second-order factors represents a higher degree of generality than any of the first-order factors. (Only about 8 second-order factors have been reliably identified in the psychometric abilities domain.)

The second-order factors are also intercorrelated, but only a single *third-order* factor can be extracted from them, as no reliable structured variance remains after extraction of the third-order factor. No replicable higher-order factors beyond the third order have been identified yet. Thus the third-order factor is the apex of the triangle and the most general of all factors (therefore called the *g* factor). It is so general that unlike every other factor, it has some degree of "loading" in each of the factors below it in the hierarchy and in each of the specific tests at the base of the hierarchy. The *g* factor is often identified as "intelligence," because it has its highest loadings in tests of abstract reasoning and problem solving, but the word "intelligence" is too fraught with excess and misleading meanings to be useful in scientific discourse. Besides, it is entirely superfluous in this context.

The existence of g is not only an empirical fact but a theoretical necessity, if one is to account for the well-established phenomenon that all varieties of mental abilities that show individual differences in the general population are positively correlated with one another. In fact, g accounts for much more of the total variance in all mental tests than any other factor or combination of factors independent of g. It is also more highly correlated with many performance criteria of mental capability in education and work than any other first-order or second-order factor, or any combination of factors independent of g. The g factor is the chief active ingredient of the predictive validity of the tests used in education, personnel selection, and selection for specialized training programs in the armed services.

It is therefore most significant that, as Professor Braden has pointed out, being born deaf does not affect g. Among the major factors, it affects only the development of verbal ability. (The development of musical ability is, of course, also affected.) It must be understood that, as yet, there is no pure psychometric test of g. We can test only with a vehicle that is loaded with g but also carries non-g factors. Verbal tests, such as vocabulary, synonyms-antonyms, verbal analogies, sentence completion, and reading comprehension all reflect a verbal ability factor besides g. Therefore, if used to assess mental ability in deaf people, they may seriously misrepresent the person's level on g, the most important and most general factor of ability. The assessment of g in deaf people must depend on a variety of tests that are highly g-loaded but have minimal loadings on the verbal factor, whatever other factors may be present. On some ostensibly nonverbal tests, performance is helped by verbally mediated thought processes. In a hierarchical factor analysis, such a test will have a significant loading on a verbal factor in addition to g (and possibly other non-g factors).

As Professor Braden has noted, the differences between deaf and hearing people on various psychometric tests are nearly the exact opposite of the average differences between the black and white populations in terms of their factor composition. The deaf-hearing difference is entirely a difference in the verbal factor, with no difference in g. However, blacks and whites, on average, do not differ at all on the verbal factor (independent of g), but differ markedly on the g factor (about 1.2 standard deviations, or equivalent to 18 points on the IQ scale). The varying size of the black-white difference on various tests is best predicted by the degree to which the tests are g-loaded, whereas the deaf-hearing difference on various tests is best predicted by the tests' loadings on the verbal factor. Although the verbal factor typically figures strongly in schooling and higher education, a deficiency in verbal ability, given a normal level of g, is much less educationally and occupationally disabling than is a comparable deficiency in g. More important, however, is the fact that verbal ability is not exclusively dependent on sensory acuity, that is, the ability to *hear* spoken language, or the ability to use language vocally. Language can be learned and used, and the verbal mediation of thinking developed, through other media. The lesser efficiency of non-auditory and non-vocal communication probably accounts for the early lag in verbal skills in children who are born deaf, and it accounts for their eventual catching up in late adolescence, provided the appropriate experiences for developing verbal skills (not necessarily speech) have persisted continuously to adulthood. The deaf adult then is able to fully express his or her level of *g*, or general intelligence, in verbally demanding activities, such as reading comprehension and writing.

The hierarchical structure of abilities, in terms of their generality shown by the factor analysis of a great variety of mental tests obtained from population samples, leads to a further question: How is this factor structure related to the brain mechanisms involved in mental abilities within a single individual? Also, why are the abilities seen in individuals all positively intercorrelated across individuals, making for a general factor, or *g*, common to all abilities? Deaf persons show a marked discrepancy between their level on two special abilities (in this case, verbal and musical), and their level on *g*.

The opposites of this are idiot savants, who show an extreme discrepancy between a particular narrow ability and all other abilities, usually showing the greatest inconsistency between some specialized skill, which is highly developed, and the savant's level of *g*, which is usually quite low. Some savants are too severely retarded to take care of themselves, yet can perform feats of mental calculation, or play the piano by ear, or memorize pages of a telephone directory, or draw objects from memory with nearly photographic accuracy. The modularity of these abilities is shown by the fact that rarely, if ever, does one find a savant with more than one narrow type of average or superior ability, always limited within a single first-order factor or a single module.

In striking contrast, there are persons whose level of *g* is within the normal range, yet who, because of a localized brain lesion, show a severe deficiency in some particular ability, such as face recognition, receptive or expressive language dysfunctions (aphasia), or inability to form long-term memories. Again, modularity is shown by the fact that these functional deficiencies are quite isolated from the person's total repertoire of abilities. In persons with a normally intact brain, a module's efficiency for processing its own class of information can be enhanced through extensive experience and practice in the particular domain served by the module.

This evidence in no way contradicts the existence of *g*, as is often mistakenly believed. The presence of a general factor shows that the workings of the various modules, though distinct in their functions, are all affected to some degree by some brain characteristics in which there are individual differences, such as chemical neurotransmitters, neural conduction velocity, amount of dendritic branching, degree of myelination of axons, and general cortical arousal. Hence individual differences in the specialized mental activities associated with different modules are correlated.

A simple analogy might help to explain the theoretical compatibility between the positive correlations among all mental abilities (hence the existence of g) and the existence of modularity in mental abilities. Imagine a dozen factories (persons), each of which manufactures the same five different gadgets (modular abilities). Each gadget is produced by a different machine (module). The five machines are all connected to each other by a common gear chain which is powered by one motor. But each of the factories uses a different motor to drive the gear chain, and each factory's motor runs at a different constant speed than the motors of every other factory. This will cause the factories to differ in their rates of output of the five gadgets (scores on five different tests). The factories will be said to differ in overall efficiency or capacity (g), because the rates of output of the five gadgets are positively correlated. If the correlations between output rates of the gadgets produced by all of the factories were factor analyzed, they would yield a large general factor (g). The output rates of gadgets would be positively correlated, but not *perfectly* correlated, because the sales demand for each gadget differs for each factory, and the machines that produce the gadgets with the larger sales are better serviced, better oiled, and kept in consistently better operating condition than the machines that make low-demand gadgets. Therefore, even though the five machines are all driven by the same motor, they differ in their efficiency and consistency of operation, making for less than a perfect correlation between their rates of output. Then imagine that in one factory the main drive-shaft of one of the machines breaks, so it cannot produce its gadgets (e.g., localized brain damage affecting a single module, but not of g). Or imagine a factory where there is a delay in the input of the raw materials from which one of the machines produces gadgets (analogous to a deaf child not receiving auditory verbal input). In still another factory, the gear chain to all but one of the machines breaks and they therefore fail to produce gadgets. But one machine remains powered by the motor receives its undivided energy and produces gadgets faster than if the motor had to run all the other machines as well (e.g., an idiot savant).

Going beyond the limits of this simple analogy, it is likely that modules (which are not sensory capacities, but cerebral mechanisms) have different initial selective sensitivities to various environmental inputs, such as certain kinds of visual and auditory stimuli, in different individuals. This would result in individual differences in the amount of attention paid to different aspects of the environment, creating a positive feedback to the module that promotes its development. At the same time, the efficiencies of all the modules are affected by certain aspects of cerebral functioning that are common to every module's operation, and in which there are individual differences. These could be such characteristics as neural condition velocity and the general level of cortical arousal, which uniformly affect the whole cerebrum. Some such hypothesis is needed to account for the g factor.

It can be likened to the central processing unit (CPU) of a computer. A computer with a CPU that operates at a speed of 66 MHz does all its operations—word processing, computing, retrieval of information from "memory"—more quickly than a CPU with a speed of 50 MHz, given the same software programs. But if each computer is provided with a different program for executing a specific routine, the programs could possibly differ in design such that the 50 MHz CPU is enabled to perform this specialized function more efficiently than the 66 MHz CPU.

   I believe that such a model of human abilities, which accords with most of the established facts in this domain, affords a basis for understanding much of the empirical knowledge about the psychology of deafness that Professor Braden has reviewed. It also may suggest empirically testable hypotheses that lead to corrections and elaborations that could have heuristic value for future research on the education of deaf children.

ARTHUR R. JENSEN

Professor of Educational Psychology
University of California, Berkeley

References

Adler, A. J. (1985). Ray's adaptation of the Wechsler Intelligence Scale for Children-Revised for the Deaf with hearing and hearing impaired students. *Dissertations Abstract International, 47*, 121A (Order No. DA8529575).

Allen, T. E. (1986). Patterns of academic achievement among hearing-impaired students: 1974 and 1983. In A. N. Schildroth & M. A. Karchmer (Eds.), *Deaf children in America* (pp. 161–206). San Diego, CA: College Hill Press.

Altshuler, K. Z. (1974). The social and psychological development of the deaf child: Problems and treatment. In P. J. Fine (Ed.), *Deafness in infancy and early childhood* (pp. 55–86). New York: Medcom.

Amoss, H. (1936). *Ontario School Ability Examination.* Toronto: Ryerson.

Anderson, R. J., & Sisco, F. H. (1977). *Standardization of the WISC-R Performance Scale for deaf children* (Office of Demographic Studies Publication Series T, No. 1). Washington, DC: Gallaudet College.

Anthony, D. (1966). *Seeing essential English.* Unpublished thesis, University of Michigan, Ypsilanti, MI.

Balow, I. H., & Brill, R. G. (1975). An evaluation of reading and academic achievement levels of 16 graduating classes of the California School for the Deaf, Riverside. *Volta Review, 77*, 255–266.

Bangert-Drowns, R. L., Kulik, J. A., & Kulik, C. L. C. (1984, Aug.). *The influence of study features on outcomes of educational research.* Paper presented at the annual meeting of the American Psychological Association, Toronto.

Bardos, A. N., & Weber, M. (1988). *WISC-R, MAT-EF, DAP and SAT with hearing-impaired children.* Paper presented at the annual convention of the Ohio School Psychologists.

Barron, C. W. (1940). Studies in the psychology of the deaf (No. 1). *Psychological Monographs, 52* (1, Whole No. 323).

Batkin, S., Groth, H., Watson, J. R., & Ansperry, M. (1970). The effects of auditory deprivaton in the development of auditory sensitivity in albino rats. *Electroencephalography and Clinical Neurophysiology, 28*, 351–359.

Batson, T. W., & Bergman, E. (Eds.), (1973). *The deaf experience: An anthology of literature by and about the deaf.* Washington, DC: Gallaudet College.

Bellugi, U. (1972). Studies in sign language. In T. O'Rourke (Ed.), *Psycholinguistics and total communication: A state of the art* (pp.). Silver Springs, MD: American Annals of the Deaf.

Bellugi, U. (1989, July). *Keynote address for the Second International Symposium on Cognition,*

Education, and Deafness. Paper presented at the Second International Symposium on Cognition, Education, and Deafness, Gallaudet University, Washington, DC.

Belmont, J. M., Karchmer, M. A., & Bourg, J. W. (1983). Structural influences on deaf and hearing children's recall of temporal/spatial incongruent letter strings. *Educational Psychology, 3*, 261–276.

Bender, N. N. (1980, April). *Self-instruction and impulsivity control by deaf children*. Paper presented at the annual meeting of the American Educational Research Association, Boston, MA.

Berk, R. A. (Ed.) (1982). *Handbook of methods for detecting test bias*. Baltimore, MD: John Hopkins University Press.

Bernstein, B. (1961). Social class and linguistic development: A theory of social learning. In A. H. Halsey, J. Floud, & C. A. Anderson (Eds.), *Education, economy, and society* (pp. 288–314). New York: Holt.

Bernstein, B. (1970). Education cannot compensate for society. *New Society, 387*, 344–347.

Binet, A., & Simon, T. (1910). Oral and manual methods of teaching the deaf. *American Annals of the Deaf, 55*, 4–33.

Birch, J. R., & Birch, J. W. (1951). The Leiter International Performance Scale as an aid in the psychological study of deaf children. *American Annals of the Deaf, 96*, 502–511.

Birch, J. R., & Birch, J. W. (1956). Predicting school achievement in young deaf children. *American Annals of the Deaf, 101*, 348–352.

Birch, J. R., Stuckless, E. R., & Birch, J. W. (1963). An eleven year study of predicting school achievement in young deaf children. *American Annals of the Deaf, 103*, 236–240.

Bishop, H. M. (1936). Performance Scale tests applied to deaf and hard of hearing children. *Volta Review, 38*, 447, 484–485.

Blair, F. (1957). A study of the visual memory of deaf and hearing children. *American Annals of the Deaf, 102*, 254–267.

Blood, I. M., & Blood, G. W. (1982). Classroom teachers' impressions of hearing impaired and deaf children. *Perceptual and Motor Skills, 54*, 877–878.

Bolton, B. (1978). Differential ability structure in deaf and hearing children. *Applied Psychological Measurement, 2*, 147–149.

Bond, G. G. (1987). An assessment of cognitive abilities in hearing and hearing-impaired preschool children. *Journal of Speech and Hearing Disorders, 52*, 319–323.

Bone, F., & Delk, L. (1988). *Final report Model Secondary School for the Deaf annual profile 1987–1988*. Center for Curriculum Development, Training & Outreach, Pre-College Programs. Washington, DC: Gallaudet University.

Bonham, S. J. (1963). *Predicting achievement for deaf children*. Dayton City School District. Ohio Department of Education, Columbus, OH. (ERIC Document Reproduction Service No. ED 015 572).

Bowe, F. G. (1971). Non-white deaf persons: Educational, psychological, and occupational considerations. *American Annals of the Deaf, 116*, 357–361.

Bracken, B. A. (1985). A critical review of the Kaufman Assessment Battery for Children (K-ÙÙABC). *School Psychology Review, 14*, 21–36.

Braden, J. P. (1984). The factorial similarity of the WISC-R Performance Scale in deaf and hearing samples. *Journal of Personality and Individual Differences, 5*, 403–409.

Braden, J. P. (1985a). The relationship between choice reaction time and IQ in deaf and hearing children (Doctoral dissertation, University of California, 1985). *Dissertations Abstracts International, 46*, 2622A. (University Microfilms No. DES85–24895).

Braden, J. P. (1985b). The structure of nonverbal intelligence in deaf and hearing subjects. *American Annals of the Deaf, 131*, 496–501.

Braden, J. P. (1985c). WISC-R deaf norms reconsidered. *Journal of School Psychology, 23*, 375–382.

Braden, J. P. (1987). An explanation of the superior Performance IQs of deaf children of deaf parents. *American Annals of the Deaf, 132*, 263–266.

Braden, J. P. (1988). Understanding IQ differences between groups: Deaf children as a natural experiment in the nature-nurture debate. In D. H. Soklofske & S. B. Eysenck (Eds.), *Individual differences in children and adolescents: International research perspectives* (pp. 265–277). London: Hodder & Stoughton.

Braden, J. P. (1989a, July). *Deafness as a natural experiment: A meta-analytic review of IQ research.* Invited address, Second International Symposium on Cognition, Education, and Deafness, Gallaudet University, Washington, DC.

Braden, J. P. (1989b). Fact or artifact? An empirical test of Spearman's Hypothesis. *Intelligence, 13*, 149–155.

Braden, J. P. (1989c). *A meta-analytic investigation of the cumulative deficit phenomenon using deaf subjects.* Manuscript in preparation for submission.

Braden, J. P. (1990a). The criterion-related validity of the WISC-R Performance Scale and other nonverbal IQ tests for deaf children. *American Annals of the Deaf, 134*, 329–332.

Braden, J. P. (1990b). Do deaf persons have a characteristic psychometric profile on the Wechsler Performance Scales? *Journal of Psychoeducational Assessment, 8*, 518–526.

Braden, J. P. (1992). Intellectual assessment of deaf and hard of hearing people: A quantitative and qualitative research synthesis. *School Psychology Review, 21*, 82–94.

Braden, J. P., Maller, S. J., & Paquin, M. M. (1993). The effects of residential versus day placement on the Performance IQs of children with hearing impairment. *Journal of Special Education, 26*, 423–433.

Braden, J. P., & Paquin, M. M. (1985). A comparison of the WISC-R and WAIS-R Performance scales in deaf adolescents. *Journal of Psychoeducational Assessment, 3*, 285–290.

Braden, J. P., & Zwiebel, A. (1990). *The structure of nonverbal intelligence in deaf children: A study of environmental effects.* Manuscript under review.

Brasel, K. E., & Quigley, S. P. (1977). Influence of certain language and communication environments in early childhood on the development of language in deaf individuals. *Journal of Speech and Hearing Research, 20*, 95–107.

Bridgman, O. (1939). The estimation of mental ability in deaf children. *American Annals of the Deaf, 84*, 337–349.

Brill, R. G. (1960). A study in adjustment of three groups of deaf children. *Exceptional Children, 26*, 464–466, 470.

Brill, R. G. (1962). The relationship of Wechsler IQ's to academic achievement among deaf students. *Exceptional Children*, 315–321.

Brill, R. G. (1969). The superior I.Q.'s of deaf children of deaf parents. *The California Palms, 15*(2), 1–4.

Brinich, P. M. (1981). Relationship between intellectual functioning and communicative competence in deaf children. *Journal of Communication Disorders, 14*, 429–434.

Brooks, C. R., & Riggs, S. T. (1980). WISC-R, WISC, and reading achievement relationships among hearing-impaired children attending public schools. *Volta Review, 82*, 96–102.

Brown, A. W. (1930). The correlations of non-language tests with each other, with school achievement, and with teachers' judgments of the intelligence of children in a school for the deaf. *Journal of Applied Psychology, 14*, 371–375.

Brown, S. C. (1986). Etiological trends, characteristics, and distributions. In A. N. Schildroth and M. A. Karchmer (Eds.), *Deaf children in America* (pp. 33–54). San Diego, CA: College Hill.

Burchard, E. M. L., & Myklebust, H. R. (1942). A comparison of congenital and adventitious deafness with respect to its effect on intelligence, personality and social maturity—Part II: Social maturity. *American Annals of the Deaf, 87*, 241–251.

Capwell, D. F. (1945). Performance of deaf children on the Arthur Point Scale. *Journal of Consulting Psychology, 9,* 91–94.

Chambers, J. F. (1971). Predicting the academic achievement level of deaf students. *Dissertations Abstract International, 31,* 6396A (Order No. 71–15, 924).

Chastain, R. L. & Reynolds, C. R. (1984, August). *An analysis of WAIS-R performance by sample stratification variables used during standardization.* Paper presented at the Annual Convention of the American Psychological Association, Toronto, Onatrio, Canada. (ERIC Document Reproduction Service No. ED 249 409)

Chess, S., & Fernandez, P. (1980). Neurologic damage and behavior disorder in rubella children. *American Annals of the Deaf, 125,* 998–1001.

Clarke, B. R., & Leslie, P. T. (1971). Visual-motor skills and reading ability of deaf children. *Perceptual and Motor Skills, 33,* 263–268.

Clegg, S. J., & White, W. F. (1966). Assessment of general intelligence of negro deaf children in a public residential school for the deaf. *Journal of Clinical Psychology, 22,* 93–94.

Cokely, D., & Gawlick, R. (1975). Childrenese as pidgin. *Sign Language Studies, 5,* 72–81.

Commission on Education of the Deaf (1988). *Toward equality: A report to the President and the Congress of the United States.* Washington, DC: U.S. Government Printing Office.

Conrad, R. (1979). *The deaf schoolchild: Language and cognitive function.* London: Harper & Row.

Conrad, R., & Weiskrantz, B. C. (1981). On the cognitive ability of deaf children with deaf parents. *American Annals of the Deaf, 126,* 995–1003.

Cornett, R. O. (1975). What is cued speech? *Gallaudet Today, 5*(2), 1–3.

Courtney, A. S., Hayes, F. B., Couch, K. W., & Frick, M. (1984). Administration of the WISC-R Performance Scale to hearing-impaired children using pantomimed instructions. *Journal of Psychoeducational Assessment, 2,* 1–7.

Cowan, W. M. (1970). Anterograde and retrograde transneural degeneration in the central and peripheral nervous system. In W. J. H. Nauta & S. O. E. Ebbeson (Eds.), *Contemporary research methods in neuroanatomy* (pp. 217–251). Berlin: Springer.

Craig, H. B., & Gordon, H. W. (1988). Specialized cognitive function and reading achievement in hearing-impaired adolescents. *Journal of Speech and Hearing Disorders, 53,* 30–41.

Crown, P. J. (1970). *The effects of race of examiner and standard vs. dialect administration of the Wechsler Preschool and Primary Scale of Intelligence on the performance of Negro and white children.* Unpublished doctoral dissertation, Florida State University, Tallahassee, FL.

Davis, J. M., Elfenbein, J., Schum, R., & Bentler, R. A. (1986). Effects of mild and moderate hearing impairments on language, educational, and psychosocial behavior of children. *Journal of Speech and Hearing Disorders, 51,* 53–62.

Day, H. E., Fusfeld, I. S., & Pintner, R. (1928). *A survey of American schools for the deaf.* Washington, DC: National Research Council.

De Marco, W. (1969). The scatter of intellectual abilities of the hard of hearing as assessed by the Wechsler Intelligence Scale for Children. *Dissertations Abstract International, 30,* 3383B-3384B (Order No. 70–830).

Diderot, D. (1875). Lettre sur les Sourds et les Muets. *Oeuvres Completes par J. Assezat, 1,* 343–428.

Drever, J., & Collins, M. (1928). *Performance tests of intelligence: A series of non-linguistic tests for deaf and normal children.* Edinburgh: Oliver & Boyd.

Du Toit, J. M. (1954). Measuring the intelligence of deaf children. *American Annals of the Deaf, 99,* 237–251.

Ensor, A. (1988, March). *WAIS-R Performance as a predictor of achievement for deaf adolescents.* Paper presented at the annual meeting of the National Association of School Psychologists, Boston, MA.

Ensor, A., & Phelps, L. (1989). Gender differences on the WAIS—R Performance Scale with young deaf adults. *Journal of the American Deafness and Rehabilitation Association, 22,* 48–52.

Evans, L. (1960). Factors related to listening and lipreading. *Teacher of the Deaf, 58*, 417–423.

Evans, L. (1966). A comparative study of the Wechsler Intelligence Scale for Children (Performance) and Raven's Progressive Matrices with deaf children. *Teacher of the Deaf, 64*, 76–82.

Evans, L. (1980). WISC Performance Scale and Coloured Progressive Matrices with deaf children. *British Journal of Educational Psychology, 50*, 216–222.

Evans, W. D. (1984, Aug.). Families and deaf children. Address given to New Parent Orientation of the California School for the Deaf, Fremont, CA.

Falberg, R. M. (1983). Psychological assessment of the verbal functioning of postsecondary educational program applicants: Improving predictive validity. In D. Watson, G. Anderson, P. Marut, S. Ovellette, & N. Ford (Eds.), *Vocational evaluation of hearing-impaired persons: Research and practice*. Warm Springs: University of Arkansas.

Farrant, R. H. (1964). The intellective abilities of deaf and hearing children compared by factor analyses. *American Annals of the Deaf, 109*, 306–325.

Feuerstein, R., Rand, Y., & Hoffman, M. B. (1979). *The dynamic assessment of retarded performers: The learning Potential Assessment Device, theory instruments, and techniques*. Baltimore: University Park Press.

Fletcher, S. G., Smith, S. C., & Hasegawa, A. (1985). Vocal/verbal response times of normal-hearing and hearing-impaired children. *Journal of Speech and Hearing Research, 28*, 548–555.

Flynn, J. R. (1986). Massive IQ gains in 14 nations: What IQ tests really measure. *Psychological Bulletin, 101*, 171–191.

Forde, J. (1977). Data on the Peabody Picture Vocabulary Test. *American Annals of the Deaf, 122*, 38–43.

Frisby, C. L., & Braden, J. P. (1992). Feuerstein's dynamic assessment approach: A semantic, logical, and empirical critique. *Journal of Special Education, 26*, 281–301.

Frishberg, N. (1975). Arbitrariness and iconicity: Historical change in American Sign Language. *Language, 51*, 696–719.

Frisina, D. R. (1965). A psychological study of the mentally retarded deaf child. *Dissertation Abstracts International, 15*, 2288A (Order No. 13,084).

Fromkin, V., Krashen, S., Curtiss, S., Rigler, D., & Rigler, M. (1974). The development of language in Genie: A case of language acquisition beyond the "critical period." *Brain and Language, 1*, 81–107.

Fuller, C. W. (1959). A study of the growth and organization of certain mental abilities in young deaf children. *Dissertation Abstracts International, 20*, 2382A (Order No. 59–4794).

Funderberg, R. S. (1975). The relationship of short-term visual memory and intelligence to the manual communication skills of profoundly deaf children. *Dissertation Abstracts International, 36*, 3564A (Order No. 26,932).

Furth, H. G. (1966). *Thinking without language*. New York: Free Press.

Fusfeld, I. S. (1940). Research and testing at Gallaudet College. *American Annals of the Deaf, 85*, 170–183.

Galenson, E., Miller, R., Kaplan, E., & Rothstein, J. (1979). Assessment of development in the deaf child. *Journal of Child Psychiatry, 18*, 128–142.

Gamble, H. W. (1987). A national survey of programs for intellectually and academically gifted hearing-impaired students. *American Annals of the Deaf, 132*, 231–236.

Gardner, R. A., & Gardner, B. T. (1969). Teaching sign language to a chimpanzee. *Science, 165*, 664–672.

Gaskill, P. (1957). Tests of abilities and attainments: Pilot experiments in selection and guidance. In A. W. G. Ewing (Ed.), *Educational guidance and the deaf child* (Chap. 9, pp. 188–212). Manchester, UK: Manchester University Press.

Georgia Department of Public Health. (1967). *A health survey of negro students, Georgia School for the Deaf, 1964 Part II*. Atlanta, GA: Author.

Giangreco, C. J. (1966). The Hiskey-Nebraska Test of Learning Aptitude (Revised) compared to several achievement tests. *American Annals of the Deaf, 111*, 566–577.

Gibbins, S. (1988, April). *Use of the WISC-R Performance Scale and K-ABC Nonverbal Scale with deaf children: A cross cultural study.* Paper presented at the annual convention of the National Association of School Psychologists, Chicago, IL.

Gibson, J. M. (1984). Field dependence of deaf students: Implications for education. In D. S. Martin (Ed.), *International symposium on cognition, education, and deafness: Working papers.* (ERIC Document Reproduction Service No. 247-709). Washington, DC: Gallaudet University College of Education.

Glowatsky, E. (1953). The verbal element in the intelligence scores of congenitally deaf and hard of hearing children. *American Annals of the Deaf, 98*, 328–335.

Goetzinger, C. P., & Rousey, C. L. (1957). A study of the Wechsler Performance Scale (Form II) and the Knox Cube Test with deaf adolescents. *American Annals of the Deaf, 102*, 388–398.

Goetzinger, M. R., & Houchins, R. R. (1969). The 1947 Colored Raven's Progressive Matrices with deaf and hearing subjects. *American Annals of the Deaf, 114*, 95–101.

Goodlet, C. B., & Greene, V. R. (1940). The mental abilities of twenty-nine deaf and partially deaf Negro children. *West Virginia State College Bulletin, 4*(1).

Goss, R. N. (1970). Language used by mothers of deaf children and mothers of hearing children. *American Annals of the Deaf, 115*, 93–96.

Gould, S. J. (1981). *The mismeasure of man.* New York: Norton.

Graham, E. E., & Shapiro, E. (1953). Use of the Performance Scale of the Wechsler Intelligence Scale for Children with the deaf child. *Journal of Consulting Psychology, 17*, 396–398.

Greenberg, J. (1970). *In this sign.* New York: Holt, Rinehart & Winston.

Greenberger, D. (1889). Doubtful cases. *American Annals of the Deaf, 34*, 93.

Habbe, S. (1936). *Personality adjustments of adolescent boys with impaired hearing* (Teachers' College Contributions to Education No. 697). New York: Bureau of Publications, Teachers' College, Columbia University.

Hagborg, W. (1987). Hearing-impaired students and sociometric ratings: An exploratory study. *Volta Review, 89*, 221–229.

Hall, P. (1929). Results of recent tests at Gallaudet College. *American Annals of the Deaf, 74*, 389–395.

Hannah, M. E., & Midlarsky, E. (1985). Siblings of the handicapped: A literature review for the school psychologist. *School Psychology Review, 14*, 510–520.

Harris, R. I. (1978). The relationship of impulse control to parent hearing status, manual communication, and academic achievement in deaf children. *American Annals of the Deaf, 123*, 52–67.

Hayes, G. M., & Griffing, B. L. (1966). *Current status of psychological and achievement testing of deaf minors enrolled in special day classes at the secondary level (Grades 7–12) for the school year 1964–65).* Sacramento, CA: State Department of Education. (ERIC Document Reproduction Service No. ED 017 078).

Haywood, H. C., & Switzky, H. N. (1986). The malleability of intelligence: Cognitive processes as a function of polygenic-experiential interaction. *School Psychology Review, 15*, 245–255.

Heider, F., & Heider, G. (1941). Studies in the psychology of the deaf (No. 2). *Psychological Monographs, 53*(1, Whole No. 242).

Herrnstein, R. J. (1982, August). IQ testing and the media. *The Atlantic Monthly,* pp. 68–74.

Hine, W. D. (1970). The abilities of partially hearing children. *British Journal of Educational Psychology, 40*, 171–178.

Hirshoren, A., Kavale, K., Hurley, O. L., & Hunt, J. T. (1977). The reliability of the WISC-R Performance Scale with deaf children. *Psychology in the Schools, 14*, 412–415.

Hirshoren, A., Hurley, O. L., Kavale, K. (1979). Psychometric characteristics of the WISC-R Performance Scale with deaf children. *Journal of Speech and Hearing Disorders, 44*, 73–79.

Hirshoren, A., Hurley, O. L., & Hunt, J. T. (1977). The WISC-R and the Hiskey-Nebraska Test with deaf children. *American Annals of the Deaf, 122*, 392–394.

Hiskey, M. S. (1941). A new performance test for young deaf children. *Educational and Psychological Measurement, 1*, 217–232.

Hiskey, M. S. (1956). A study of the intelligence of deaf and hearing children through a comparison of performances on the separate standardizations of the Nebraska Test of Learning Aptitude. *American Annals of the Deaf, 101*, 329–339.

Hiskey, M. S. (1966). *Hiskey—Nebraska Test of Learning Aptitude*. Lincoln, NE: College View Printers.

Hofler, R. (1927). Ueber die bedeutung der abstraktion fur die giestige entwickelung des tabstummen kindes. *Z. Kinderforsch, 33*, 414–444.

Holland, B. F. (1936). A study of the reactions of physically normal, blind, and deaf children to questions in a verbal intelligence test. *The Teachers Forum, 9*(1), 2–10.

Howard, J. O. (1969). A comparison of the Revised Stanford-Binet Intelligence Scale, Form L-M, and the Nebraska Test of Learning Aptitude, 1966 Revision, with groups of mentally retarded, deaf, and normal children. *Dissertation Abstracts International, 30*, 3322A (Order No. 69–17,732).

Humphries, T., & Padden, C. (1988). *Deaf in America: Voices from a culture*. Cambridge, MA: Harvard University Press.

Hurley, O. L., Hirshoren, A., Kavale, K., & Hunt, J. T. (1978). Intercorrelations among tests of general mental ability and achievement for black and white deaf children. *Perceptual and Motor Skills, 46*, 1107–1113.

Jacobs, L. (1974). *A deaf adult speaks out*. Washington, DC: Gallaudet College Press.

James, R. P. (1984). A correlational analysis between the Raven's Matrices and the WISC-R Performance Scale. *Volta Review, 86*, 336–341.

Jensen, A. R. (1969). How much can we boost IQ and scholastic achievement? *Harvard Educational Review, 39*, 1–123.

Jensen, A. R. (1977). Cumulative deficit in IQ of blacks in the rural South. *Developmental Psychology, 13*, 184–191.

Jensen, A. R. (1978). Genetic and behavioral effects of nonrandom mating. In R. T. Osborne, C. E. Noble, & N. Weyl (Eds.), *Human variation: The biopsychology of age, race, and sex* (Chap. 4, pp. 51–105). New York: Academic Press.

Jensen, A. R. (1980). *Bias in mental testing*. New York: Free Press.

Jensen, A. R. (1985). The nature of black-white differences on various psychometric tests: Spearman's hypothesis. *The Behavioral and Brain Sciences, 8*, 193–219.

Jensen, A. R., & Reynolds, C. R. (1982). Race, social class and ability patterns on the WISC-R. *Personality and Individual Differences, 3*, 423–438.

Johnson, E. H. (1947). The effect of academic level on scores from the Chicago Non-Verbal Examination for Primary Pupils. *American Annals of the Deaf, 92*, 227–233.

Johnson, R. E., Liddell, S. K., & Erting, C. J. (1989). *Unlocking the curriculum: Principles for achieving access in deaf education* (Gallaudet Research Institute Working Paper 89–3). Washington, DC: Gallaudet University.

Jonas, B., & Martin, D. S. (1984). Cognitive improvement of hearing-impaired high school students through instruction in Instrumental Enrichment. In D. S. Martin (Ed.) *International symposium on cognition, education, and deafness: Working papers*. (ERIC Document Reproduction Service No. 247–725).

Jordan, I. K. & Karchmer, M. A. (1986). Sign language use of children enrolled in educational programs. In A. N. Schildroth & M. A. Karchmer (Eds.), *Deaf children in North America* (pp. 83–103). San Diego, CA: College Hill.

Kaltsounis, B. (1971). Differences in creative thinking of black and white deaf children. *Perceptual and Motor Skills, 32*, 243–248.

Karchmer, M. A., Trybus, R. J., & Paquin, M. M. (1977, April). *Early manual communication, parental hearing status, and the academic achievement of deaf students*. Paper presented at the annual convention of the American Educational Research Association, Montreal.

Katz, I. (1969). A critique of personality approaches to Negro performance, with research suggestions. *Journal of Social Issues, 25*, 13–27.

Katz, I., & Greenbaum, C. (1963). Effects of anxiety, threat and racial environment on task performance of Negro college students. *Journal of Abnormal and Social Psychology, 66*, 562–567.

Katz, I., Epps, E. G., & Axelson, L. J. (1964). Effect upon Negro digit-symbol performance of anticipated comparison with whites and with other Negroes. *Journal of Abnormal and Social Psychology, 69*, 77–83.

Kaufman, A. S., & Kaufman, N. L. (1983). *Kaufman Assessment Battery for Children*. Circle Pines, MN: American Guidance Service.

Kearney, J. E. (1969). A new performance scale of cognitive capacity for use with deaf subjects. *American Annals of the Deaf, 114*, 2–14.

Kelly, M., & Braden, J. P. (1990). Criterion-related validity of the WISC-R Performance Scale with the Stanford Achievement Test-Hearing Impaired Edition. *Journal of School Psychology, 28*, 147–151.

Kendall, D. C. (1957). Mental development of young deaf children. In A. W. G. Ewing (Ed.), *Educational guidance and the deaf child* (Chap. 3, pp. 44–62). Manchester, UK: Manchester University Press.

Keys, N., & Boulware, L. (1938). Language acquisition by deaf children as related to hearing loss and age of onset. *Journal of Educational Psychology, 29*, 401–412.

Kirk, S. A., & Perry, J. (1948). A comparative study of the Ontario and Nebraska tests for the deaf. *American Annals of the Deaf, 93*, 315–323.

Kisor, H. (1990). *What's that pig outdoors?: A memoir of deafness.* New York: Hill and Wang.

Kitson, H. D. (1915). Psychological tests for lip-reading ability. *Volta Review, 17*, 471–476.

Klansek-Kyllo, V., & Rose, S. (1985). Using the Scale of Independent Behavior with hearing-impaired students. *American Annals of the Deaf, 130*, 533–537.

Kluwin, T. N. (1981). The grammaticality of manual representations of English in classroom settings. *American Annals of the Deaf, 126*, 417–421.

Konigsmark, B. W., & Gorlin, R. J. (1976). *Genetic and metabolic deafness.* Philadelphia, PA: Saunders.

Kostrubala, C., Reed, J., & Braden, J. P. (1993, August). *Are deaf children bright or just fast on nonverbal intelligence tests?* Poster presented at the annual meeting of the American Psychological Association, Toronto, Ontario, Canada.

Kusche, C. A., Greenberg, M. T., & Garfield, T. S. (1983). Nonverbal intelligence and verbal achievement in deaf adolescents: An examination of heredity and environment. *American Annals of the Deaf, 128*, 458–466.

Kyle, J. G. (1978). The study of auditory deprivation from birth. *British Journal of Audiology, 12*, 37–39.

Lane, H. (1977). *The Wild Boy of Aveyron.* London: Allen & Unwin.

Larr, A. L. & Cain, E. R. (1959). Measurement of native learning abilities of deaf children. *Volta Review, 61*, 160–162.

Lavos, G. (1950). The Chicago Non-Verbal Examination. *American Annals of the Deaf, 95*, 379–388.

Lavos, G. (1954). Interrelationships among three tests of nonlanguage intelligence administered to the deaf. *American Annals of the Deaf, 99*, 303–313.

Lavos, G. (1962). W.I.S.C. psychometric patterns among deaf children. *Volta Review, 64*, 547–522.

Levine, B., & Roscoe, I. (1955). The Progressive Matrices (1938), the Chicago Non-Verbal and the Wechsler Bellevue on an adolescent deaf population. *Journal of Clinical Psychology, 11*, 307–308.

Levine, E. S. (1960). *The psychology of deafness.* New York: Columbia University.

Levitt, E., & Cohen, S. (1976). Attitudes of children toward their handicapped peers. *Childhood Education, 52*, 171–173.

Liben, L., Nowell, R., & Posnansky, C. (1978). Semantic and formational clustering in deaf and hearing subjects' free recall of signs. *Memory and Cognition, 6,* 599–606.

Light, R. J., & Pillemer, D. B. (1984). *Summing up: The science of summarizing research.* Cambridge, MA: Harvard University Press.

Loehlin, J. C., Lindzey, G., & Spuhler, J. N. (1975). *Race differences in intelligence.* San Francisco: Freeman.

Love, J. K. (1907). The classification of deaf pupils in Denmark. *American Annals of the Deaf, 52,* 114–116.

Luetke-Stahlman, B. (1988). Documenting syntactically and semantically incomplete bimodal input to hearing-impaired subjects. *American Annals of the Deaf, 133,* 230–234.

Lyons, V. W., Stein, S., Levin, A., Johnson, E., Fogwell, D., & Brown, A. W. (1933). Report of the 1931 survey of the Illinois School for the Deaf. *American Annals of the Deaf, 78,* 157–175.

Maller, S., & Braden, J. P. (1993). The criterion validity of the WISC-III with deaf adolescents. *Journal of Psychoeducational Assessment Monograph Series Advances in Psychoeducational Assessment: Wechsler Intelligence Scale for Children: Third Edition* (pp. 105–113).

MacKane, K. (1933). *A comparison of the intelligence of deaf and hearing children* (Teachers' College Contributions to Education No. 585). New York: Bureau of Publications, Teachers' College, Columbia University.

MacMillan, D. P., & Bruner, F. H. (1906). *Children attending the public day schools for the deaf in Chicago* (Special report of the Department of Child Study and Pedagogic Investigation). Chicago, IL: Chicago Public Schools.

MacPherson, J. G., & Lane, H. S. (1948). A comparison of deaf and hearing on the Hiskey Test and on Performance Scales. *American Annals of the Deaf, 93,* 178–184.

Madden, R. (1931). *The school status of the hard of hearing child.* (Teachers' College Contributions to Education, No. 499). New York: Bureau of Publications, Teachers' College, Columbia University.

Mayer, P. & Lowenbraun, S. (1990). Total communication use among elementary teachers of hearing-impaired children. *American Annals of the Deaf, 135,* 257–263.

McCrone, W. P. (1979). Learned helplessness and level of underachievement among deaf adolescents. *Psychology in the Schools, 16,* 430–434.

McIntire, M. L. (1977). Acquisition of American Sign Language hand configurations. *Sign Language Studies, 16,* 247–266.

McLelland, P. E. (1968). A comparative study of the reasoning ability of two groups of hearing impaired children in a residential school. *Dissertation Abstracts International, 29,* 3005A–3006A (Order No. 68–18,224).

Meacham, F. R. (1984). A comparative study of the WISC-R and WAIS-R Performance IQ scores of 16-year-old hearing impaired students in a residential program. *Dissertation Abstracts International, 45,* 2042A–2043A (Order No. DA8423502).

Meadow, K. P. (1968). Early manual communication in relation to the deaf child's intellectual, social, and communicative functioning. *American Annals of the Deaf, 113,* 29–41.

Mercer, J. R. (1979). In defense of racially and culturally non-discriminatory assessment. *School Psychology Digest, 8,* 89–115.

Miller, M. S. (1984, July). *Experimental use of signed presentations of the Verbal Scale of the WISC-R with profoundly deaf children: A preliminary report of the sign selection process and experimental test procedures.* Paper presented at the International Symposium on Cognition, Education, and Deafness, Washington, DC. (ERIC Document Reproduction Service No. ED 170 082).

Mindel, E. D., & Vernon, M. (Eds.), (1987). *They grow in silence: Understanding deaf children and adults.* Boston, MA: College Hill Press.

Mira, M. P. (1962). The use of the Arthur Adaptation of the Leiter International Performance Scale and the Nebraska Tests of Learning Aptitude with preschool deaf children. *American Annals of the Deaf, 107*, 224–228.

Montgomery, G. W. G. (1968). A factorial study of communication and ability in deaf school leavers. *British Journal of Educational Psychology, 38*, 27–37.

Moog, J., & Geers, A. (1985). EPIC: A program to accelerate academic progress in profoundly hearing-impaired children. *Volta Review, 87*, 259–277.

Moores, D. F. (1970). An investigation of the psycholinguistic functioning of deaf adolescents. *Exceptional Children 36*, 645–652.

Moores, D., Kluwin, T., Johson, R., Cox, P., Blennerhassett, L., Kelly, L., Sweet, C., & Fields, L. (1987). *Factors predictive of literacy in deaf adolescents with deaf parents* (Project No. NIH-NINCDS-83–19, Contract No. NO1–NS-4–2365). Washington, DC: National Institute of Neurological and Communicative Disorders and Stroke.

Morrison, W. J. (1946). Personal communication reported in R. Pintner, J. Eisenson, & M. Stanton, *The psychology of the physically handicapped* (p. 116). New York: Crofts.

Mott, A. J. (1900). A comparison of deaf and hearing children in their ninth year-II. *American Annals of the Deaf, 45*, 33–39; 93–109.

Murphy, K. P. (1957). Tests of abilities and attainments: Pupils in schools for the deaf aged twelve. In A. W. G. Ewing, (Ed.), *Educational guidance and the deaf child* (Chap. 11, pp. 252–277). Manchester, UK: Manchester University Press.

Murphy, L. J. (1957). Tests of abilities and attainments: Pupils in schools for the deaf aged six to ten. In A. W. G. Ewing (Ed.), *Educational guidance and the deaf child* (Chap. 10, pp. 213–251). Manchester, UK: Manchester University Press.

Myklebust, H. R. (1946). A study of the usefulness of objective measures of mechanical aptitude in guidance programs for the hypoacoustic. *American Annals of the Deaf, 91*, 123–152.

Myklebust, H. R. (1964). *The psychology of deafness* (2nd ed.). New York: Grune & Stratton.

Myklebust, H. R., & Burchard, E. M. L. (1945). A study of the effects of congenital and adventitious deafness on the intelligence, personality, and social maturity of school children. *Journal of Educational Psychology, 36*, 321–343.

Naglieri, J. A., & Jensen, A. R. (1987). Comparison of black-white differences on the WISC-R and the K-ABC: Spearman's hypothesis. *Intelligence, 11*, 21–43.

Nance, W. E., & Sweeney, A. (1975). Genetic factors in deafness in early life. *Otolaryngologic Clinics of North America, 8*, 19–48.

Newlee, C. E. (1919). A report of learning tests with deaf children. *Volta Review, 21*, 216–223.

Neyhus, A. (1962). *The personality of socially well-adjusted adult deaf as revealed by projective tests.* Unpublished doctoral dissertation, Northwestern University.

Norden, K. (1975). *Psychological studies of deaf adolescents.* Lund, Norway: CWK Geerup.

Ogbu, J. U. (1982). Origins of human competence: A cultural-ecological perspective. *Annual Progress in Child Psychiatry and Child Development*, 113–140. New York: Brunner/Mazel.

Ogbu, J. U. (1988). Cultural diversity and human development. *New Directions for Child Development, 42*, 11–28.

Oleron, P. (1953). Conceptual thinking of the deaf. *American Annals of the Deaf, 98*, 304–310.

Oleron, P. (1960). An experimental study of the psychological development of deaf children. In A. Ewing (Ed.), *The modern educational treatment of deafness: Report on the International Congress* (pp. 3–56). Manchester, UK: Manchester University Press.

Osborne, R. T. (1980). *Twins: Black and white.* Athens, GA: Foundation for Human Understanding.

Paquin, M. M. (1992). *The superior nonverbal intellectual performance of deaf children of deaf parents: An investigation of the genetic hypothesis.* Unpublished doctoral dissertation, California School of Professional Psychology, Alameda, CA.

Paquin, M. M., & Braden, J. P. (1990). The effect of residential school placement on deaf children's Performance IQ. *School Psychology Review, 19*, 350–355.

Parnasis, I. (1981, March). *The effects of parental deafness and early exposure to manual communication on the cognitive skills, English language skill and field-independence of young deaf adults.* Paper presented at the annual meeting of the American Educational Research Association, Los Angeles, CA.

Parnasis, I., & Drury, A. (1983, April). *Parental hearing status and age of exposure to manual communication: Influences on cognitive and English language skills of young deaf adults.* Paper presented at the annual meeting of the American Educational Research Association, Montreal, Canada.

Parnasis, I., & Long, G. (1979). Relationships among spatial skills, communication skills, and field independence in deaf students. *Perceptual and Motor Skills, 49,* 879–887.

Parnasis, I., & Samar, V. J. (1982). Visual perception of verbal information by deaf people. In D. Sims, G. Waiter, & R. Whitehead (Eds.), *Deafness and communication: Assessment and training* (pp. 53–71). Baltimore: Williams & Wilkins.

Peterson, E. G. (1936). Testing deaf children with Kohs Block Designs. *American Annals of the Deaf, 81,* 242–254.

Phelps, L., & Branyan, B. J. (1988). Correlations between the Hiskey, K-ABC Nonverbal Scale, Leiter and the WISC-R Performance Scale with public school deaf children. *Journal of Psychoeducational Assessment, 6,* 354–358.

Phelps, L., & Branyan, B. J. (1990). Predicting the academic achievement of public school deaf children. *Psychology in the Schools, 27,* 210–217.

Phelps, L., & Ensor, A. (1986). Concurrent validity of the WISC-R using deaf norms and the Hiskey-Nebraska. *Psychology in the Schools, 23,* 138–141.

Phelps, L., & Ensor, A. (1987). The comparison of performance by sex of deaf children on the WISC-R. *Psychology in the Schools, 24,* 209–214.

Pickles, D. G. (1966). The Wechsler Performance Scale and its relationship to speech and educational response in deaf slow-learning children. *The Teacher of the Deaf, 64,* 382–393.

Pintner, R. (1924). Results obtained with the Non-Language Group Test. *Journal of Educational Psychology, 15,* 473–483.

Pintner, R. (1925). Group tests after several years. *Journal of Educational Psychology, 16,* 391–395.

Pintner, R. (1928). A mental survey of the deaf. *Journal of Educational Psychology, 19,* 145–151.

Pintner, R., & Brunschwig, L. (1936). Some personality adjustments of deaf children in relation to two different factors. *Journal of Genetic Psychology, 49,* 377–388.

Pintner, R., Eisenson, E. H., & Stanton, M. B. (1946). *Psychology of the physically handicapped.* New York: Crofts.

Pintner, R., & Lev, J. (1939). The intelligence of the hard of hearing school child. *Journal of Genetic Psychology, 55,* 31–48.

Pintner, R., & Paterson, D. G. (1915a). The Binet Scale and the deaf child. *Journal of Educational Psychology, 6,* 201–210.

Pintner, R., & Paterson, D. G. (1915b). A class test with deaf children. *Journal of Educational Psychology, 6,* 591–600.

Pintner, R., & Paterson, D. G. (1916a). The form board ability of young deaf and hearing children. *The Psychological Clinic: A Journal for the Study and Treatment of Mental Retardation and Deviation, 9,* 234–237.

Pintner, R., & Paterson, D. G. (1916b). Learning tests with deaf children. *Psychological Monographs, 20,* (Whole No. 88).

Pintner, R., & Paterson, D. G. (1917). Psychological tests of deaf children. *Volta Review, 19,* 661–667.

Pintner, R., & Paterson, D. G. (1918). Some conclusions from psychological tests of the deaf. *Volta Review, 20,* 10–14.

Pintner, R., & Reamer, J. F. (1920). A mental and educational survey of schools for the deaf. *American Annals of the Deaf, 65,* 451–472.

Poizner, H., Klima, E. S., & Bellugi, U. (1987). *What the hands reveal about the brain.* Cambridge MA: MIT Press.

Porter, L. J., & Kirby, E. A. (1986). Effects of two instructional sets on the validity of the Kaufman Assessment Battery for Children-Nonverbal Scale with a group of severely hearing impaired children. *Psychology in the Schools, 23,* 37–43.

Porteus, S. D. (1918). The measurement of intelligence: Six hundred and fifty three children examined by the Binet and Porteus tests. *Journal of Educational Psychology, 9,* 13–31.

Quay, L. C. (1971). Language, dialect, reinforcement, and the intelligence test performance of Negro Children. *Child Development, 42,* 5–15.

Quay, L. C. (1972). Negro dialect and Binet performance in severely disadvantaged black four-year-olds. *Child Development, 43,* 245–250.

Quay, L. C. (1974). Language, dialect, age, and intelligence-test performance in disadvantaged black cihldren. *Child Development 45,* 463–468.

Rainer, J. D., & Altshuler, K. (Eds.), (1967). *Psychiatry and the deaf.* Washington, DC: Department of Health, Education, and Welfare.

Raven, J.C., Court, J. H., & Raven, J. (1983). *Manual for Raven's Progressive Matrices and Vocabulary Scales.* London: H. K. Lewis.

Raviv, S., Sharan, S., & Strauss, S. (1973). Intellectual development of deaf children in different educational environments. *Journal of Communication Disorders, 6,* 29–36.

Ray, S. (1979). *An adaptation of the 'Wechsler Intelligence Scales for Children-Revised' for the deaf.* Natchitoches, LA: Author.

Ray, S. (1982). Adapting the WISC-R for deaf children. *Diagnostique, 7,* 147–157.

Ray, S. (1988). *Comparison of the means and standard deviations of deaf children with deaf parents, deaf children with hearing parents and the total sample.* Unpublished manuscript.

Rayson, B. (1987). Deaf parents of hearing children. In E. D. Mindel & M. Vernon (Eds.), *They grow in silence: Understanding deaf children and adults* (pp. 103–110). Boston, MA: College Hill Press.

Reamer, J. C. (1921). Mental and educational measurements of the deaf. *Psychological Monographs, 29* (3, Whole No. 132).

Reich, C., Hambleton, D., & Houldin, B. K. (1977). The integration of hearing impaired children in regular classrooms. *American Annals of the Deaf, 122,* 534–542.

Reynolds, C. R. (1982). Methods for detecting construct and prediction bias. In R. A. Berk (Ed.), *Handbook of methods for detecting test bias* (pp. 199–259). Baltimore, MD: Johns Hopkins University Press.

Reynolds, C. R., & Brown, R. T. (Eds.). (1984). *Perspectives on bias in mental testing.* New York: Plenum.

Reynolds, H. N. (1976). Development of reading ability in relation to deafness. *Proceedings of the Seventh World Congress of the World Federation of the Deaf.* Silver Spring, MD: National Association of the Deaf.

Ries, P. W., & Voneiff, P. (1974). Demographic profile of hearing impaired students. *PRWAD Deafness Annual, 4,* 17–42.

Roach, R. E., & Rosecrans, C. J. (1971). Intelligence test performance of black children with high frequency hearing loss. *Journal of Auditory Research, 11,* 136–139.

Roach, R. E., & Rosecrans, C. J. (1972). Verbal deficit in children with hearing loss. *Exceptional Children, 38*(5), 395–399.

Rose, S. P., Conneally, P. M., & Nance, W. E. (1977). Genetic analysis of childhood deafness. In F. H. Bess (Ed.), *Childhood deafness: Causation, assessment, and management* (pp. 19–35). New York: Grune & Stratton.

Ross, G. (1953). Testing intelligence and maturity of deaf children. *Exceptional Children 20,* 23–24, 42.

Roth, S. D. (1938). Survey of the psychological examination given by Dr. Stella M. Bowers, May 1937. *West Virginia Tablet, 61*(7), 1–6.

Scarr, S., & Weinberg, R. A. (1983). The Minnesota Adoption Studies: Genetic differences and malleability. *Child Development, 54*, 260–267.

Schein, J. D. (1975). Deaf students with other disabilities. *American Annals of the Deaf, 120*, 92–99.

Schein, J. D., & Delk, M. (1974). *The deaf population in the United States.* Silver Spring, MD: National Association for the Deaf.

Schick, H. F. (1934). *A performance test for deaf children of school age.* Paper presented at a meeting of the Society of Progressive Oral Advocates, St. Louis, MO.

Schick, H. F., & Meyer, M. F. (1932). The use of the Lectometer in the testing of the hearing and the deaf. *American Annals of the Deaf, 77*, 292–304.

Schildroth, A. N. (1976). *The relationship of nonverbal intelligence test scores to selected characteristics of hearing impaired students.* Unpublished manuscript, Office of Demographic Studies, Gallaudet College.

Schildroth, A. N. (1986). Residential schools for deaf students: A decade in review. In A. N. Schildroth & M. A. Karchmer (Eds.), *Deaf children in North America* (pp. 83–103). San Diego, CA: College Hill.

Schildroth, A. N., & Karchmer, M. A. (Eds.). (1986). *Deaf children in North America* (pp. 83–103). San Diego, CA: College Hill.

Schlesinger, H. S., & Meadow, K. P. (1972). *Sound and sign: Childhood deafness and mental health.* Berkeley, CA: University of California.

Schonemann, P. H. (1985). On artificial intelligence. *Behavioral and Brain Sciences, 8*, 241–242.

Scyester, M. (1936). Summary of four years' experiment with preschool deaf children at the Illinois School for the Deaf. *American Annals of the Deaf, 31*, 212–230.

Seiler, R. D. (1985). Signed vs. gestured administration of the WISC-R Performance Scale and the K-ABC Nonverbal Scale as predictors of achievement with hearing impaired students. *Dissertation Abstracts International, 47*, 844B-845B (Order No. DA8609069).

Shirley, M., & Goodenough, F. L. (1932). A survey of intelligence of deaf children in Minnesota schools. *American Annals of the Deaf, 77*, 238–247.

Siger, L. (1968). Gestures, the language of signs, and human communication. *American Annals of the Deaf, 113*, 11–28.

Siple, P., Fischer, S., & Bellugi, U. (1977). Memory for nonsemantic attributes of American Sign Language signs and English words. *Journal of Verbal Learning and Verbal Behavior, 16*, 561–574.

Sisco, F. H. (1982). Sex differences in the performance of deaf children on the WISC-R Performance Scale. *Dissertation Abstracts International, 43*, 6A. (University Microfilms No. DA8226432).

Sisco, F. H., & Anderson, R. J. (1980). Deaf children's performance on the WISC-R relative to hearing status of parents and child-rearing experiences. *American Annals of the Deaf, 125*, 923–930.

Snijders, J., & Snijders Oomen, N. (1959). *Non-verbal intelligence tests for deaf and hearing subjects (A manual).* Groningen, Holland: J. B. Wolters.

Snyderman, M., & Rothman, S. (1986). Science, politics, and the IQ controversy. *The Public Interest, 83*, 79–97.

South Dakota (1938). *Seventh Biennial Report of the State Commission for the Control of the Feebleminded, for Period Ending June 30, 1938.* Unpublished manuscript. Devils Falls, SD: Author.

Spearman, C. (1927). *The abilities of man.* New York: Macmillian.

Springer, N. N. (1938). A comparative study of the behavior traits of deaf and hearing children of New York City. *American Annals of the Deaf, 83*, 255–273.

Springer, N. N. (1938). A comparative study of the intelligence of a group of deaf and hearing children. *American Annals of the Deaf, 83*, 138–152.

Steer, M. D., Hanley, T. D., Spuehler, H. E., Barnes, N. S., Burk, K. W., & Williams, W. G. (1961).

The behavioral and academic implications of hearing losses among elementary school children. Purdue Research Foundation Project Number P. U. 0240. Lafayette, IN: Purdue University.

Stein, B. E., & Schuckman, H. (1973). Effects of sensory restriction upon the responses to cortical stimulation in rats. *Journal of Comparative and Physiological Psychology, 82*, 182–187.

Stevens, G., & Carlson, J. (1978). Formal operational thought in deaf and hearing adults. In R. Weismann, P. J. Brown, & P. A. Levinson (Eds), *Piagetian theory and its implications for the helping professions* (Vol. 1, pp. 67–92). Los Angeles, CA: University of Southern California Press.

Stevenson, E. A. (1964). A study of the educational achievement of deaf children of deaf parents. *California News, 80*, 1–3.

Stewart, J. H. (1981). Wechsler Performance IQ Scores and social behaviors of hearing-impaired students. *Volta Review, 83*, 215–222.

Stinson, M. S. (1974). Relations between maternal reinforcement and help and the achievement motive in normal-hearing and hearing-impaired sons. *Developmental Psychology, 10*, 348–353.

Stokoe, W. C. (1960). Sign language structure: An outline of the visual communication systems of the American Deaf. *Studies in Linguistics: Occasional Papers, 8* (University of Buffalo).

Streng, A., & Kirk, S. A. (1938). The social competence of deaf and hard of hearing children in a public day-school. *American Annals of the Deaf, 83*, 244–254.

Strunkard, A. J., Sorensen, T. I. A., Hanis, C., Teasdale, T. W., Chakraborty, R., Schull, W. J., & Schulsigner, F. (1986). An adoption study of human obesity. *The New England Jornal of Medicine, 314*(4), 193–198.

Stuckless, E. R., & Birch, J. W. (1966). The influence of early manual communication on the linguistic development of deaf children. *American Annals of the Deaf, 111*, 452–460, 499–504.

Sullivan, P. M. (1982). Administration modifications on the WISC-R Performance Scale with different categories of deaf children. *American Annals of the Deaf, 127*, 780–788.

Sullivan, P. M., & Vernon, M. (1979). Psychological assessment of hearing impaired children. *School Psychology Digest, 8*, 271–290.

Templin, M. C. (1950). *The development of reasoning in children with normal and defective hearing.* Westport, CN: Greenwood Press.

Thoday, J. M. (1973). Educability and group differences. *Nature, 245*, 418–420.

Tomlinson-Keasey, C., & Kelly, R. R. (1978). The deaf child's symbolic world. *American Annals of the Deaf, 123*, 452–458.

Treacy, L. (1952). *A study of social maturity in relation to factors of intelligence in acoustically handicapped children.* Unpublished Thesis, Northwestern University.

Trybus, R. J., & Karchmer, M. A. (1977). School achievement scores of hearing impaired children: National data on achievement status and growth patterns. *American Annals of the Deaf, 122*, 62–69.

Ulissi, S. M., Brice, P. J., & Gibbins, S. (1988). *The use of the Kaufman-Assessment Battery for Children with the hearing impaired.* Unpublished manuscript.

Ulissi, S. M., & Gibbins, S. (1984). Use of the Leiter International Performance Scale and the Wechsler Intelligence Scale for Children-Revised with hearing-impaired children. *Diagnostique, 9*, 142–153.

Upshall, C. C. (1929). *Day schools vs. institutions for the deaf* (Teachers' College Contributions to Education No. 389). New York: Bureau of Publications, Teachers' College, Columbia University.

Urbach, P. (1974). Progress and degeneration in the 'IQ Debate.' *British Journal of Philosophy of Science, 25*, 99–135, 235–259.

Vandell, D. L., Anderson, L. D., Ehrhart, G., & Wilson, K. S. (1982). Integrating hearing and deaf preschoolers: An attempt to enhance hearing children's interactions with deaf peers. *Child Development, 53*, 1354–1363.

Vernon, M. (1967a). Characteristics associated with post-rubella deaf children: Psychological, educational, and physical. *Volta Review, 69*, 176–185.

Vernon, M. (1967b). Meningitis and deafness: The problem, its physical, audiological, psychological, and educational manifestations in deaf children. *Laryngoscope, 10*, 1856–1874.

Vernon, M. (1967c). Relationship of language to the thinking process. *Archives of General Psychiatry, 16*, 325–333.

Vernon, M. (1967d). Rh Factor and deafness: The problem, its psychological, physical, and educational manifestations. *Exceptional Children, 34*, 5–12.

Vernon, M. (1967e). Tuberculous meningitis and deafness. *Journal of Speech and Hearing Disorders, 32*, 177–181.

Vernon, M. (1969). Sociological and psychological factors associated with hearing loss. *Journal of Speech and Hearing Research, 12*, 541–563.

Vernon, M., & Brown, D. W. (1964). A guide to psychological tests and testing procedures in the evaluation of deaf and hard-of-hearing children. *Journal of Speech and Hearing Disorders, 29*, 414–423.

Vernon, M., & Koh, S. D. (1970). Early manual communication and deaf children's achievement. *American Annals of the Deaf, 115*, 527–536.

Vernon, P. E. (1982). *The abilities and achievements of Orientals in North America*. New York: Academic Press.

Vonderhaar, W. F. (1977). A comparative study of Performance Scale IQs and subtest scores of deaf children on the Wechsler Intelligence Scale for Children and the Wechsler Intelligence Scale for Children-Revised. *Dissertation Abstracts International, 38*, 1312A–1313A (Order No. 18,671).

Vonderhaar, W. F., & Chambers, J. F. (1975). An examination of deaf students' Wechsler Performance subtest scores. *American Annals of the Deaf, 120*, 540–543.

Wahl, J., & de Paola, T. (1978). *Jamie's tiger*. New York: Harcourt, Brace, Jovanovich.

Waldman, J. L., Wade, F. A., & Aretz, C. W. (1930). *Hearing and the school child: Hearing, school progress, and achievement of public school children*. Philadelphia, PA: Temple University.

Watson, B. U., & Goldgar, D. E. (1985). A note on the use of the Hiskey-Nebraska Test of Learning Aptitude with deaf children. *Language, Speech, and Hearing Services in Schools, 16*, 53–57.

Watson, B., Goldgar, D. E., Kroese, J., & Lotz, W. (1986). Nonverbal intelligence and academic achievement in the hearing impaired. *Volta Review, 88*, 151–157.

Watson, B. U., Sullivan, P. M., Moeller, M. P., & Jensen, J. K. (1982). Nonverbal intelligence and English language ability in deaf children. *Journal of Speech and Hearing Disorders, 47*, 199–204.

Wechsler, D. (1974). *Wechsler Intelligence Scale for Children-Revised*. New York: Psychological Corporation.

Wechsler, D. (1981). *Wechsler Adult Intelligence Scale- Revised*. New York: Psychological Corporation.

White, A. H., & Stevenson, V. M. (1975). The effects of total communication, manual communication, oral communication and reading on the learning of factual information in residential school deaf children. *American Annals of the Deaf, 120*, 48–57.

Williams, R. L. (1974, May). Scientific racism and IQ: The silent mugging of the black community. *Psychology Today*, 32–41.

Willis, D. J., Wright, L., & Wolfe, J. (1972). WISC and Nebraska performance of deaf and hearing children. *Perceptual and Motor Skills, 34*, 783–788.

Wilson, J. J., Rapin, I., Wilson, B. C., & Van Denburg, F. V. (1975). Neuropsychologic function of children with severe hearing impairment. *Journal of Speech and Hearing Research, 18*, 634–652.

Wolf, A. N. (1986). *Meta-analysis*. Beverley Hills, CA: Sage University Paper Series in the Quantitative Sciences.

Wolff, A. B., & Harkins, J. E. (1986). Multihandicapped students. In A. N. Schildroth & M. A. Karchmer (Eds.), *Deaf children in America* (pp. 55–81). San Diego, CA: College Hill Press.

Wolk, S. R., & Zieziula, F. R. (1985). Reliability of the 1973 edition of the SAT-HI over time: Implications for assessing minority students. *American Annals of the Deaf, 130*, 285–290.

Woodward, J. C. (1973). Some characteristics of pidgin sign English. *Sign Language Studies, 3*, 39–46.

Wright, R. H. (1955). The abstract reasoning of deaf college students. *Dissertation Abstracts International, 15,* 1911A (Order No. 13,151).

Youniss, J. A. (1974). A Piagetian perspective on thinking and language. *Journal of Education, 156,* 43–51.

Zeckel, A., & van der Kolk, J. J. (1939). A comparative intelligence test of groups of children born deaf and of good hearing, by means of the Porteus Test. *American Annals of the Deaf, 84,* 114–123.

Zwiebel, A. (1987). More on the effects of early manual communication on the cognitive development of deaf children. *American Annals of the Deaf, 134,* 16–20.

Zwiebel, A. (1988). *Intellectual structure of hearing impaired children and adolescents: A follow up study.* Manuscript submitted for review.

Zwiebel, A., & Mertens, D. M. (1985). A comparison of intellectual structure in deaf and hearing children. *American Annals of the Deaf, 130,* 27–31.

Index

Academic achievement, 9, 67, 78–80, 89, 90, 93, 94, 95, 102, 104, 122, 123, 124–127, 128, 137, 143, 144, 147, 150, 152, 154, 156, 158–160, 163, 165, 166, 167, 172, 176, 178, 181, 189, 190, 191, 195, 196, 198
  Stanford Achievement Test, 78
Administration of tests, 83–84, 88, 117–118, 119, 134, 135, 136, 138, 154–155
  oral, 14, 83–84, 103, 117–118, 135, 136
  other, 83–84, 117–118
  Ray's method, 117–118
  signed, 83–84, 138
  total communication, 83–84, 117–118
  written, 83–84, 117–118, 135, 136
American Sign Language (ASL) 36–37, 38, 40, 46, 56, 57, 79, 100, 102, 105, 132, 143, 151, 153, 163, 164
Assortative mating, 101, 103, 173, 174
Audiological information
  audiogram, 17–18, 19
  decibel (dB), 18, 19
  Hertz (Hz), 17, 18, 19
  Pure Tone Average (PTA), 18–19, 21
  Speech Detection Threshold (SDT), 18, 19, 21, 22
  Speech Reception Threshold (SRT), 18, 19, 20, 21, 22
Auditory Agnosia, 22
Auditory Deprivation, 15–21, 140
  effect on brain, 24, 140

Binet, Alfred, 5, 35

Compensation, 111, 129–134, 136, 137, 198
Consanguineous mating, 177
Cross-sectional studies, 89–90, 97, 158
Cumulative Deficit Phenomenon, 89–91, 104, 157–160, 176–177, 189, 191

Deaf children of deaf parents, 55–60, 132, 135, 151, 164, 171–174, 176, 182, 187, 197
  intelligence of, 98–103, 105, 152, 174, 181
Deaf children of hearing parents versus others, 52, 61, 164, 171, 174, 176, 182, 187, 197
  intelligence of, 98–103, 105, 152, 174, 181
Deaf children of hearing parents with a deaf sibling, 52–55, 165, 171–174, 176, 177–178, 197
  intelligence of, 98–103, 105, 173, 177
Deafened, 25, 33
Deafness
  as a minority group, 62, 143–145, 148, 153, 163–165, 181, 194, 200
  definition, 21–22, 25
  versus hearing impaired, 25, 26
  prelingual, 20–21, 25
  postlingual, 20–21
Descartes, René, 3, 4

Residential schools, versus day programs, 6, 95–97, 104–105, 134–135, 197
Restricted versus elaborated codes, Bernstein's theory of, 151–153
Rochester Method, 34

Socioeconomic status (SES), 46, 58, 59, 61, 101, 146, 149–150, 151, 157, 165–166, 167, 194

Socrates, 1, 2, 3

Test bias
evidence of, 122–124, 126–129, 136, 142–144, 145–147, 198
fallacious definitions of, 108–111
in normal-hearing groups, 13, 107, 142–145
polemic theories of, 143–145, 189

ISBN 0-306-44686-3